The Complete Book of Perfect Phrases for Job Seekers

Michael Betrus
and
Carole Martin

New York Chicago San Francisco Lisbon
London Madrid Mexico City Milan New Delhi
San Juan Seoul Singapore Sydney Toronto

1 2 3 4 5 6 7 8 9 0   FGR/FGR   0 1 4 3 2 1 0 9 8

ISBN: 978 0-07-148566–1
MHID: 0-07-148566–X

This is a compilation of previously published McGraw-Hill books:

Michael Betrus, *Perfect Phrases for Cover Letters*, (0-07-145406–3) © 2005

Michael Betrus, *Perfect Phrases for Resumes*, (0-07-145405–5) © 2005

Carole Martin, *Perfect Phrases for the Perfect Interview*, (0-07-144982–5) © 2005

McGraw-Hill books are available at special quantity discounts to use as premiums and sales promotions, or for use in corporate training programs. To contact a representative please visit the Contact Us pages at www.mhprofessional.com

The Complete Book of Perfect Phrases for Job Seekers

Contents

Section One

Perfect Phrases for Cover Letters

Michael Betrus

Section Contents

Part I: Cover Letter Basics 5

Part II: Perfect Management Phrases 59

Part III: Individual Performance Phrases 75

Part IV: Job-Search-Related Phrases 103

Additional Resources 127

Part I

Cover Letter Basics

Introduction

I hear it all the time as both a hiring manager and a career coach: "Cover letters? Résumés? That stuff is of the past. Now it's all about e-mail, job postings, and networking." I've interviewed hundreds of candidates for middle- and upper-level management for some giant firms, and this is what they tell me.

I interview candidates for six-figure jobs and some have absolutely horrendous résumés and cannot draft a well-written letter. I never understand it.

Now, some others do a great job on their letters and résumés. You know what? Simply because they have a well-written letter or résumé will get them recognized amidst a sea of responses that make *Mad* magazine (dating myself here) look like the *Wall Street Journal*. A great letter or résumé will get looked at just because it stands out.

My group has passed on some great candidates who have good pedigrees but such poorly written letters (e-mails, actually) or résumés that I cannot fathom them sending me a coherent weekly report.

Writing great letters and résumés is important because it is the first opportunity a recruiter or hiring manager gets to see an example of the work you can perform. If the résumé or letter has a typo or is not grammatically correct, that's not a great sign. I promise, I decline to meet with anyone who takes such little care.

This book will provide you with the best concept for cover letters, the consultative sales approach. This principle teaches you to spin your job search around the needs of the employer, not your skills or background. It will also provide you with many sample letters, letter formats, and guidelines, and thousands of phrases you can use when crafting that letter or e-mail to respond to an opportunity. Crafting a great letter or e-mail will get you noticed.

I have been involved in this type of work for years. In college, I wrote an article to help give my fellow college students at Michigan State University tips on getting hired when not pursuing the on-campus recruiting channel. As an accounting graduate, I had no more aptitude for getting published than anyone else. But even before I ever thought of writing that first book on résumés or cover letters, I did write effective cover letters and took a lot of time to spin my key messages around the needs of the employers.

Your attention to detail sends a message far beyond the words used in your response to a posting or a contact you are making through a colleague. Please pay attention to what you write! You will never know how many doors are closing because of imperfect writing; you just may not get the callbacks.

Formatting a Cover Letter and E-mail

I. Heading

To include name, address, phone number, fax number, e-mail, etc.

Patrick D. Dudash
1801 West Cortney Street
West Palm Beach, FL 33409
Phone: (561) 555–1234 / Fax: (561) 555–4321
Pdudash@xxx.com

The heading does not have to include all of the items listed here. Name, address, and telephone are critical, but fax number and e-mail address are optional. If you include your e-mail address, make sure you check it often. If you list a fax number, make sure you check it as well. And of all things, do not use your current employer's fax or e-mail address unless you have their approval.

E-mail note: You do not need to use this heading if you're sending an e-mail. Place this information at the signature line on an e-mail.

II. Date

September 5, 2009
E-mail note: You do not need to type in the date, since it will be time stamped anyway.

III. Name, Title, Company Name, and Address of Recipient

Ms. Maria Lane, Executive Vice President
PGR Industries, Inc.
1011 Dame Kate
Nashville, TN 23244

The only critical thing here is to make sure you include the company name and the recipient's title, if you know it.

E-mail note: Like the Heading, this is not required in an e-mail. However, in the "Subject" line in the e-mail, reference the specific position and recipient's name (if known). If you are responding to a Marketing Manager position, type in "Marketing Manager Candidate Dudash" in the subject line, to make it easier for the recipient to open and file and forward.

IV: Salutation

Dear Ms. Lane:

V. Power Introduction

Attention grabber—generating interest—why you are writing this employer.

Over the last few months I've noticed your firm moving into consulting with several health-care firms. After speaking with Mike Kiryn, I am aware that you are bidding on the upcoming opening of two new Columbia hospitals. You will no doubt need significant health-care industry expertise to drive this account. Health care can really get complicated when trying to balance aggressive marketing and sales techniques along with a more public entity image.

I have been working in marketing and public relations for nine years, most recently with Humana in Florida. We successfully opened 11 new hospitals over the last six years, and even experienced a storm when we opened the one in Orlando. That one opened in the midst of a major citywide controversy about the rising cost of health care, and much criticism was directed our way in the media. Under my direction, Humana successfully overcame that encounter and now that hospital is one of the most successful in the region.

Notice how the letter opens giving Ms. Lane an understanding that the applicant knows her business, and then ties her needs into Mr. Dudash's background.

VI. Purpose of the Letter

After working with Humana for several years, I feel I need a change. I have informed our regional director that I will be relocating to the Northeast, and would like to move into the consulting arena, supporting the health-care industry. After 15 years in the industry in key public relations roles, and after seeing the explosion in the industry with too many green managers making fundamental mistakes, I know I can share a wealth of knowledge to

improve their operations. As well, I have many key contacts in the industry, but am not interested in starting up
a consulting operation of my own. I can provide a solid
lead list to broaden your client list.

VII. Critical Messages

I offer your consulting service the following skills:

- 15 years in public relations
- 15 years in the health-care industry
- Expertise in new launches and crisis management
- Key contacts within the industry

VIII. Call to Action

You must initiate the next steps.

Please expect my telephone call in the next week so that
we might be able to set a time to meet and discuss
employment possibilities that would serve our mutual
interests.

IX. Close

Thanks for your consideration. I look forward to meeting
with you soon.

Sincerely,
Patrick Dudash

As with any letter, you can use a block style paragraph format
(shown here) or indent the first line. Both are equally acceptable,
though the block style is used more in business.

This letter does a comprehensive job of illustrating the way to draw the connection between the applicant's skills and the company's needs. Even in e-mail format, it works brilliantly.

Broadcast Letters

The broadcast letter is a hybrid between a résumé and cover letter and coveys much of your credentials without a résumé.

The broadcast letter looks more like a letter than a résumé, so the reader may be apt to give it more attention. This is especially true when a screening authority—a Human Resources recruiter or administrative assistant—is screening candidates. They may be more apt to pass on a "letter" to the boss but might more readily redirect a "résumé" to Personnel or Human Resources.

Suppose you're employed but do not want to take any chances that your current employer might find out you are looking for a job. Certainly you will not want to send out a résumé that names your current employer. This would be a good time to consider creating a broadcast letter.

The broadcast letter may offer less information than your résumé, but can hold more sizzle. More so than a résumé, it is an exercise in creativity, and it needs to be written very well or the strategy can backfire and not be advantageous.

Most broadcast letters today are sent in e-mail form and therefore need to contain short paragraphs and use bullets for key points. You need to keep them short and powerful in the introductions and in the closing.

Sample Introductions

Dear Mr. Grant:

Maria Lane provided me with your name and thought it might be beneficial if we got together and discussed your medical research program.

I set up the medical research program at the UNC, and today, 10 years after its inception, the program is considered one of the best in the country. I would like to make your program the benchmark for all others to emulate. Below are a few career highlights:

[Career highlights in bullet form follow.]

Dear Mr. Connors:

Paul Anners, probation officer for Hillsborough County, gave me your name and suggested I call you. I am a highly experienced locksmith, and though I have no formal training, there is very little I don't know about the business. In fact, I am working with Paul because I became too good at my trade.

Paul told me that you work with people who have experienced some trouble with the law ONLY if they are committed to total rehabilitation and work hard to get ahead. I have a wife and three children. I made a horrific mistake two years ago and will never do anything to jeopardize my future again.

I offer you the following:

[Career highlights in bullet form follow.]

Dear Mr. Regal:

I spearheaded the successful turnaround of three Fortune 100 companies and nine nationally recognized firms since 1981. Though my name is not a household word nor have I been CEO, COO, or president of any of the organizations that I have helped rehabilitate, I have been the strategic financial tactician behind some of the most successful reengineering efforts in the past quarter century in high-tech environments.

Your executive recruiting firm is recognized worldwide as the leader in helping top corporations secure visionary leaders and senior-level executives. Following 17 years of consultative prominence with three of the nation's leading consulting firms, I would like now to identify a company that would be interested in my leadership qualities on a long-term basis in a top position as President, CEO, COO, or CFO.

[Career highlights in bullet form follow.]

Dear Mr. Louega:

A few months ago, I completed the sale of Thurner Industries, Inc., a company that, in four years of leadership, I successfully turned into a highly profitable and much desired operation. Although I have been offered a similar role for another subsidiary of Thurner Industries, I would like to explore career opportunities building technology-based organizations. In anticipation of opportunities you may have for a Senior Operations or Manufacturing Executive, I enclose my résumé for your consideration. Recent accomplishments include:

[Career highlights in bullet form follow.]

Dear Ms. Lourdes:

If your staff could benefit through the addition of an eminently qualified senior sales professional, then I suggest it could prove to our mutual benefit to establish a dialogue. While secure in my present post, I am confidentially exploring new opportunities to which I could increase my span of control and have a greater contribution to overall sales results.

As my background reflects, my track record of performance demonstrates consistent advancement in the sales field over the past 14 years within the high-tech and prototype manufacturing environments. Of specific note may be the following indicators of the sales results I've produced for my employers:

[Career highlights in bullet form follow.]

Dear Mr. Kroll:

As a medical/pharmaceutical account manager and area trainer, managing a $5.5 million New York metro-region territory, I offer quantifiable expertise directly related to an 18-year background with Beecham Laboratories, a Fortune 200 leader in health-care solutions.

In recent years, I have produced over $18 million in sales in only 48 months, have attained three Beecham "Quota Buster" awards, and have been appointed to Beecham's prestigious "Presidential Team." Customers appreciate my extensive product knowledge, training abilities, and thorough follow-up. Beecham has recognized my creative marketing, innovative product launches, and comprehensive new-hire mentoring.

Representative accomplishments in specific medical/pharmaceutical areas include:

(Career highlights in bullet form follow.)

Dear Ms. Siegal:

As current Vice President of Finance for a Fortune 500 industrial leader, and former CFO of two mid-sized manufacturers, I have been instrumental in the origination of highly imaginative and highly profitable financial management programs achieved through motivational leadership blended with sound financing and creative thinking.

The following accomplishments reflect the absolute value that I can bring to Cerion's current and long-term business ventures:

[Career highlights in bullet form follow.]

Dear Mr. Dixon:

Recognized as a dynamic management executive, I possess a career in successfully building and leading companies to profitability and growth. My expertise includes new business development, strategic sales and marketing campaigns, team leadership and operational management.

- For the past three years, I have served as ...
- I was recruited to plan and implement an aggressive sales and marketing plan to establish worldwide sales and ...
- Prior, I served as the Vice President, Sales and Marketing for ...

Closing Phrases

- would like to stop by and introduce myself and share my portfolio with you. Would next week be convenient? I will contact you this Thursday at 11:00 A.M. to determine if such arrangements would interest you. Thank you for your time and consideration.

- If you believe, as I do, that my qualifications and credentials merit further review on how I can best serve your community center's cultural needs, I would appreciate the opportunity of meeting with you. Please expect my telephone call in the coming week to arrange such a meeting. Thank you for your consideration.

- I will be meeting with Janine next Monday at 10:00 A.M. and will plan to call you from her office. If you need any further information about me, she suggested you call her at (555) 555–5678. I thank you for your time and trust in Janine and me. I will not let you down!

- As a follow-up to this correspondence, I will call you next week to determine if my qualifications meet your needs at this time. As I have not yet discussed my plans with Thurner, I would appreciate your discretion in this matter.

- If you are looking for a senior manager who will make an immediate and positive impact upon operations, revenue streams, and profit margins, I would like to explore the opportunity. I look forward to speaking with you soon.

Consultative Sales Approach

Marketing principles revolve around the four Ps: product, place, promotion, and price. Your self-marketing principles should revolve around the same principles. Thus, it makes sense to draw the parallels even further.

Marketers attempt to create and position a product to meet the needs of their target sales segment. You should position yourself in a manner that meets the needs of your targeted employers. Once marketing does its thing, it is up to sales to complete the process. This is the place—the distribution element of the marketing mix. Your sales element is in full force when you are in the interviewing stage, but even before that you need to set up the stage for a strong sell.

Enter consultative sales, which requires you to understand the needs of the customer (or your prospective employer) and sell the customer on the idea that you have a product to meet those needs. To rise above the pack in the job search process, you need to demonstrate to the prospective employer that you clearly understand its needs and you can fill the gap in its organization to meet those needs.

Here are a few examples of things to look for in an organization. You should understand and research them before beginning the process of writing the cover letter and sending your résumé so you can address those items in your communications, just as in sales and marketing.

- Existing products
- New products
- Geographic presence
- Climate of the industry
- Competitive products and companies
- Emerging trends in the industry and within the organization
- Profile of the current staff
- Profile of the desired staff skill set
- The company's key business or market drivers

There are many others, but you get the point. You need to learn about these things. Then you can better position yourself as someone who can help the company achieve its goals, rather than someone who needs a job. The research should take place before you send the cover letter and résumé so that you can customize them to meet the needs you uncovered.

You can learn about these things in several ways. When you have uncovered that information, you can use it in two ways. In your résumé you should position, spin, or highlight your accomplishments to make them consistent with the company's overall goals. Your cover letter is the vehicle to address what you've learned and how you can help them meet their goals.

The Formula

Here is the basic formula for a consultative cover letter:

PART 1. Based on research you've completed, this first section of the letter is where you state the needs of the company or hiring manager. The purpose is to demonstrate your understanding of their situation and business. If nothing else, it shows the reader you know something about his or her situation and needs.

PART 2. This is the bridge. Draw the connection between what the business's needs are and how its people resources address them. You can see multiple examples of this on the following pages.

PART 3. Now you begin to present information about yourself. You've stated the company's needs and how people will meet those needs. Now you need to connect yourself to the solution. Write just a couple statements about how your skills and accomplishments will solve the company's problems and meet its needs.

Take a look at the sample letters section and look for the ways each letter opens, demonstrating an understanding of where the company is and where it is going. Then look for the way the writers are connecting the company's needs with their skills. If you can master this concept, you will be successful not just in your job search, but also in your overall career.

Opening Phrases

- Lisa Councilman provided me with your name and suggested I contact you regarding summer employment this season. Apparently, Lisa has worked for you for the past three summers, but she will be in Europe this year and thought I might work in her place.

- After completing much research on [prospective employer] the industry over the last few months, it has become apparent that [your company] holds a unique position in the market.

- Your marketing director, Jeff Kilpatrick, mentioned you are looking for an MIS director. He told me some very interesting things about GB and I am impressed, not only with the growth and profitability, but in the similarities between GB and Diversified Centers, my current employer. GB has added 23 new training centers in the U.S. With that much widespread activity, MIS needs must surely be exploding.

- Melissa Sumner at Touchstone recently informed me that you are overseeing costumes and makeup for the new film, "The Nutty Professor." Melissa shared with me some of the effects that you are planning to use to transform the lead character between the thin professor and the very overweight professor. In order to pull this off, you will undoubtedly need artists skilled in this field.

- Over the last few months I've noticed your firm moving into consulting with several health-care firms. After speaking with Patrick Workley, I am aware you are bidding on the upcoming opening of two new Columbia hospitals. You will no doubt need significant health-care industry expertise to drive this account …

- I have been researching HP and their play in the integrated services offerings for some time. I was intrigued to read about the upcoming VoiP announcement that is currently scheduled for this fall. VoiP is reportedly going to converge data and voice transport products into a single, more cost-effective transport that can support virtually unlimited bandwidth demands.

- The *Chicago Times* ran an article last month indicating UPS was expanding its call center operations in the Chicago area and that a benchmarking effort was going to be made to bring the center back in-house after many years of contracting the service. Now that the talk of strike has been put to bed, I am sure you will be focusing attention again on this project. I believe I can help!

Middle Section Phrases

- In order to meet your aggressive growth goals of launching this market by next fall, you will certainly need a strong RF team that has experience in the CDMA platform. Specifically, you will need a team that has experience optimizing the Lucent and Nortel base stations. As a consultant, I …

- With that much national activity, you must need each site to be networked with your home office for both voice and data transport, as well as establish a WAN to improve real-time connectivity. As well, the design aspect of the business must eat up a lot of bandwidth in data transport, so it would surely help if you could share information more quickly and efficiently, while maintaining your privacy firewall.

- Experience with plastics, makeup, special wraps, and the various maskings take a great deal of skill to apply in a way that is transparent to the viewer. I know; I was the lead artist for several movies and clips, including Michael Jackson's *Thriller* video, *Halloween H$_2$0*, and in several *Tales from the Crypt* episodes.

- In order to pull this off, you will surely need to have strong relationships in place with the CLECs or ILECs in given markets. For in the short run that is the only way you can provide the local access "last mile." I have a lot of experience working with Bell Atlantic/Nynex and Bell South in xDSL …
- Some of my career highlights include the following, which actually tie in closely with the emerging needs at UPS:

  - Personnel management and team-building; directing a team to consistently exceed organizational expectations

  - Systems and operational benchmarking; developing systems of operations that can be replicated in other operations

  - A highly competitive but jovial manager who inspires success while demanding results

  - Strong finance/budget management skills; bottom-line oriented

- I understand you are looking for people who have experience in retail environments, are customer-service oriented, are loyal and dependable, have working knowledge of point-of-sales computer technologies, and are drug free. Retail environments like this can be so difficult to find good people. I am in my third year at UCLA majoring in Business Administration and have five years retail experience (The Body Shop, Wolfe Camera, and The Gap) and am very familiar with POS computer systems.

Closing Phrases

- My experience appears to be in perfect line with your needs right now and what you will need after launch. I will give you a call next week to set up some time for us to talk further.

- It appears that my accomplishments with Diversified Centers are in line with your MIS needs at GB. I will give you a call next week to set up a meeting to talk further.

- My experience is very consistent with what you will need for your upcoming film. Please review my attached résumé for the specifics of my film credits. You will see that I would be a good fit for helping you with all of the makeup and related preparations for the demanding transformation scenes. I will call you next Tuesday and set up a time to stop by the studio to meet you.

- I am sure that you see connection between my four areas of strength above and the criteria by which UPS evaluates potential managers. I know your time is extremely valuable, and so is mine. Therefore I would enjoy speaking with you for a few moments over the telephone to determine if an in-person meeting might be beneficial to us both. Please expect my call next Monday afternoon. If this is not a good time to chat for a few minutes, we can arrange another time that is mutually convenient.

- Bob mentioned that you are presently looking for a retail manager to direct operations at your flagship location. I would be interested in meeting with you to discuss this exciting opportunity. I have one more week to finish up things with FSS and then I am available to meet with you in Nashville. I will call you tomorrow to discuss this fax.

- I will be off for the summer as of May 29. However, I will be home for spring break (April 7–15) and would like to stop by and introduce myself to you. We can both be sure that Maria would not have introduced us to each other if she didn't feel I could fill her shoes in a way that measures up to your high standards.

Consultative Approach Cover Letters

MELISSA SUMNER

9981 Southern Boulevard, West Palm Beach, Florida 33409

(561) 555–5719

March 29, 20__

Ms. Theresa Mascagni

Vice President Technical Operations

4800 Oakland Park Boulevard

Fort Lauderdale, FL 33341

Dear Ms. Mascagni:

After completing much research on the wireless communications industry over the last few months, it has become apparent that NextWave holds a unique position in the market. NextWave has secured multiple C-Block licenses across the country and when built out will have a national presence comparable to AT&T and Sprint.

In order to meet your aggressive growth goals of launching this market by next fall, you will certainly need a strong RF team that has experience in the CDMA platform. Specifically, you will need a team that has experience optimizing the Lucent and Nortel base stations.

As a consultant, I led RF teams from network design to launch with both PrimeCo and Sprint PCS in the Chicago and Dallas MTAs, both of which were on a Lucent platform. I can provide excellent references from both. I think NextWave is a cutting-edge operation, one in which ingenuity, creativity, and drive can make a material impression. I want to be a part of your team.

My experience is in perfect line with your needs right now and what you will need after launch. I will give you a call next week to set up some time for us to talk further.

Sincerely,
Melissa Sumner

GLENNA HAZEN
2357 Golf Drive Lane, Coppell, TX 75220
(817) 555–5974

June 9, 20__
Mr. Grant D. Powers
CEO Golden Bear International
Golden Bear Plaza
11712 U.S. Highway 1
North Palm Beach, FL 33412

Dear Mr. Powers:

Your Controller, Mr. Gerald Haverhill, told me over golf a few weeks ago that you are looking for an MIS director. He told me some very interesting things about GB, and I was impressed, not only with the growth and profitability, but with the similarities between GB and Diversified Centers, my current employer. GB has added 23 new training centers in the U.S., as well as overseen the design of all Jack Nicklaus courses. With that much widespread activity, MIS needs must surely be exploding.

With that level of national activity, you must need each site to be networked with your home office for both voice and data transport, as well as establish a WAN to improve real-time connectivity. As well, the design aspect of the business must eat up a lot of bandwidth in data transport, so it would surely help if you could share information more quickly and efficiently, while maintaining your privacy firewall. My current operation is quite similar. I have built a very efficient network for our many regional locations to communicate. Diversified Centers builds and manages strip mall shopping centers for Tom Thumb grocery stores. Our network enables each regional office to stay in touch via e-mail and shared drives through our WAN, as well as utilize the Sprint ION network for real-time communications of high bandwidth development plans, similar to your use of golf course designs.

It appears that my accomplishments with Diversified Centers are in line with your MIS needs at GB. I will give you a call next week to set up a meeting to talk further.

Looking forward to meeting you,
Glenna Hazen

P.S. Gerald told me you are quite close with Mr. Nicklaus. Please congratulate him on his fine Masters showing!

CAROLYN KELLENBURGER
5534 College Parkway
Cape Coral, FL 33410
(941) 555–9753

March 15, 20__
Ms. Kimberly Houston
Paramount Pictures
4800 Hollywood Boulevard
Santa Monica, CA 90211

Dear Ms. Houston:

Jim Talley at Touchstone recently informed me that you are overseeing costumes and makeup for the new film *The Nutty Professor*. Jim shared with me some of the effects that you are planning to use to transform the lead character between the thin professor and the very overweight professor. In order to pull this off, you will undoubtedly need artists skilled in this field.

Experience with plastics, makeup, special wraps, and the various maskings takes a great deal of skill to apply in a way that is transparent to the viewer. I know; I was the lead artist for several movies and clips, including Michael Jackson's *Thriller* video, *Halloween H$_2$0* and several *Tales from the Crypt* episodes.

My experience is very consistent with what you will need for your upcoming film.

Please review my attached résumé for the specifics of my film credits. You will see that I would be a good fit for helping you with all of the makeup and related preparations for the demanding transformation scenes. I will call you next Tuesday and set up a time to stop by the studio to meet you.

Sincerely,
Carolyn Kellenburger

MISTI DeORNELLAS
45227 Michigan Avenue, Chicago, IL 64197
(312) 555–3125

March 9, 1999
Ms. Maria Lane, Executive Vice President
Hyde and Smithson Public Relations, Inc.
1800 Scenic Way
Mountain View, VT 19877

Dear Ms. Lane:

Over the last few months I've noticed your firm moving into consulting with several health-care firms. After speaking with Tom Aimee, I am aware that you are bidding on the upcoming opening of two new Columbia hospitals. You will no doubt need significant health-care industry expertise to drive this account.

Health care can really get complicated when trying to balance aggressive marketing and sales techniques along with a more public entity image.

The two new locations in Portsmouth and Springfield will be delicate openings given the amount of bad press Columbia has received in the last year or two.

Columbia has been in trouble with both the IRS and the FBI for tampering with federal aid and overbilling Medicare. They will undoubtably need good advice on how to position their openings to get off on the right foot.

I have been working in marketing and public relations for nine years, most recently with Humana in Florida. We successfully opened 11 new hospitals over the last six years, and even experienced a storm when we opened the one in Orlando.

That one opened in the midst of a major citywide controversy regarding the for-profit nature of Humana versus the for-the-good-of-the-people persona hospitals have maintained. Under my direction Humana successfully overcame that encounter, and now that hospital is one of the most successful in the region.

My skills are very much in line with the needs of both your firm and your clients:

- 15 years in public relations
- 15 years in the health-care industry
- Expertise in new launches and crisis management
- Key contacts within the industry

Please expect my telephone call in the next week so that we might be able to set a time to meet and discuss employment possibilities that would serve our mutual interests.

Sincerely,
Misti DeOrnellas

WALT JOHNSON
2357 Indiana Lane
Indianapolis, Indiana 49877
(317) 555–5687

September 8, 20__
Ms. Christy Garcia
Director Sales and Marketing
AT&T Data Services
3333 Westwood One
Indianapolis, IN 49557

Dear Ms. Garcia:

I have been researching AT&T and their play in the integrated services offerings for some time. I was intrigued to read about the upcoming INC announcement that is currently scheduled for this fall. INC is reportedly going to converge data and voice transport products into a single, more cost-effective transport that can support virtually unlimited bandwidth demands.

In order to pull this off, you will surely need to have strong relationships in place with the CLECs or ILECs in given markets. In the short run that is the only way you can provide the local access "last mile." I have a lot of experience working with Bell Atlantic/Nynex and Bell South in xDSL. Surely xDSL will be your plan for last mile access when it is built out, and you will need skilled network data engineers to optimize and design that integration.

Please take a look at my résumé, which reflects the broad experience I have developed in data transport and xDSL technology. I will call you next week for an appointment when we can review this further.

Sincerely,
Walt Johnson

CHARLENE W. PARKER
668 West Hannover Boulevard, Chicago, IL 60623
Phone: (773) 555–2486
E-mail: Fivestar10@Main.net

July 9, 20___
Mrs. Grace Billings, Customer Service Manager
United Parcel Service
1000 State Street
Chicago, IL 60602

Dear Mrs. Billings:

Congratulations on the recent contract between the pilot's union and management. The recent strike was surely devastating, not only to UPS, but the nation as a whole who depend on and trust UPS. The agreement signed last week ensures that the good name of and extraordinary service provided by UPS will not be tarnished.

I read in the Business section of the *Chicago Times,* over a month ago, that UPS was expanding its call center operations in the Chicago area and that a benchmarking effort was going to be made to bring the center back in-house after many years of contracting the service. Now that the talk of a strike has been put to bed, I am sure you will be focusing attention again on this project. I believe I can help!

I work as a Call Center Manager for Sears Roebuck and Company here in Chicago. They too once contracted out their call center/customer service operations and made the decision to bring it in-house six years ago. I was one of nine team leaders responsible for the strategic planning and implementation of the conversion from contracted to in-house call center operations for Sears.

Some of my career highlights include the following, which actually tie in closely with the emerging needs at UPS:

- Personnel management and team building; directing a team to consistently exceed organizational expectations
- Systems and operational benchmarking; developing systems of operations that can be replicated in other operations
- A highly competitive but jovial manager who inspires success while demanding results
- Strong finance/budget management skills; bottom-line oriented

I am sure that you see the connection between my four areas of strength above and the criteria by which UPS evaluates potential managers. I know your time is extremely valuable, and so is mine.

Therefore, I would enjoy speaking with you for a few moments over the telephone to determine if an in-person meeting might be beneficial to us both.

Please expect my call next Monday afternoon. If this is not a good time to chat for a few minutes, we can arrange another time that is mutually convenient.

Thank you for your time and consideration.

Sincerely,
Charlene W. Parker

CYNTHIA E. GOODMAN
2121 East 75th Street, Fort Lauderdale, FL 33304
(954) 555–5945

March 21, 20__
Mr. Howard Finelaw, President
Valet Services of South Florida
9205 Dixie Highway, Suite 200-B
Pompano Beach, FL 33360

Dear Mr. Finelaw:

Our paths have met on at least two occasions, and I was truly impressed each time. Please allow me to explain. I attended the Executive Women's Association gala event three weeks ago at the Cypress Creek Marriott, where more than 400 people attended. When I drove my car to the valet, I was awestruck by the professionalism of the attendants, the uniforms, and the courtesies extended, not only to me, but to everyone. I mean to say that the valet service was so exceptional, it was the talk of the evening!

When I asked to speak to the hotel manager to rave about the valet service, he told me that it had nothing to do with the Marriott. I found out that your company is responsible for this level of service. Last Saturday night my husband and I went to the Kravis Center to see *Phantom of the Opera*. Needless to say, half of South Florida was there—and so were you! Again, I could not believe the level of service provided—simply exceptional.

So our paths have met on two occasions over the past four to five weeks—and I'd like to propose a third. I am a highly successful sales professional, and I will represent only companies with top-rated products and services. I would like to propose a meeting to discuss how I can best help your company grow and prosper even beyond the success you have had to this point.

After completing some research online, I discovered your Web site. I noticed that your company has plans to expand into Broward and Martin Counties. I know I can use my plethora of corporate contacts to help you build your company. And if you decide you want to go regional, state, or national, I have the experience and verifiable track record to assist in this area as well.

And here's the best part—I enjoy being compensated for results, and I guarantee results. I do not require a high base salary compensation plan, but actually prefer an attractive commission program. I am a six-figure earner and am compensated only when I bring in the business. My past sales experience has been focused on hospitality-oriented business, so I have key contacts with companies that can use professional valet services. In fact, I have spent the last three evenings studying the valet business and have familiarized myself with the competition, past and future trends, and growth/profit potential. Based on my preliminary findings, you are in a niche market with almost unlimited potential.

I have enclosed a detailed résumé of my qualifications and will contact you early next week to discuss possible scenarios for future employment with your company.

Thanks for taking the time to read this letter. I do hope we can meet in the next week or so.

Sincerely,
Cynthia E. Goodman

HELEN R. HENDERSON
21 Village Street
San Francisco, CA 99465
(302) 555–6102

February 22, 20__
Ms. Alice Greene
Center Plaza Hallmark
201 Broadway, Center Plaza
San Francisco, CA 99427

Dear Ms. Greene:

Bonnie Taylor provided me with your name and suggested I contact you regarding summer employment this season. Apparently, Bonnie has worked for you for the past three summers but will be in Europe this year and thought I might work in her place.

I understand you are looking for people who have experience in retail environments, are customer-service oriented, are loyal and dependable, have working knowledge of point-of-sales computer technologies, and are drug free. In retail environments like this it can be so difficult to find good people. The retail stores I have worked with at school have really struggled to get good, bright, and courteous people on staff.

I am in my third year at UCLA, majoring in Business Administration. As well, I have five years of retail experience (The Body Shop, Wolfe Camera, and The Gap) and am very familiar with POS computer systems.

I will be off for the summer as of May 29. However, I will be home for spring break (April 7–15) and would like to stop by and introduce myself to you. We can both be sure that Bonnie would not have introduced us to each other if she didn't feel I could fill her shoes in a way that measures up to your high standards.

I will call you next week to see if we can arrange an interview during my spring break. Thanks in advance for your consideration.

Sincerely,
Helen R. Henderson

Sample Letters for All Occasions

Letter Targeting a Specific Employer

PAULINA TAYLOR

June 4, 20__
Patti Coury
PCR Firm
Los Angeles, CA 90211

Dear Ms. Coury:

After contributing to the growth and success of AMEX Financial Services for 12 years, I am seeking new challenges with an enterprising company in need of someone with exceptional planning, leadership, and analytical qualities. One of your colleagues, Bill Stephens, and I met for lunch earlier this week, and Bill recommended that I contact you regarding prospective opportunities in your department.

As evidenced in the enclosed résumé, my experience encompasses all aspects of corporate business development and operations, strategic planning, budget administration, systems integration, internal management consulting, resource utilization, and project management. My ability to analyze needs and develop unique programs designed to yield a profitable outcome has proven to be one of my greatest assets.

Credited with significantly impacting bottom-line profitability and reducing operational costs at AMEX Financial, I excel at modeling complex situations in order to generate investment/costing details for new business ventures. I am technologically proficient, with direct experience in remittance, imaging, and systems design and development. My record of achievements is exemplary, as I have successfully directed and managed complex assignments while meeting or exceeding anticipated scheduling and budgetary projections.

Characterized by others as visionary and decisive, I possess keen instincts and offer strategies to quickly effect change and improvement. I am equally at ease working as a team member or independently, and enjoy a leadership role where I can foster motivational and mentoring relationships with colleagues and subordinates.

I am most interested in an opportunity where I can provide strong corporate leadership and vision. I would welcome the chance to discuss with you personally the value I offer Hamilton Company. If you feel such a discussion would be beneficial, please contact me at (310) 555–1212.

Sincerely,
Paulina Taylor

Broadcast Letter Samples (Sent as E-mail)

Dear Mrs. Curri:

I have a solid record for bringing in advertising dollars to prestigious, upscale publications from Aspen, Beverly Hills, and Palm Beach, to Newport, Rhode Island, and San Diego. As a top producing sales professional, I am certain I can be a contributing member of your advertising sales team.

Key Strengths:

- Presentation and closing skills
- Networking; building key alliances
- Graphic art and production management
- Concept development
- Customer service & retention management
- High ethical/professional standards

Past Employment (1990–2005):

Aspen Monthly, Aspen, CO	Sales Supervisor
Beverly Hills Illustrated, Beverly Hills, CA	Sales Associate
The LaJolla Magazine, San Diego, CA	Sales Associate
Palm Beach Illustrated, Palm Beach, FL	Advertising Sales Associate
The Newport News, Newport, RI	Sales Associate

I would like to stop by and introduce myself and share my portfolio to you. Would next week be convenient? I will contact you this Thursday at 11:00 A.M. to determine if such arrangements interest you.

Thank you for your time and consideration.

Sincerely,
Stephen Kayl

August 2, 20___
Mr. Holland L. Regal, President
Beltway Technologies, Ltd.
6300 Hunter Way
Waltham, MA 12197

Dear Mr. Regal:

I spearheaded the successful turnaround of three Fortune 100 companies and nine nationally recognized firms since 1981. Though my name is not a household word nor have I been CEO, COO, or president of any of the organizations that I have helped rehabilitate, I have been the strategic financial tactician behind some of the most successful reengineering efforts in the past quarter century in high-tech environments.

Your executive recruiting firm is recognized worldwide as the leader in helping top corporations secure visionary leaders and senior-level executives. Following 17 years of consultative prominence with three of the nation's leading consulting firms, I would like now to identify a company that would be interested in my leadership qualities on a long-term basis in a top position as President, CEO, COO, or CFO.

Three employers over the past 17 years:

1. Arthur Anderson
2. Mackenzie & Associates
3. Corporate Dynamics International

Twelve notable client companies (accompanied by outstanding references) that I have consulted for:

1. General Electric
2. Hewlett Packard
3. Cisco Systems
4. Compaq Computer
5. Intel
6. Softkey International
7. GBC
8. Digital Equipment
9. Delta Airlines
10. Lucent Technologies
11. LaserTools, Inc.
12. Ford Motor Company

My educational qualifications:

MBA Stanford University, 1980
Bachelor of Science: Industrial Engineering/Business Management, Tufts University
Faculty Staff Member: Peter Drucker Worldwide Training and Educational Academy

Maximizing shareholder earnings/growth management/financial integrity:

These are the three critical strengths I bring to the table. I am well-connected with Wall Street and have been personally involved with positioning three companies in the past four years to go public (including drafting a 230-page financial summary and pro forma). Finally, I have spent 60 percent of my time over the last five years in the international, global arena—helping position companies to maximize foreign market potential.

Certainly I do not want to waste precious time for either of us. Should you feel that you might come across a client seeking executive-level leadership that could take advantage of my qualifications and verifiable track record, feel free to contact me and I will forward a detailed, highly confidential résumé with supporting documentation. I would be seeking a position with a minimum compensation package of $200,000 and equity stock options based on performance.

Thank you for taking the time to review this letter. I look forward to hearing back from you if you feel an opportunity might exist that would benefit one of your client companies.

Sincerely,
Cliff W. O'Brien

Networking Letter Samples

NIKA NIKSIRAT
215 Hartman Drive, Portsmouth, NH 03801
(603) 555–4606

June 2, 20__
Mr. Benjamin Chang
Technical Director, Cisco Systems
4399 Central Avenue
Boston, MA 18002

Dear Mr. Chang:

Dave Tinker from Cellcorp suggested I contact you. He said you "know more about the network router business than anyone this side of the Mason-Dixon line." I knew you would be someone I had to meet.

Though I am employed with Bell Atlantic, I have decided to make a career move toward a more entrepreneurial upstart operation. I am not writing you for a position, but rather to get some industry advice from you. Companies that are just starting out are usually well capitalized but may be short on technical or operational expertise.

Having been involved with several major product launches with Bell Atlantic, I feel I have been through it all. However, going forward I think I can make a greater impact with a start-up. A start-up will be able to utilize my experience, and it could be a good situation for them and me.

I will call you next week to talk to you for a few minutes. Don't worry, I only want some advice, and if you have the time, I would love to take you to lunch. Thanks in advance for all your time!

Sincerely,
Nika Niksirat

DEBBIE McMULLAN
1215 Phillips Drive
New York, NY 10001
(212) 555–9555

December 3, 20__
Ms. Beth Pasterz
Robert Half International
1222 Park Avenue
New York, NY 10012

Dear Ms. Pasterz:

Thanks for speaking with me on the phone earlier. I agree that there probably isn't a good match between me and your current positions to fill. However, you did mention that based on our phone interview you thought my credentials were strong, and it got me thinking.

Would you still mind if we met? I am new to the New York area, as my husband was just transferred, and it looks like we'll be here for quite a while. You seemed to be fairly well connected and in the know as to what's going on here. I would love to meet just to get your advice on which firms I might avoid, which might be good, and what the overall climate is like in New York.

I realize you are probably quite busy, and I'd be happy to buy you breakfast or lunch just to talk for a few minutes. I promise I won't monopolize your time. You never know, maybe I will be calling you soon to help me recruit my new accounting staff.

I will call you on Friday and try to set something up. Thanks, I really enjoyed talking with you today.

Best regards,
Debbie McMullan

Internet Job Posting Responses

I have some friends who have posted for dozens of positions over the Internet, on sites like careerbuilder.com or monster.com, never getting one response.

Here is what happens on the other side, speaking from my personal experience. Hiring managers or recruiters get so many unqualified responses that they give very little time to any one résumé or letter. Letters never get read, by me anyway, if they are more than three lines per paragraph and appear not to be germane to the position applied.

Internet Job Posting Letter Tips

1. Short paragraphs, no more than three lines.
2. Hard space returns so the layout is broken up on the viewer's page.
3. Relevance! The letters should closely align to the job requirements.
4. Bullets: easier to read and to the point.

An ineffective letter is much worse than no letter. Below are some phrases that will help you respond to Internet job postings. Look at this for structure and layout, not the actual words. With e-mail letters and Internet postings, structure has as much to do with the letter effectiveness as the letter.

Internet Posting Letter Response Structure

1. Quick reference to job you are applying for.
2. Three to four bullets summarizing why you are the right candidate. These should absolutely mirror the posting's job requirements.
3. Quick, nonwordy closing.

Dear Microsoft:

I am very interested in speaking with you about your national accounts position, as it is described as a perfect fit for my experience.

I do offer [and then list their position criteria spun around your career highlights]:

- Ten years experience in national account sales targeting Fortune 500 accounts
- Nine years training and development experience
- Consultative sales approach
- Negotiating, RFP and RFQ expertise

Please see my professional career highlights on my résumé below.

As a team member of your organization, I can provide:

- Effective applications solutions for financial and business operations
- Analysis, needs determination, and project management
- Powerful team leadership
- Technical instruction and business support for end users and clients on business issues and application implementation

My enclosed résumé clearly shows I have qualifying skills and abilities compatible with this position. Briefly, they are:

- Considerable industry-related experience augmented by a formal education and refined by specialized training
- A proven record of success achieved through diligence, hard work, attention to detail, and my belief in a consistent application of the fundamentals
- A sincere desire to contribute to the continued growth and success of your company

After you have the opportunity to review my résumé, I would like to meet with you to discuss how effectively I can contribute. Should you have any questions before scheduling an appointment I may be reached through the number listed above.

Part II

Perfect Management Phrases

Coaching Phrases

Coaching in business can deliver dramatic results and drive significant financial impact for an organization. Today's values-based organizations employ coaching to inspire performance, develop their current and future leaders, and ensure the success of the people within. Success in anything is always about people and successful execution, in anything.

If coaching ability is important to your prospective employer, then you have to be able to effectively articulate that in a believable manner in your cover letter and in your résumé. If you just say you're a coach with nothing to back it up, the interviewer will see through it and disregard you in that way. Be specific and use examples!

Perfect Letter Phrases for Coaching

- My consulting engagements center on Executive Coaching and Leadership Development: partnering with various business executives to coach them regarding their business challenges; helping them to improve their performance and achieve their business goals. I even coached a Fortune 250 CEO regarding how his behaviors influenced his organizational culture and environment.
- As a group manager in marketing, I created and implemented "Coaches Corner Tips" to cross-pollinate sales/service scripting, improve product knowledge and soft skills, and increase sales techniques.
- While working as a project manager supporting multiple internal disciplines, we conducted 360-degree feedback sessions to gain a better understanding of our strengths and development needs. The consensus from this report

identified coaching across and down as a strength for me. I have a copy of the 360 review and would be happy to bring it to our next meeting.

- I developed our group to meet and exceed company goals through coaching techniques, training, and corrective action. Our group assumed an advocate role developing and writing training courses based on development opportunities within the company.

- As the director of the call center, I supervise an average of 40 Senior Specialists, listening and coaching on an average of 20 to 25 calls daily. Providing immediate feedback is the cornerstone to effective coaching, both for great behaviors and for opportunities.

- My coaching activities focused on organizational processes, coaching/motivating staff, and dealing with problem behaviors resulted in an estimated 7 percent increase in overall productivity while our staff realized a reduction of 4 percent in the same time frame.

- I am a seasoned professional with over 15 years experience leading coaching, training, documentation, and staff development in the following areas:

  - Career Development

  - Coaching and Performance Consulting

  - Training Management/Delivery

  - Distance Learning Administration

- My success in working well with those who do not report to me lies in effectively coaching through solutions with peers and other departments to reach a common goal. For example, while working on billing system changes,

I had to motivate the sales organization to work with me while it was definitely outside their core competency and the behavior they were paid to exhibit.

- While at PepsiCo, I developed a program on coaching, behavioral interviewing, and retail selling. This included:

  - Designing, facilitating, and implementing intensive training lectures, seminars, and course curriculum; career excellence and personal coaching abilities.

  - Classes on anger management, budgets and financial counseling, diversity in the workplace, conflict resolution, team-building, and personal coaching techniques.

Perfect Letter Phrases for Driving Performance

- Coaching a team is mandatory to high performance. My group led in calls processed and in monitored calls of excellence. We accomplished this by holding weekly one-on-one reviews and setting daily goals and expectations, and by recognizing when those goals were met or exceeded.

- Sustaining high and consistent sales for my organization made my group the highest performing within the organization. My approach to driving performance begins with people. Assessing talent and hiring great people is my cornerstone to success.

- The accounting department I managed had the highest employee satisfaction survey rating. The independent surveyor estimated that this translated to 21 percent increased productivity.

- The workforce is a key value driver that is crucial to increasing shareholder value. In a study of 191 senior executives at major U.S. corporations, 92 percent believe human assets have a great effect on the ability of a company to achieve customer satisfaction, 82 percent see the impact of employees on profitability, and 72 percent see an impact on innovation and new product development.

- According to one of *Fortune* magazine's "Most Desirable Companies to Work For," hiring great people is the first requirement for high performance. One great person is equal to three good people, and one good person is equal to three average people.

- Setting goals establishes a performance target for each activity, whether it is a daily sales goal, an annual one, or even the number of inquiries a call center processes. While general manager at PepsiCo, I set weekly targets of productivity for my team, and they responded by achieving a top four of 130 districts national ranking.

- Driving high performance begins with leading by example. By leading the key activities for our success myself, my team both learned how to execute and that they needed to in order to be a true part of the team.

- The "high-performance" organization owes its success to its employees. It is an indication of a learning organization that provides training in the following areas: redesign of business processes, delegation of work, teamwork, companywide communication, shared vision, and advanced technology skills. A high-performance business improves faster than its competition and sustains that rate, while satisfying all its stakeholders.

- Our marketing organization identified the most critical factors to delivering the greatest possible total return to shareholders over an extended period of time—the hallmark of a high-performance business.

- Performance-driven organizations are characterized by above-average results, usually measured in financial terms, such as profit, earnings per share, revenue growth, return on invested capital, product costs, and asset utilization. Strong financial performance is an indicator of excellence elsewhere in the organization; actually, these companies outperform their competitors in customer service and satisfaction, product quality, innovation, and productivity.

- My organization led improvements in five key areas, resulting in a 53 percent increase in market value. My team's workforce management practices include:

  - Implementing focused HR technology

  - Opening up communications between management and employees

  - Establishing a collegial, flexible workplace

  - Creating a total rewards and accountability orientation

  - Attaining excellence in recruitment and retention

- Teams invariably contribute significant achievements in business, charity, schools, government, communities, and the military. Overcoming barriers to performance is how groups become teams.

- Managers and others often should pay more attention to helping team leaders perform. Assuming that the team approach really is the best option, the key to getting unstuck lies in addressing the particular obstacles confronting the team with a strong performance focus. There is no incremental performance expectation beyond that provided by individual executives working within their formal areas of responsibility.

- The bottom line of performance is that organization success depends on how well the expectations of key stakeholders are met (customers, investors, employees, suppliers, and the public).

- The ABC division led performance at Goodwyn, a Fortune 75 company. Our operating redesign included the following issues:

  - Benchmarking high-performance organizations; learning about high performance

  - Assessing current organization strengths and weaknesses

  - Creating an organization operating philosophy

  - Designing the work system, including jobs, roles, and responsibilities

  - Designing a performance measurement and management plan

  - Creating a capability building plan: training, development experiences

  - Developing a transition plan to manage the change

  - Providing for continual renewal to ensure adapting to the changing environment

Managing Conflict

Conflict is not always negative. In fact, it can be healthy when effectively managed. Healthy conflict can lead to:

- Growth and innovation
- New ways of thinking
- Additional management options

There are five steps to managing conflict:

- Analyze the conflict
- Determine management strategy
- Prenegotiation
- Negotiation
- Postnegotiation

You need to position yourself as one who manages conflict well, who grows teams, keeps morale high, and drives your team or projects to "strive, stretch, and reach."

Perfect Letter Phrases for Managing Conflict

- Recruited as a contracted trainer for specialized workshop programs, I led programs including stress management, interpersonal communication skills, career management, customer service skills, conflict resolution, understanding and managing change, team-building, assertiveness/self-esteem, and "Who Moved My Cheese?"
- As you mentioned the importance of bridging ideas to a successful conclusion, I acted as liaison between executives, tenants, brokers, and corporation, managing conflict and ensuring shared understanding, accountable for coordination of final agreements.

- As a project leader managing several department contributions, I resolved conflicts between departments to ensure personnel were available for flights, conducted team leader meetings, and resolved all customer problems.
- I developed and led conflict resolution programs in schools linking leadership program with life skills awareness within a Baldridge in Education framework.
- I created an annual culture survey and consulted with management teams on potential suggestions to enhance/improve culture. This resulted in:

  - My organization was responsible for driving change and managing new staffing models utilizing the "workout" change model by leading a team of 30 cross-functional managers:

  - Facilitated several conflict resolution sessions between operations and functional groups

  - Facilitated new manager assimilation sessions

  - Facilitated change management work-out sessions

- Managing conflict successfully has more to do with acting as a coach, not a cop.
- My past successes demonstrate strengths in managing diverse job processes, building and maintaining relationships throughout an organization, motivating staff and colleagues, assessing and developing high potential talent, and managing corporate objectives through major change.
- I attended the following classes in the effort to hone my coaching and interpersonal management skills:

- Managing Conflict: AT&T School of Business, Course MS6431, completed

- Managing People and Performance: AT&T School of Business, Course MD7601, completed October 1993

- Certifications: Numerous technical and managerial courses: Managing People and Performance, Managing Conflict, Communications Workshop, Leadership for the Future, Achieving Communication Effectiveness, and Labor Relations (AT&T School of Business & Technology)

- Conflict can be constructive, but if left to "work itself out," the outcomes are seldom acceptable to all parties. Not only will mismanaged conflict disrupt the best of plans, it also dissipates energy and distracts from your goals.

- A key requirement of any great internal success coach prepares training materials and leads workshops on Stress Management, Understanding and Managing Change (incorporating "Who Moved My Cheese?" materials), Career Development and Advancement.

- In 2006, I was selected local facilitator for the nationwide training broadcasts, Coaching Skills for Managers, Planning and Organizing, Oral Communications and Listening Skills, Training Aids, and Training Technology Update. I am a certified facilitator for group feedback sessions for managerial and support staff who completed the "Performance Development System's" training assessment instrument.

High Employee Satisfaction

High employee satisfaction is essential in recruiting and hiring a quality workforce. Tracking the attitudes and opinions of employees can identify problem areas and solutions related to management and leadership, corporate policy, recruitment, benefits, diversity, training, and professional development. A comprehensive employee satisfaction study can be the key to a more motivated and loyal workforce.

Good managers and good companies realize a happy employee is a productive employee. Poor managers might lead by intimidation, fear, or be too far the other way and appear lackadaisical. A good sports coach knows that to squeeze out that extra level of performance, the athlete must be motivated and driven.

Driven and motivated employees will be more creative and work harder to solve problems because they care about their careers and about the company or organization with whom they work.

For your part in this, you want to be the manager or employee who creates this drive for excellence, who is able to get the team to perform high by being highly satisfied. With your cover letters, if this is an important trait of the hiring manager, you definitely want to address it in a letter or e-mail.

Consider the following phrases for articulating that you have and can create high employee satisfaction.

Perfect Letter Phrases Demonstrating High Employee Satisfaction

- I organized and participated as a lead in task forces set up by management to improve employee satisfaction in 2003, and the results showed a much better rating in 2004.

- Facilitating employee growth through a culture of openness, continuous feedback, and a practice of prompt decision making (most employee concerns addressed within one working day) has made CPG a "Top Company to Work For," according to *Fortune* magazine's 2005 annual review.

- We started employee involvement groups to improve morale and safety, which resulted in one recorded and no loss-time injuries this past year. Our CEO states that morale has never been higher. Employee turnover decreased from 35 to 5 percent.

- As general manager I implemented a performance management process, which created a strong overachieving team with high employee satisfaction and a less than 5 percent turnover rate.

- In 2006, I won the Award of Excellence in recognition of exceptional employee relations for six consecutive years, as voted on by management. This exemplifies the important characteristics of high integrity, loyalty, and dedication.

- Increased productivity 25 percent overall with reduced staff turnover and high employee satisfaction by creating a positive, teamwork environment, setting goals and sharing the vision.

- We consistently achieved high employee satisfaction, resulting in minimal employee attrition numbers. We also maintained a 90 percent or better rate of retention for the senior seasonal staff team, and zero percent turnover for full-time staff for two consecutive years.

- As a Human Resources director, I have always resolved employee/employer issues fairly and effectively, which contributed to high employee satisfaction.
- Our call center productivity improved at least 40 percent and achieved a high employee satisfaction rating as evidenced by an independent study by planning, managing, and monitoring personnel, labor relations, and training.
- The HR organization I led managed a $1 million project that increased office morale, customer service, and diversity ratings, according to T.D. Finley Rating Survey, by 50 percent.
- In 2004 we introduced employee financial/award incentives that improve productivity and reduce absenteeism, resulting in a 15 percent increase in gross profits. That year we achieved the highest percentage of employee advancement in the organization.
- In order to improve employee loyalty and satisfaction, we worked with management to create a program offering free, in-house, leading industry certifications. This program offered employees optional classes in the evenings within our shop for courses leading to certifications such as MCSE and CNE. There were visible improvements with employee satisfaction, and we had a less than 2 percent turnover during the program's two years.
- I have always provided face-to-face contact needed to resolve sensitive employee issues, including terminations, violence in the workplace issues, harassment/discrimination investigations, and labor relations issues. I even partnered with Senior/Executive

➡

Business Leaders to deploy business initiatives and to improve employee satisfaction.

- As the corporate culture champion, I am responsible for department and centerwide employee satisfaction results. Achieved improvement in employee satisfaction through implementation of employee-focused initiatives.

Part III

Individual Performance Phrases

Cost Reduction

It's no coincidence that the most effective cost cutters are companies like Wal-Mart Stores Inc. or Dell Inc., which use technology to keep processes such as inventory management at the cutting edge. Cost reduction in general is a big part of business. It has always had its place, but more since the economic climate softened in 2000. Events since then have compounded the economic instability, and countless companies have made drastic measures to reduce costs to remain viable.

In the telecom industry in particular, cost reduction, not limited to but impacted by workforce reduction, has been paramount for survival.

Here is what you need to be aware of: Cost reduction always has value. You need to position the cost reduction measures in your discipline in association with improved performance of some kind, not just eliminating a workforce or particular product or function. Associate reduction of costs with improved performance and then you'll really have something to talk about.

The phrases below are to be used as a template for articulating a more substantive description of how you drove reduction in costs. You won't be able to use all these exact phrases because some are specific to the given candidate's accomplishments. Use them as a guideline to be more specific rather than general. Don't be vague!

Perfect Letter Phrases for Cost Reduction

■ As the call center director, I reduced costs by redesigning front and back office call center processes for a

$100 million-plus annual inbound operations, which led to a cost reduction of 18 percent per member in FY06.

- I took on an extracurricular project to rewrite and implement a new safety handbook resulting in an immediate 25 percent reduction in workers' compensation claims.

- My finance organization led to the reduction in direct labor cost by $2.5 million on an annual budget of $12 million. We even drove employee incentive programs, which cost-reduced operation by $1 million.

- My team led a successful turnaround from a $1.5 million loss to $.5 million profit in one year; reduced breakeven cost by more than 30 percent, and delivered a 50 percent quality improvement. I led the development of a growth plan for equity investment and refinancing, and implemented key operational changes that drove profitability improvements. We exceeded cost reduction goals by more than 245 percent, delivering over $100,000 in savings in the first year.
[*Note: try to be specific when describing so your message is not vague and does not appear fake or made up. Even this could be more specific.*]

- The transitional team I lead developed the business case for an inbound telemarketing acquisition vehicle, leading to a significant reduction in acquisition costs (14 percent) and to an incremental 2 million annual registrations.

- As plant manager, I supervised the printing plant production and performed efficiency studies of equipment and operations that resulted in waste reduction from 8 to 3.5 percent, and production increases of 15 percent. Customer complaints reduced to zero.

- I led cost reduction and efficiency activities during revenue downturn, improving the bottom line 5 percent despite 13 percent revenue reduction.

- I was assigned as project manager for the PRI, working with "Global Shared Services," to reduce total cost of ownership of digital output devices (printers-copiers-faxes), establishing processes, standards, and enabling Web access and usage monitoring for cost containment and reduction of nonbusiness activities by minimizing unauthorized use. A 10 to 15 percent cost reduction was projected after a complete cost/benefit analysis and equipment inventory was completed.

- We accomplished the reduction of inventory by 24 percent, utilizing MRP [Management Resource Planning], JIT [Just in Time], and Value Managed Partnerships with suppliers.

- I created the first Corporate Inventory Reduction Program, achieving 15 percent reduction in inventories, reducing carrying costs and interest charges.

- My group implemented cost containment strategies for medical and workers' compensation programs.

- As chief negotiator, I lead in negotiations with the UAW and URW. Major achievements in latest UAW contract (6–03) include COLA savings of $1 million and 30 percent reduction in medical absenteeism, saving $2 million.

- While balancing the requirements to have a cost-effective marketing and distribution system with a progressive organization capable of generating explosive growth, I identified cost containment and restructuring opportunities that led to a total 75-basis-point decrease in sales acquisition cost, a 32 percent

➡

reduction while increasing sales $2.3 billion, almost a 50 percent increase. Cost reductions have allowed for additional promotional opportunities, increased price competitiveness, and a self-financed expansion into new distribution channels.

- My leadership over an executive team was responsible for the reduction of over $65 million in annual expenses prior to the purchase of Ameritech by SBC.

Negotiation

Negotiation skills are an important part of business and life. You negotiate every day without even knowing. I negotiate every morning with my wife or son and don't even notice, losing too many to my son, which encroaches on time management, another section!

The strength of your agreements, understandings, and relationships can mean the difference between success and failure. Weak agreements with companies and individuals always break down. They bring nagging dissatisfaction and aggravation into your business and personal lives. Strong agreements help you reach and exceed your own objectives, and leave the other party gaining more satisfaction at the same time.

Negotiating is important for everyone, but particularly for those who work in sales, purchasing, legal, or for any senior level manager.

When you do craft a message around your negotiating skills, be specific. Just saying you have excellent negotiating skills says nothing. You need to offer some specifics to lend credibility.

Perfect Letter Phrases for Negotiating

- Managing $200 million in government contracts and $600 million in proposal efforts required skillful negotiating skills. I led full-life-cycle negotiation and administration of federal government solicitations and contracts for AT&T's government service offerings.
- As a client executive, I negotiated enterprise and nonenterprise agreements with major software and

consulting services suppliers that resulted in substantial cost savings, cost avoidance, and risk mitigation.

- With limited available negotiation leverage, my team renegotiated software support agreements that resulted in dramatic decreases in total costs of ownership for software support and maintenance agreements. In 2006, I attended the Karrass Effective Negotiating Techniques seminar.

- Having led negotiations in both vertical and horizontal environments, I am adept in developing alternative language and resolving disagreements during negotiations with customers, partners, and vendors in international, commercial, and government markets.

- A financial pricing director must be an accomplished contract negotiator and manager, with international work-location experience, and over 10 successful years developing, drafting, negotiating, and managing sales and other customer-related contracts. Typical contracts include: distribution, reseller, OEM, and government.

- In 2004, I negotiated all-time charter business with major oil companies and traders. This included supervising all spot charter negotiations in conjunction with operations, legal, engineering, insurance, financial, and personnel departments. My group negotiated eight overseas new building construction contracts in excess of $400 million.

- I am a professionally certified and highly experienced sourcing, contracts, and procurement manager with diverse and comprehensive domestic and international procurement, strategic sourcing, contract, project

➡

management, logistics management, subcontract management, supplier management, and negotiations experience.

- As the senior contract administrator at Masco, the fifth largest company in Miami, I was responsible for drafting, reviewing, negotiating, and administering contracts relating to commercial aviation; researching federal, state, and international laws and regulations; and making recommendations to senior management on creating compliant company procedures and contractual terms.

- From 1999 to 2004, I was the number three national accounts manager at IBM, servicing existing accounts and developing new accounts, making presentations and negotiating agreements, and closing sales. As a top national accounts manager, negotiating agreements that would breed mutual satisfaction was my strongest suit. In fact, I once negotiated an $18-million agreement with a Wachovia VP over a dinner napkin to close our region's largest sale in 2003.

- As a contract specialist for P&G, I drafted and managed RFPs, RFIs, and RFQs, even working with Legal to create our first boilerplate.

- As the head of legal counsel, I am the lead negotiator for corporate contracts, statements of work, amendments for outsourcing of IT and Finance and Accounting services, and acquisition of information technology and professional services.

- I participated on the negotiating team on the largest alliance in company history: Chrysler strategic alliance ($800-million investment in company as part of overall agreement).

➡

- Reviewed over 200 proposals and worked on 10 teams focused on specific deals (partnerships, strategic equity investments, acquisition, etc.).
- Represented Chrysler corporate development as an advisor to business units and Internet team—targeting, reviewing, negotiating, performing due diligence on projects related to the Internet, devices, applications, and new partnerships and technologies.
- Managed transaction and project pipeline process as well as the unsolicited proposal evaluation process based on Chrysler's strategic priorities for all business units and business development activities.

Oral Presentations

Oral communication skills are critical to the success of individuals and their organizations. This is equally true whether you are communicating one-to-one or one-to–250. A good presentation has the power to deliver your message and the emotional force to move your audience to new ways of thinking and/or behaving.

Delivering oral presentations or having excellent oral presentation skills is important to any position, but perhaps more vital to those in training, sales, marketing, consulting, and to senior management in general. In almost every letter I read, the candidate writes "excellent oral [or presentation] skills." Fine. So what? Everything you write should answer the question, "So what?"

Consider modeling your phrases the way the following more specific phrases are written.

Perfect Letter Phrases for Oral Presentations

- As a trainer for ACR, I develop and deliver presentations that excite and inform. Excellence in training skills include developing and delivering training curriculum, including the presentations and workbooks.
- My experience as an engaging speaker and seminar leader, sales presenter, and technical management liaison has made me the most skilled motivator in the organization. I have a natural ability to work with others, influence C-level decision making, and promote company products and services to a wide range of targeted prospects, alliance partners, and vendor leaders.

➡

- I have presented to more than 30 Fortune 500 CXOs in the effort to practice consultative sales techniques, uncovering the needs of the client, and developing valuable solutions.
- I have effectively promoted company products through oral presentations in a variety of venues, including trade shows and conferences, to create exciting "buzz." I am regularly requested to speak at industry trade conferences [*you might be more specific here*] and global billing and trade shows.
- I have delivered over a thousand lectures, primarily for Ford Motor Company, Fidelity, and Anderson Consulting, and am recognized by *Marketing and Sales* magazine as one of the top 10 speakers in the United States. In 1999, I was recognized by the WTC in Dallas as "America's number one motivational technology speaker."
- In 2005, I wrote the keynote speech for a motivational speaker. I doubled the original content through extensive research and interviews, and made countless revisions to make the tone and texture of the language sound consistent with the speaker's personal style. The presentation received excellent audience feedback and a repeat invitation from the speaker for the 2006 CTIA show.
- As a marketing and motivational speaker, I participated in training classes through the delivery of entertaining and informative lectures to middle and high school students. Topics include those that encourage and support self-confidence, social skills, etc. The audience number ranged from 30 to 300 plus.

➡

- Communication includes effective speaking and writing skills. As an experienced public speaker: I conducted training seminars for candidates, volunteers, and party activists; served as a liaison between different personality types; am comfortable and effective communicating with both superiors and staff.
- You mentioned team-building is critical to success in this position. At my current employer, I am an organizational leader, trainer, and educator recognized for my ability to merge dissimilar people into cohesive teams with common focus.

Organizational Skills

I interviewed a candidate named Steve some time ago and hired him based on his ability to manage multiple projects simultaneously. His résumé listed: "Excellent organizational skills." Then I worked with him, and within 90 days it proved to be blatantly untrue. Steve could not plan or manage multiple projects or issues simultaneously. Sometimes I wondered how I missed it during the interview. I was faked out. I now discount that phrase "excellent organizational skills" as a hiring manager unless it is supported.

That's the key—to support the skill with some backup, so it seems credible, and not with cover letter fluff. Consider the following phrases and how they are supported. Notice that the actual phrase "organizational skills" is not always present; it is implied, which is perhaps even more powerful.

Perfect Letter Phrases Demonstrating Organizational Skills

- My 15 years experience in managing multiple projects simultaneously, including the ability to work under pressure, meet tight deadlines, and utilize problem-solving skills to ensure projects met stated goals and objectives, is a very good fit for your operations management position.
- My success lies in leading revenue generation programs with particular skill in managing multiple projects simultaneously from concept to completion.
- I consistently bring projects to a successful finish on time and on budget by successfully managing multiple projects simultaneously and effectively managing my time.

➥

- In 2005, I was promoted to lead the Project Management Team. I managed all aspects of the division's business and systems projects by preparing and managing project plans, scheduling and facilitating status meetings, and evaluating and analyzing cost-benefit relationships.

- As a principle at Arrow Consulting, project management for marketing programs is a cornerstone of successful engagements and in building a client base. I am experienced in all areas of targeted marketing, retail management, and ad production and printing, and at managing multiple projects simultaneously.

- My organization led a strategic marketing plan for the company, researched and evaluated new safety software, provided detailed case research and accident reconstruction support for ongoing litigation, and published press releases, all of which contributed to a successful IPO in 2006.

- Working with cross-functional teams, I achieve win-win outcomes through strong organizational skills with an acute attention to detail, ability to manage multiple projects simultaneously, and excellent analytical, follow-through, and decision-making skills.

- As managing account executive, I am responsible for marketing, coordinating, and managing vendor services for large corporate accounts. My group represented multiple regional vendor services, specializing in workers' compensation, auto, medical malpractice, and disability insurance, requiring excellent organizational skills and project planning.

- I was recruited to provide risk, logistics, inventory, facility and warehouse operations management, including

➡

personnel supervision, for a leading remanufacturer of consumer electronic products. This position requires excellent organizational skills in order to manage all functional areas properly. Responsibilities included coordinating international logistics between multiple manufacturing and refurbishment centers, and establishing and managing the reverse logistics department, handling over 15,000 units per year.

- At Cisco Systems, I managed the partner program support, including the production and distribution of Electronic Partner Packages, multiple collateral projects (data sheets and Division Overview brochure), trade show collateral, and signage requirements.

- A successful coordinator effectively manages integrated marketing programs with limited resources from development and implementation to program reporting and analysis. I am experienced at consulting with teams to understand their needs, uncovering opportunities, and recommending creative ideas and solutions. I also have proven skills in organizing, prioritizing, and managing multiple projects simultaneously on time and budget.

- My sales support organization interfaced with three regional sales centers and with field marketing to develop projects targeting installed customers to increase customer loyalty. Under my leadership we developed and managed integrated marcom projects from concept to completion.

- I managed the creative development of sales literature, including product software specification sheets, brochures, reference guides, and case studies. Success lay

➡

in ensuring completion of projects on time and within budget guidelines. I worked with various agencies regarding copywriting, design, and print production, managing multiple projects simultaneously.

- I was recruited to develop a communication strategy to ensure that group goals were being tracked and that they met project deadlines. While I was the managing partner, I developed streamlined project tracking processes that resulted in acquisitions of over $53 million, while managing multiple projects simultaneously with outside vendors.

- The plant for which I was responsible increased production efficiency by an average of 14 percent annually for three years. I accomplished this by managing multiple projects simultaneously, including client relations, schedules, and deadlines.

Problem Solving

A manager's primary function is to solve problems. A manager's understanding of the problem-solving style he or she most often uses is an essential early step to becoming a more effective and creative problem solver.

Managers tend to deal with problems in one of three ways:

1. **Avoid them.** Refuse to recognize that a problem exists. Not quite the strongest managers, but I have had the pleasure of knowing some of these folks. Some people just don't understand most problems do not self-correct.

2. **Solve them as necessary.** Deal with the urgent. Better, but still not senior management material.

3. **Seek them out.** Anticipate, to avoid the problems becoming urgent. You want to be here! This is where you need to position yourself and represent your skills on your résumé and during the interview.

Perfect Letter Phrases for Problem Solving

- I have always been a creative problem solver. My experience moving beyond limiting questions and nurturing problem-solving ideas through each of four phases of creative problem solving has resulted in a very solid foundation.

- As a hospital administrator, success has included strategic thinking and 10 years of solving design, communication, and process problems.

- Having been promoted to account management with Chiat-Day, a leading advertising firm, I managed all print and presentation projects, exceeding a 95 percent on-time rate. I handled project tracking, system/file management, estimating, budget/billing, vendor billing, and liaisons with all clients.

- A veteran production manager, I am experienced with quality assurance, problem solving, streamlining processes, and optimizing production work flow. Succeeding in my position requires extensive experience in project management, creating intuitive business collateral, Internet promotion, and developing proactive marketing strategies.

- My strength is a problem-solving ability: analyzing the symptoms, identifying what is wrong, and finding the solution.

- At Ford Motor, I implemented the following structured programs and methods into the engineering department: Advanced Quality Planning, Dimensional Control Plan Plus, Failure Mode and Effects Analysis, Design of Experiments, Quality Operating System, 8-D Problem Administration, and Planning & Problem Solving.

- A core strength of mine is overseeing multiple tasks with varying priorities, working with many departments within an organization to ensure smooth operation, identifying areas of improvement, as well as researching, developing, and implementing improved procedures. An example includes … [*Use one relevant to the target company's business.*]

- My vice president has always recognized my ability in problem solving, with a strong background in methods and time studies for setting production standards. This is

➡

particularly relevant in assessing and resolving employee conflicts and organizational problems, allowing for increased productivity.

- I developed strategic relationships with various department heads and suppliers, which significantly improved communication and problem-resolution capabilities within the organization.

- I have applied strong interpersonal and communication skills in working with a wide range of personnel at all levels to gain valuable insight, avoid potential problems, and facilitate the timely completion of projects.

- As a claims manager, I successfully implemented customer deductions programs, which identified problem areas within the corporation and reported results. I then made recommendations to senior management on a daily basis in written review summaries.

Time Management

Time management is a vital skill for a successful person, in any discipline. No question. So many people think they have it and so few do. I had a vice president several years ago who used to say, "Give me someone smart, passionate, and who knows how to use their time, and we can give them the experience." Same with time management for me. It's vital to success. If you can convey that you effectively manage multiple projects simultaneously, you will be much more valuable to your prospective employer. Then call me because I want you working with me!

Don't let anyone steal your time. It is priceless and should be guarded with care. Benjamin Franklin once said, "Dost thou love life? Then do not squander time, for that is the stuff life is made of." More recently, Henry Kissinger, former Secretary of State said, "There cannot be a crisis next week. My schedule is already full." Needless to say, the most valuable commodity in the world is time. It is easily wasted and can never be replaced; therefore, time management is essential.

Consider the following phrases, employed to convince employers that these candidates use their time effectively.

Perfect Letter Phrases for Time Management

- While a district manager with Lane Bryant, sales and time management skills were required for success:

  - Conducted training needs assessments for 23 stores to determine training shortfalls and needs

  - Attended several sales and time management courses (i.e., Covey, Franklin, Career Path)

- Developed and conducted specific training courses that addressed the needs of our business

- Provided consultation services in time management training to four other peer district managers

- Excelling as a plant manager in a large-scale production environment requires excellent time management skills and the ability to meet deadlines and work under pressure. My team led productivity targets by leading the floor, training the staff, and anticipating problems before they occurred.

- [Hiring manager], you mentioned being successful in this role requires strong time management skills. While general manager for Aramark, my success required finding out how much time is worth, concentrating on the right things, deciding work priorities, planning to solve a problem, tackling the right tasks first through prioritized "to do" lists, and executing the plan timely.

- As advertising account manager I utilized extensive project coordination, prioritization, and details/time management techniques to keep all schedules on track and time sensitive projects on time and on budget.

- I am certified in time management through the Franklin Covey Education series.

- At SE Toyota, I sponsored an 80:20 program, which argues that typically 80 percent of unfocused effort generates only 20 percent of results. The remaining 80 percent of results are achieved with only 20 percent of the effort. This led to a new initiative to improve time management skills of 670-plus employees. The company estimates we improved productivity by 17 percent the first year, very high by industry standards.

- I assisted in the implementation of SAP R/3 as the time management deployment lead, and directed the implementation of the time management module at each factory site. I also assumed the lead site payroll and HR personnel with data mapping and conversion, and instructed site power users and end users in time management training classes.

- Having been promoted to senior project manager, I demonstrated how to prioritize tasks, organize and coordinate activities, manage time, set and achieve goals, meet deadlines, develop relationships, and establish procedures.

- I assisted the production coordinator by leading the floor, training the staff, and pulling statistics. Skills used include: time management, ability to meet strict deadlines, and the ability to work under pressure.

- Your [position] requires an organized, detail-oriented, and self-motivated professional with excellent time management, prioritization, and multiple task/project coordination skills. I have demonstrated that in my past two positions, and my ability to manage time effectively was the main reason I earned an internal promotion.

- My current role as project manager enabled me to become certified in an active listening course, Decker Communication Course, and Franklin Time Management.

- Time management to me is the ability to manage multiple assignments and maintain quality of service under fast-paced conditions.

- I trained the clients' project team and determined the global template functionality for the global project team

➡

in the U.S. Duties included project plan preparation, progress reporting, training of local project team, determining local requirements, identification and specification of system interfaces, final configuration of the system, and system and acceptance testing. Modules configured and implemented were PA, PD, Training and Events, Recruitment, and Time Management.

- Effective time management required me to list out tasks, prioritize them, and map out execution of them all. I do not procrastinate, but rather use my time wisely, plan exceptionally, and employ the Covey planning system.

Written Skills

Having written a dozen books on topics like this book, I am biased concerning the importance of writing in business. I majored in accounting and never thought about the importance of writing early in my career. In fact, pride had more to do with my attention to detail in writing than anything: I never wanted to be caught with a typo or obvious incorrect grammar and have the reader think I was less professional or not queued to be promoted.

Good writing skills are an absolute reflection on your professional skills. Much of it is in proofreading and some attention to detail. I'll tell you this: When you write poorly, people think less of you professionally.

Demonstrating excellent writing skills begins with writing letters and e-mails. What follows are some phrases to consider to prove that you do in fact have excellent writing skills. Note how detailed and specific some of the descriptions are written. As a hiring manager, I would not doubt the writing skills of candidates like these.

Perfect Letter Phrases for Writing Skills

- In preparation for the 2006 CES Show, I wrote preview briefs for two clients that were used at industry seminars.
- As a product manager, I built briefing books for clients utilizing information obtained from various sources.
- My accomplishments include validating other consultants' plans, thoughts, and presentations for their clients. I provide consulting, business plan and market plan assistance, preparation for multiple presentations,

➡

marketing brochures, and mailing programs for a diversity of companies.

- I worked with creative directors and training managers to develop, implement, create, and design staff instruction manuals, newsletters, Web pages, policy and procedure manuals, and announcements to publicize various training programs using Excel, PowerPoint, Word, and Lotus Notes.

- I led the layout, design, and production of printed materials, including newsletters, brochures, slides, graphs, and other visual PowerPoint presentation materials. I created Excel/Access spreadsheets, database, word processing, and graphics computer software programs.

- My support role requires being highly resourceful, possessing strong merchandising and visual presentation skills, and strong attention to detail. I also have a keen sense of color, balance, and scale. Past accomplishments include drafting the sales boilerplate, presentations, and statement of work outlines.

- As a client manager, I led the client communications, product branding, product rollouts (creative and tactical implementation), communication templates, proposal style guides, process documentation, and ad campaign development.

- A successful marketing communications copywriter writes copy for marketing pieces, including but not limited to product sheets, press releases, brochures and flyers, ad copy, board reports, and client communications, which I have done with much success for PepsiCo for the past two years.

➡

- Currently I am senior technical writer under contract to Sprint. There, I developed the Sprint Proposal Library, which included writing and editing proposal materials, proposal boilerplate, forms, templates, technical manuals, technical requirements, and design reports.
- I served as Web editor responsible for writing and maintaining content, including service offering descriptions, value propositions, FAQs, news items, and seed content for online community. Key accomplishments include:

  - Manage content administration for Web site, including updates, revisions, and posting of new material (ATG/Interwoven content management system).
  - Redevelopment of Web sites, including page design, site structure, and navigation.
  - Researched, developed, and wrote Web-based, interactive business training (included instructional story and material); quizzes and tutoring; expert interviews and audio; glossary and FAQs; conceptualized and worked with tech staff to develop multimedia component that reinforced instructional material.
  - Developed informational resource articles on work/life issues; identified new areas and ideas for development, including resources, tools, and potential alliance partners.

Part IV

Job-Search-Related Phrases

Follow-Up Letters

I interviewed a regional manager candidate about a year ago and was on the fence: He was amply qualified—maybe too qualified—and I questioned his desire and commitment. I decided to wait it out and see what he did following the interview. I never heard from him, and moved forward with another candidate.

In many cases, the difference between success and failure is follow-up. Most people send out a résumé and expect that someone will call. It is not a strategy that breeds accomplishment. The mission is to produce actions—interviews and meetings. Follow-up letters are tools to inspire such action when original tactics fall short of expectation.

Perfect Phrases for Follow-Up Letters

- After reviewing my notes from our conversation, it is evident that you require a dynamic person who will not only generate sales revenue, but also play an integral part in maintaining International's position as a "leading edge" supplier of world-class packaging equipment. In my present role, I do this every day.

- After reviewing my résumé, perhaps you may think that I am overqualified and my compensation exceeds the level of pay anticipated for this particular position. To put your concerns to rest, the opportunity to join your group is an opportunity I do not want to pass by. Although my compensation has averaged $115,000, my salary requirements are flexible, considering future opportunities for growth within the organization. I would welcome a personal interview to further discuss the search and am confident that the outcome would be beneficial to future

➡

KPMG business results. I appreciate you passing this information along.

- Again, thank you for meeting with me and affording an opportunity to discuss the position with you and Ms. Jennings. If I can answer any further questions, please feel free to contact me at the telephone number listed above. I look forward to speaking with you soon.

- I am confident that my strengths will help you to create a greater customer focus, which will in turn boost earnings and raise morale. Could we speak soon about my possible contributions to Smyth Insurance? Thank you for your time; I eagerly await the opportunity to meet with you in person.

- Our meeting at the end of the day revealed that my technical capabilities could fit into a number of areas at Dartwalsh. My conversation with Mike Tarmew concerning laser technology and high-speed through-put leads me to believe that this is an area where you may have a need I can fill. However, I remain open to exploring a variety of opportunities to find the best match. I will call you next Friday morning to set up another meeting.

- I am writing to follow up on the letter and résumé I sent you on February 16 last year. You were recruiting for a product manager with experience in voice and data integration and experience selling in the Fortune 250 arena. I am a product manager with IBM with four years of product sales experience and have presented to over 30 CXOs from the Fortune 250.

- I want to thank you for your candor in explaining why you did not choose me for the position I interviewed for two years ago. I understand that you wanted someone with

➡

more than my one year of experience in health-care administration. I now have three years of experience.

- Nearly a year ago you and I met to discuss an opening in your sales department. We were in the process of setting up a second meeting when I called to let you know that I had accepted a position at Haverty's.

- May I ask whether you are still recruiting for your accounting office, for which I applied on January 30?

- I know you have been away on business, but I am wondering if you received my letter of January 7. I sent you a brief business plan outlining what I would do if given the opportunity to lead the new marketing initiative we discussed.

- In response to your district manager posting of August 18, I forwarded my résumé, two references, and a cover letter. Since I have received no response, I am wondering if my materials failed to reach you. My background is a very close fit with the position requirements described.

- As a follow-up to our telephone conversation of May 16, here is an updated copy of my résumé.

- During our telephone conversation yesterday afternoon you offered to forward my résumé to your Springfield office. Here is an updated copy that I would appreciate you sending. Thank you very much for your help.

Internal Job Search

Pursuing job opportunities internally is much different than pursuing them externally. The biggest difference is spin and positioning. While you should always be truthful when representing your qualifications externally, your spin is severely limited, communicating internally versus externally.

Externally, no one really knows if you were the nerve center behind Apple's resurgence with the iPod or not. However, if you work for Apple, well, your qualifications are much more widely known and can be validated.

There are pluses and minuses to each form of communication. With an internal communication, you need to leverage two things: relationships and accomplishments. Internal sponsorship is critical to moving around internally or particularly in getting promoted internally. I recall my first director position, which I took several years ago. When I interviewed with the vice president, he expressed two potential concerns before bringing me on.

Once I understood them, I rallied all my supporters from within the organization and scripted them with key messages to offset his concerns. Some were written in e-mail form and some were voice mail. The point is to leverage relationships.

Below are some great introductory phrases for internal letters, usually e-mails.

Perfect Phrases for Internal Job Search

- Mr. Levin, Lisa Pearman suggested I contact you about the new senior engineering manager position in your group. I have worked for Lisa for two years and she speaks very highly of you and encouraged me to contact you, thinking it would be a great mutual fit.

- As you know, I have worked with you for two years as Marketing Manager of P&G's soap division. As we discussed yesterday, I am ready to move on to the Group Manager position in the family products group. As my director, you have been able to observe that contribution firsthand. But I felt it would be a good idea to take inventory of my achievements.

- I am writing to formally express interest in being considered as a candidate for the Field Service Revenue Administration Manager. I have attached an up-to-date copy of my résumé as well as a memo detailing salient project accomplishments over the past 18 months. I present the following highlights …

- As a seasoned sales manager with Wagner and Poles (four years as Sales Manager, seven years total), I am armed with extensive expertise in developing new business, turning around sluggish sales, and significantly impacting growth and profits. I believe I am well qualified for the position of National Key Account Manager within our organization, and have enclosed a résumé outlining my highlights and contributions with regard to Wagner and Poles.

Networking

Networking is widely recognized as the most effective technique in securing employment opportunities. Networking is the process of engaging your network of family, friends, and associates to help you identify and obtain the job you desire. I think of networking as connecting dots, creating your own six degrees of separation.

The networking cover letter is a letter communicating to your network of contacts that you are seeking advice and information, not a job as the short-term objective. The letter clearly defines your skills, what types of opportunities you are seeking, and specific organizations you'd like to work for. It is still true, like it or not, that it is not so much *what* you know that counts but *who* you know.

An effectively written networking letter will help you (1) to take full advantage of your network of contacts or (2) to begin developing/improving a network to expand your influence.

Below are some terrific phrases designed to help you craft a great networking letter that will help you reach the decision makers in the industries and companies you target.

Perfect Phrases for Networking Letters

■ Dave Tinker from Cellcorp suggested I contact you. He said that you "know more about the network router business than anyone this side of the Mason-Dixon line." I knew you would be someone I had to meet. Though I am employed with Bell Atlantic, I have decided to make a career move toward a more entrepreneurial upstart operation. I am not writing you for a position, but rather wanted to get some industry advice from you ...

- I don't know if you will remember, but we met when your firm was doing some auditing work for Texas Oil. I was performing some legal work, as I am an attorney specializing in environmental law. I was very impressed with you and your team, and have a small favor to ask. I have been with my firm for some time and am interested in leaving in favor of a smaller firm. You seemed to know a lot about the industry as well as who's who in Dallas, and I'd like to ask your advice on the business climate here.

- Thanks for speaking with me on the phone earlier. I agree that there probably isn't a good match between your current positions and me to fill. However, you did mention that based on our phone interview you thought my credentials were strong, and it got me thinking. Would you mind if we still met? I am new to the New York area, as my husband was just transferred, and it looks like we'll be here for quite a while. You seemed to be fairly well connected and in the know as to what's going on here. I would love to meet just to get your advice on which firms I might avoid, which ones might be good, and what the overall climate is like in New York.

- May I ask your advice and assistance? As you know, for the last eight years I've been continuously challenged with new marketing assignments for PepsiCo and I've delivered impressive sales and profit gains for all of the brands I've managed. Grace, since you know my abilities and potential to contribute, would you take a moment to think about people I can contact at large manufacturing/consumer goods businesses in the Cincinnati area? I'm confident that I can bring to my next employer the same strong results I delivered for PepsiCo … In addition to any contacts you

➡

can suggest, I would greatly appreciate your insight with regard to the Cincinnati job market. To assist you in evaluating appropriate contacts and suggestions, I have enclosed a …

- I need your advice. You are a friend who has developed a fast track career, one of the company's youngest directors. I am at a career crossroads and would like to get your opinion of what you think of my current position versus a new opportunity I am considering. I'd prefer to speak to you directly about this rather than go into detail in a letter. Could we get together sometime next week to discuss my situation? I'll give you a call in the next few days to set a time. Thank you for your time.

Reference Letters

A reference letter is delivered under the writer's signature, but they will likely want your help for two reasons:

First, it takes a lot of time to sit down and create a letter like this.

Second, give them some idea of how to spin the tone and subject. Give them some information about the position or company and help them position you in the most effective light. After they write the letter, make sure you get a copy, even if they send it directly to the employer/recruiter.

In the end, however, it is recommended that you write the *outline* for the reference letter yourself. Superstars don't write the ads we see on television. The advertising agencies and marketing departments do. You are your own marketing department unless you also hire marketing professionals.

Perfect Phrases for Reference Letters

■ We have had the pleasure of associating with [you, the candidate] over the past seven years with MCI and Alcalon Systems. In my 30-plus years in the business, all with Xerox, I have never met a more professional, talented, or personable warehouse manager.

■ [Your name] is a strong and formidable negotiator. He always has the best interest of his company at heart. He is fair and always looks for a win-win solution to any negotiation.

■ [Your name] is a loyal and dedicated professional who will enhance any company. His value, when measured against his peers, is truly head and shoulders above the rest. Proctor and Gamble will be pleased to provide you with any additional information you need. Contact me at ➡

the above address, and I will quickly respond to your inquiries.

■ Any company fortunate to have [you, the candidate] as marketing manager has a true advantage in today's highly competitive economic climate. UOS has benefited from [your] expertise in management, employee, and customer relations for 12 years. [Your] independent management style allowed UOS to grow 480 percent over a 12-year period, and [you] kept his warehouse operations one step ahead of the rest of the competition.

■ We all but begged [your name] to relocate to our new headquarters, but he felt that relocation to Chicago would not be in the best interest of his family.

■ A true professional, [your name] is an indispensable asset to any organization. His team leadership skills, together with his visionary expertise, are unparalleled. Please feel free to contact me personally should you require any further information.

■ I have worked with [you] for over eight years. There is no greater team player when it comes to any type of management. He listens to all parties concerned, sees the big picture, and has the confidence and foresight to integrate everyone's ideas to come up with a comprehensive plan that works for the company. He will sacrifice his own beliefs when it comes to the good of the company. However, that does not often happen because he has such an exacting pulse on the industry specifically and in economics and business in general.

■ I was hired by [you] in 1983. Of the 12 interviews I went on, [your name] was the most professional, trustworthy, and honest hiring manager I encountered. He explained to me

➡

the pros and the cons of the job, and explicitly stated what he expected short- and long-term. He also clearly noted that he was there to train, develop, and coach us all to success.

- Apollo Dreams began operations in 1962 with zero sales. We had a new marketing concept that was different from anything existing on the market at that time. Most people resist change—not [your name]. He listened to our ideas, added some of his own, and, as a result was instrumental in assisting Apollo to its current market position as a $43 million company poised to go international and positioned for explosive growth.

- At a time when [you] could have enjoyed the relationships [you] had with other firms, [you] saw maintaining those relations was important while opening new markets. [You] got the president of his company to look at our program, negotiated a highly profitable arrangement for Vicene Horizontal, and gave us a chance. Today we sell over $3 million of our product, and [you] gave us credibility in the market.

- [You] saw the benefit to his customer and his company. He is a man of his word, a man of integrity, and a bottom-line progressive management professional. He helped make Stanford Designs what it is today and where it will go tomorrow. Anyone who hires him is truly fortunate to experience his professionalism.

Requesting Career Advice

- I am writing to ask your advice about careers in the consumer products industry. John Smith told me you have really enjoyed your career at PepsiCo and I would love to get some industry advice from you.

- I need your advice regarding whether I should take a position in management or stay in sales. Since you can view me objectively, your insight would be very valuable.

- John, Pamela Alts suggested I contact you. She shared with me the growth you and your company have experienced the past three years and, knowing me, thought I would be a good fit in that industry. I am not asking to meet with you about a current position with your company, but merely want to get some advice and learn more about the g-nome business. I will call you Thursday to try to get on your calendar.

- Michael, I know I have not worked for you in several years, but I need some advice. You know me professionally as well as anyone. I am considering a career change, from the health-care field to, of all things, managing a furniture store. Can we schedule 15 to 20 minutes to talk so I can get your advice?

- Since you have successfully changed your profession, I am hoping you can give me some advice on a career change. I understand you went through a successful career change two years ago and it has worked out well for you. Maybe it's time I leave this company too and get a fresh start. I'd love your opinion on it.

- John, I know you hate giving advice, but I need your experience on my side. I have the opportunity to buy out another fisherman's fleet at the end of the season. The trouble is, this will put us in a real bind financially next

➡

season. I hope you will come on down. I will take you to lunch and we can look at the numbers together. I trust your judgment more than my own. I look forward to hearing from you.

- Jane, you are the one person I feel I can consult on this. I just got an opportunity to move to a competitor within the same industry. It represents a management, responsibility, and salary increase, but also involves a higher risk venture. I have been at Concorp for seven years and have a lot of stability in my position, 401(k) and vacation time, etc., and am not sure if I should take the risk. May we get together over lunch this week to discuss the opportunity and your thoughts?

- Greg, I am coming to you seeking advice on a personal matter because you have known me since college and I admire your life experiences and how your career has developed at Ford. I know also that you will honor my request for confidentiality.

- I need your advice. You are a friend who seems to know the right things to do in managing your career. I have taken a more passive approach and decided to take my career into my own hands and develop a plan. I'd love to speak to you directly about this rather than go into detail in a letter. Could we get together sometime next week to discuss my situation? I'll give you a call in the next few days to set a time. Thanks in advance for your time.

- Thanks so much for the advice you offered last week. Those who learn from others' experience are usually a step ahead of the rest. I am going to take your advice and pursue another opportunity. I believe you are correct in your assessment that sometimes you need to change companies in order to get ahead.

Resignation

Over my career to date, I have resigned from four different positions. Now, everyone, especially when you are more junior in your career, dreams of walking out or leaving your previous manager, if you did not like them or the company, with short notice to pay them back for any mistreatment they may have felt.

Don't EVER do that. At each one of my resignations, I left with as much class as when I started. One, it is the right thing to do, and two, a poor exit can erase years of hard work. It is the lasting impression. If you leave with as much commitment as normal, your peers and management will marvel at your commitment and professionalism. If you start coming in late, leaving early, blowing off tasks, or leave with short notice, it will be your legacy.

Some brief tips:

- Prepare your resignation: Remove your personal items from your office, clean up your computer files (leave any important work files with guides to where they are), try to wrap up any key projects.

- Give proper notice. They may not accept two weeks, but offer it.

- Offer to help train a replacement or help recruit a replacement.

- Ask for a letter of recommendation. This may ensure a good reference if needed later.

- Say good-bye with class. No negative comments as you walk out the door.

Perfect Phrases for Resigning

- This is to inform you that an opportunity has presented itself that will enable me to work in the area of my stated preference. Therefore, I am tendering my resignation from your company. The last day of my employment will be two weeks from today, May 23, 20__. At that time I shall deliver all property of the firm in my possession. Thank you for the experience of having worked for D&G, a truly outstanding organization.

- I am sorry to inform you that circumstances dictate I must resign from my position as Division Manager. I will gladly comply with the company's request to give two weeks termination notice.

- Each year my financial obligations have increased; unfortunately, my salary here has not been able to keep up with these demands. As a result, I have been forced to reconsider my employment here and have concluded that it would be best for me to seek an employment opportunity to better meet my financial requirements. It is with mixed emotions that I have accepted a position elsewhere that carries a higher salary with possibilities for future advancement. Please accept my thanks for the opportunity to work with you. The guidance you have given me has proved invaluable and has prepared me well for my new position. I have enjoyed the challenges presented here at Doe's, and I sincerely hope that I have returned adequate service for all the benefits that I have received.

- I would be happy to help you find and train a suitable replacement. Because my projects are current and because I have left detailed instructions illustrating how to perform my job duties on my desk, my successor should have little difficulty assuming my responsibilities. Please let me know if there is anything else I can do to help make this a smooth transition.

- Please accept my regrets in resigning from my position as Marketing Manager, effective two weeks from today's date. Eager to pursue new challenges, I have decided to accept a job offer in a field more closely aligned with my course of study. My new position will put my talents and interests to work in a new and exciting area. Although I have accepted a position in another field, it does not detract from the fact that my job at AT&T has provided me pleasure as well as insight into my hopes for the future. I have enjoyed working with all of my friends here, and I want to thank everyone for their support over the years. When my resignation date arrives, I expect all my projects to be current and my obligations fulfilled. If there is anything else I can do to help make this a smooth transition, please let me know.

- Please accept this letter as official notification of my resignation from my position as Floor Manager, effective immediately. Financial considerations and a desire to further my career compel me to accept a job offer from a company that is better able to fill my present needs. Although I am disappointed that size constraints placed upon the company deny rapid upward mobility, I feel deeply indebted to you for skills I have acquired and experience I have gained. My job here has been a great source of personal satisfaction and a foundation from which I have cultivated many irreplaceable ties with coworkers.

➡

- My last day of being a manager at Square D will be two weeks from Friday, as I am resigning to accept another position. I have been offered a Human Resource position and I am anxious to make a career change. I will, however, be happy to answer any questions or concerns the new manager may have, regardless of where I am employed. Thank you for all you have done for me. I appreciate the opportunities and friendships I have enjoyed here.

- Regretfully, I must inform you that I need to resign from my position here as office manager. In accordance with company policy, I am offering two weeks notice, effective today. Please know that I am grateful for the trust and confidence that you have placed in me in the last three years. I especially appreciated the opportunity to convert the paper files in the order department to a computerized system. I believe that similar conversions in other departments, though time-consuming in the beginning, would greatly benefit the company in the long run.

- I have been offered a position as Technology Specialist in a larger company and I feel I must accept. Although the higher salary was one factor in my decision, I will also have a greater opportunity to use my degree in computer science. Of course, I will be happy to help train a replacement while I am here. The new manager is also free to call me at home or e-mail me with any questions after I leave. All of my files have been backed up on CD-R and are labeled appropriately. Please let me know if there is anything else I can do to help make this transition as trouble free as possible.

Thank-You Letters

Don't underestimate the power of a thank-you letter. Immediately after a round of interviews, always send a thank-you letter to each of your interviewers by fax, mail, or e-mail.

E-mail is the quickest way to get thank-you letters in front of interviewers, and is perfectly acceptable these days. But avoid using cutesy Net stuff, like emoticons (e.g., happy faces), shorthand and acronyms (e.g., *u* for "you" and *TIA* for "thanks in advance"). Regardless of how you send them, follow professional, business letter standards. Near the end of your interviews, ask each interviewer for his or her contact information and correct name spelling, or just ask for a business card.

Most interviewers expect you to send thank-you letters. It's also an effective interviewing strategy. For example, it:

- Shows that you are courteous, knowledgeable, and professional
- Demonstrates your written communication skills, so make sure you double-proof it and read it aloud before sending
- Helps to make you stand out in the minds of the interviewers
- Elevates you above competing candidates who didn't bother to write them
- Gives you an opportunity to reinforce your good points
- Allows you to include something important you forgot to mention during your interview
- Confirms your understanding of topics discussed and helps to avoid misunderstandings

When sending a thank-you letter to the hiring manager or recruiter, it is important to lead with a section restating your understanding of their needs: what success in this position

➡

means to them. Then you want to quickly review that your skills and experience match their needs. Then let them know of your interest and when you will contact them to follow up.

When sending would-be peers a thank-you note, make it briefer. Thank them for their time, recall a comment from the interview, and mention that you would welcome the opportunity to work with them. Then sign off.

Perfect Phrases for Thank-You Letters

- Thank you for scheduling my interviews for the engineering manager opportunity. I am pleased with the benefits Lockheed offers and impressed with its long-term outlook and programs in the works. I'd greatly appreciate the chance to contribute to its future success. After completing my interviews today, I am confident that my qualifications are in line with your requirements. As promised, I will fax my completed job application to you by tomorrow afternoon. I've double-checked with my references and they are all available to talk with you.
- Thank you for taking the time to discuss employment opportunities at GMC with me.
- I appreciate your courtesy and the time you took to answer my questions during my visit this morning.
- Thank you for the pleasant interview we had on Monday. You were very helpful in explaining the job requirements.
- Thank you for meeting with me yesterday. I appreciate your insights and advice.
- I appreciated our meeting in your office yesterday and found the interview very informative.
- Thank you for the time and courtesy you extended to me at our interview this morning.

- Meeting with you yesterday was a pleasure. I appreciate the time you took out of your busy schedule as well as the information you gave me.

- Thank you for giving me the opportunity to learn more about the management position currently available at the Platery plant.

- I appreciate the time you took yesterday to discuss the possibility of my becoming the head nurse at Columbia Health Center.

- Thank you for meeting with me today to discuss the new opportunity in your group. What CFW is doing in the new consumer markets space is indeed exciting. To successfully launch the new campaign, you will likely need someone experienced at marketing and distribution. As I mentioned in our interview, I led the team that successfully launched Frito-Lays new Star Wars campaign …

- Thank you for taking the time to interview me yesterday for the Department Secretary position. You emphasized that managing multiple projects simultaneously and attention to detail are critical needs for you. I learned a great deal about multitasking as a partner's legal secretary as well as the importance of accuracy in my work. I believe I could work well with your faculty and staff; in fact, it would be a pleasure to work with them. I will call you Friday to speak with you in more detail about the position.

- I appreciate the opportunity I had yesterday to interview with you. Our meeting reminded me of the reason I first considered your company for employment, namely, your reputation for friendly service. I believe that in today's competitive market it is friendly service that gives a competitive edge in keeping customers coming back. I gained that conviction during experience in public relations with the FGH Corporation. If hired, I promise to uphold your company's reputation for friendly, efficient service. I look forward to hearing from you.

- It was kind of you to meet with me this afternoon to discuss the group manager opportunity with Nokia. As we discussed your objectives and my background, it became clear that my knowledge, skills, and work experience have prepared me well to join your Programming Department. It would be a pleasure to work among such giants in the industry. I am certain I can replicate the success I realized at HP within your group at Nokia.

- Thanks so much for taking the time to speak with me this morning. I am very excited about the merger between Compaq and HP and the leadership position the new company will serve in the consumer space. Having managed the PR for the AWS/Cingular merger, my experience merging two technical industry giants will lend valuable experience in anticipating challenges and Wall Street perceptions as you merge these two brands and organizations.

- Thank you for interviewing me for the position of executive secretary. Because of the four years experience I have as an executive secretary, I feel I am well-suited for the job. You will find me extremely reliable, as I encourage you to follow up with my current manager. I have had a terrific tenure supporting my director, but need to leave since my husband is relocating with his position to Dallas. I am very encouraged by the new products DSC is launching and would love to join your team.

➡

- I am grateful to you for taking time yesterday to meet with me. Our interview answered many questions I had about the position and what you need to be successful. Happily, I now feel I am even better suited to the job than I had anticipated. My experience overseas has prepared me for the challenges of managing international transfers for Ford. The prospect of my association with your firm is very exciting. In addition to rewarding work and an excellent benefits package, Ford's reputation is unsurpassed.

Additional Resources

Action Verbs Used in Cover Letters

Action verbs should be used abundantly throughout your cover letters to promote your achievements, to represent you as action-oriented and make your cover letter or résumé answer the question, "So what?" when it comes to your accomplishments.

Communication/ People Skills

Addressed
Advertised
Arbitrated
Arranged
Articulated
Authored
Clarified
Collaborated
Communicated
Composed
Condensed
Conferred
Consulted
Contacted
Conveyed
Convinced
Corresponded
Debated
Defined
Developed
Directed
Discussed
Drafted
Edited
Elicited
Enlisted
Explained
Expressed
Formulated
Furnished
Incorporated
Influenced
Interacted
Interpreted
Interviewed
Involved
Joined
Judged
Lectured
Listened
Marketed
Mediated
Moderated
Negotiated
Observed
Outlined
Participated
Persuaded
Presented
Promoted
Proposed
Publicized

Reconciled
Recruited
Referred
Reinforced
Reported
Resolved
Responded
Solicited
Specified
Spoke
Suggested
Summarized
Synthesized
Translated
Wrote

Creative Skills

Acted
Adapted
Began
Combined
Composed
Conceptualized
Condensed
Created
Customized
Designed
Developed
Directed
Displayed

Drew
Entertained
Established
Fashioned
Formulated
Founded
Illustrated
Initiated
Instituted
Integrated
Introduced
Invented
Modeled
Modified
Originated
Performed
Photographed
Planned
Revised
Revitalized
Shaped
Solved

**Accounting/
Financial Skills**

Administered
Adjusted
Allocated
Analyzed
Appraised

Assessed
Audited
Balanced
Budgeted
Calculated
Computed
Conserved
Corrected
Determined
Developed
Estimated
Forecasted
Managed
Marketed
Measured
Netted
Planned
Prepared
Programmed
Projected
Qualified
Reconciled
Reduced
Researched
Retrieved

**Team Support
Skills**

Adapted
Advocated

Aided
Answered
Arranged
Assessed
Assisted
Clarified
Coached
Collaborated
Contributed
Cooperated
Counseled
Demonstrated
Diagnosed
Educated
Encouraged
Ensured
Expedited
Facilitated
Familiarized
Furthered
Guided
Helped
Insured
Intervened
Motivated
Prevented
Provided
Referred
Rehabilitated
Represented

Resolved
Simplified
Supplied
Supported
Volunteered

**Management/
Leadership Skills**

Administered
Analyzed
Appointed
Approved
Assigned
Attained
Authorized
Chaired
Considered
Consolidated
Contracted
Controlled
Converted
Coordinated
Decided
Delegated
Developed
Directed
Eliminated
Emphasized
Enforced
Enhanced

Established
Executed
Generated
Handled
Headed
Hired
Hosted
Improved
Incorporated
Increased
Initiated
Inspected
Instituted
Led
Managed
Merged
Motivated
Navigated
Organized
Originated
Overhauled
Oversaw
Planned
Presided
Prioritized
Produced
Recommended
Reorganized
Replaced
Restored

Reviewed
Scheduled
Secured
Selected
Streamlined
Strengthened
Supervised
Terminated

Organizational Skills

Approved
Arranged
Catalogued
Categorized
Charted
Classified
Coded
Collected
Compiled
Corrected
Corresponded
Distributed
Executed
Filed
Generated
Incorporated
Inspected
Logged
Maintained
Monitored

Obtained
Operated
Ordered
Organized
Prepared
Processed
Provided
Purchased
Recorded
Registered
Reserved
Responded
Reviewed
Routed
Scheduled
Screened
Submitted
Supplied
Standardized
Systematized
Updated
Validated
Verified

Analytical Skills

Analyzed
Clarified
Collected
Compared
Conducted

Critiqued
Detected
Determined
Diagnosed
Evaluated
Examined
Experimented
Explored
Extracted
Formulated
Gathered
Inspected
Interviewed
Invented
Investigated
Located
Measured
Organized
Researched
Reviewed
Searched
Solved
Summarized
Surveyed
Systematized
Tested

Coaching/ Teaching Skills

Adapted
Advised

Clarified

Coached

Communicated

Conducted

Coordinated

Critiqued

Developed

Enabled

Encouraged

Evaluated

Explained

Facilitated

Focused

Guided

Individualized

Informed

Instilled

Instructed

Motivated

Persuaded

Simulated

Stimulated

Taught

Tested

Trained

Transmitted

Tutored

Technical Skills

Adapted

Applied

Assembled

Built

Calculated

Computed

Conserved

Constructed

Converted

Debugged

Designed

Determined

Developed

Engineered

Fabricated

Fortified

Installed

Maintained

Operated

Overhauled

Printed

Programmed

Rectified

Regulated

Remodeled

Repaired

Replaced

Restored

Solved

Specialized

Standardized

Studied

Upgraded

Utilized

Section Two

Perfect Phrases for Résumés

Michael Betrus

Section Contents

Part III: Perfect Phrases by Industry and Discipline   229

Introduction

Today, résumés are more a part of a job search than ever before. They certainly are more important than they were 10 years ago, when many business experts embraced networking as the key source for finding a new position.

Okay. I do buy into that. Networking is a top source for finding a new position. But even when a candidate is brought to me through a networked source, the first thing I say is, "Have them send me their résumé and I will give them a call." Between you and I, after 10 job-search-related books and having managed hundreds of people, it's hard to not be critical of poor résumés. Still, it's table stakes for gaining an interview.

Now, in the e-mail age, all large organizations—and many small ones as well—post jobs on Web sites like careerbuilder.com and monster.com, not to mention major newspaper online job boards. What is the first thing you do when you find a job posted you like? You e-mail your résumé! You see, in the electronic age of e-mail, résumés play a bigger role than ever before.

I wish you could take the time to sift through a few hundred résumés posted on career Web sites and try to find a good candidate. The funny thing is, as difficult as it is for a job seeker, it's pretty darn difficult on the hiring side too. You would be shocked how tough on occasion that's been for me, or my recruiting department, to find good candidates.

I bet as they, and I, have mined through the career Web sites looking for candidates, we have passed on many great people. In fact, I would bet the odds are greater than Tiger winning another golf tournament.

Unfortunately, great people still write poor, unflattering résumés. Why?!!! When a hiring manager or recruiter is sifting through résumés, you have all of 10 to 30 seconds to impress them enough to read on. What makes them read on? I'm smiling at the irony as I write this, but it's *perfect phrases*. When candidates write great career summaries and great descriptors of past accomplishments, they get noticed.

That is why I wrote this book. Hopefully, it will help you craft some perfect phrases for your résumé.

Part I

Résumé Basics

On the front page of the employment section of a late 2003 Sunday edition of one of the largest newspapers in the country, there was an article debating the pros and cons of using a résumé. One commentary was that the résumé is outdated and that in today's world of electronic-based communications it will go away. It went on to say that the résumé has long evolved and that the days of using nice stock paper and matching envelopes has passed. At one point it even questioned whether hiring managers want to be bothered with reviewing résumés.

The article was partly correct. The traditional uses of a résumé have evolved. Among all the clients we have advised over the last year, none have concerned themselves with paper stock. However, hiring managers and internal and external recruiters do need résumés. What they detest are poorly written résumés that make them work to understand the profile of the candidates.

Résumés are still a huge part of the job search process. The first step in any selection process is to review the résumés of candidates, even those with inside sponsorship. In this section we want to teach you that:

- You need to create an effective and useful career summary for your résumé.
- You need to document your accomplishments in the employment history sections and make them line up as closely as possible with the requirements of the company.

People pay hundreds of dollars to have professionals teach them how to present these two things. The career summary, in particular, is crucial. If you were to poll hiring managers, human resources recruiters, and external recruiters, fewer than 10 percent would say they read every bullet describing each job a candidate had. So, if the summary section is weak or nonexistent, there's even less likelihood that the whole résumé will be read.

Consider this analogy: Recently I was traveling from Tampa to Dallas. At the Tampa airport I was looking for a couple of magazines to read on the plane. The magazine rack was large and the selection of magazines was broad. I browsed the news periodicals (like *Time*, *Newsweek*, *U.S. News & World Report*), the sports magazines, and some others. I bought two magazines after very casually perusing over 50 magazine covers.

Why did I buy those two magazines out of the whole lot? Their covers and headlines.

In most cases this is not unlike the initial résumé screening process for candidates. You can be "deselected" before you ever get to the plate. You need a good résumé—a well-presented career summary and employment history documentation—to keep your job search process open and alive with options.

A good résumé is no guarantee of obtaining a great position, but a poor one may very well result in your not getting the interview.

Being computer literate is an absolute requirement for any white-collar job today. To be considered a good prospect and a good candidate by hiring managers, good presentation skills can be critical. Hiring managers view the résumé and the cover letter as an indication of how well you may perform in the job.

The résumé is an indicator of a candidate's:

- Organization skills
- Writing skills
- Presentation skills
- Ability to "net it out" effectively—to communicate clearly in as few words as possible

Your Marketing Brochure

When you see a marketing brochure advertisement, it has been carefully crafted with several things in mind: key messaging, copy positioning, colors, graphics, and so on. Positioning is a critical part of connecting the key message of the advertisement to the instinctive viewing center of the reader.

One more reason the summary is the most important single piece of information in your résumé is because of where it rests—right in the visual center of the résumé. Imagine an 8 ½ by 11 paper. This is where the visual center of a document is and where your summary should reside:

Personal Heading
Career Summary
Job Descriptions

Each discipline or industry of perfect phrases in this book illustrates one or two examples of a career summary you can use in your résumé. Feel free to mix and match; with career summaries, you are looking for a crisp format to communicate the most information about you in the fewest words and simplest terms.

Keys to Effective Résumé Writing

Have you ever known a highly successful sales professional who didn't have a firm grasp and knowledge of his or her product? Ask any experienced salesperson what the secret to success is and he or she will say that it's knowing the product, knowing the customer, and matching the benefits of the product to the needs of the customer. This is a powerful success formula.

The job search is a sales and marketing endeavor. There is simply no way around this: *You* are the product, *you* are the salesperson, and *you* must define your customers and promote yourself to them. So, like the highly successful salesperson, the key to your success is to know your product (you) inside and out, and match the benefits of the product to the needs of your potential customers (prospective employers). In sales, we call this selling features and benefits.

Regardless of the résumé type you choose or the format you decide upon, there are five primary sections that make up a successful résumé, along with numerous subsections that can also be incorporated. The five primary sections are:

1. Heading
2. Career summary
3. Employment section
4. Education
5. Miscellaneous sections

Heading

The heading, also referred to as your *personal directory,* consists of your name, address (with full zip code), and phone number (with area code). If you carry a portable phone or pager or have a fax machine, you can include these phone numbers in your heading. We do not recommend that you include a work number. Many hiring managers do not look favorably upon furnishing a work number. They may conclude that if you use your present company's phone and resources to launch a job search campaign on company time, you might do the same while working for them.

Career Summary

Once you read the first three chapters, you'll see why I'm passionate about the value of a strong career summary.

In just a few seconds the reader should get a picture of who you are and what you have done, both functionally and by industry. Here are examples of great summaries:

Career Profile

- Twelve years experience in telecommunications industry.
- Nine years experience in sales and field management, three years in corporate marketing management.
- Created strategy behind wins with many Fortune 500 companies, including Hilton, Norsk-Hydro, National Car Rental, Outback Restaurant, and Harris Corporation.
- Achieved 100 percent plan participation with AEs by developing very creative strategic partnerships that provided alternative, nontraditional sales channels.

Specific Areas of Expertise

- Strategic sales plan development
- Strong financial background
- Establishing sponsorship at account

- Connecting customer needs to corporate solutions
- Understanding customer's business
- Developing alternative selling channels

The reader of a summary like this would need very little time to ascertain the fit of this candidate. The career summary is what gets you noticed and gets the rest of your résumé reviewed.

Employment Section

The employment section will have much influence on a prospective employer in determining if you get an interview, and ultimately, a job offer. This section highlights your professional career and emphasizes experience, qualifications, and achievements. The employment module normally begins with your most recent position and works backward (allocate the most space to the most recent positions and less space as you go back in time). Provide the following information for each employer:

1. Name of company or organization

2. City/town and state where you worked

3. Dates of employment

4. Titles or positions held

How It Should Look

When using a chronological or combination format, provide specific information for each employer you worked for and for each job you performed. Include three pieces of information for each employer/job:

1. Basic responsibilities and industry- or company-specific information

2. Special skills required to perform those responsibilities

3. Specific accomplishments

Education

Generally, the education section appears at the beginning of your résumé if you have limited work experience. A recent high school, technical school, or college graduate will, in most cases, fall into this category. As your portfolio of experience and achievements gains momentum, the education section will drop toward the end of the résumé as newly formed experiences, skills, and accomplishments begin to outweigh educational experience in the eyes of a prospective employer.

You will see examples of how these parts fit together in the 10 sample résumés that follow.

Sample Résumés

ROBERTA LYONS

320 Brandies Street • Springfield, Illinois, 62232 • (618) 555-1212 • e-mail@e-mail.com

ATHLETIC COACH
Basketball

9 Years' Successful Experience in High-Visibility Athletic Programs

"Improving Skills—Improving Character—Improving Basketball Programs"

Discipline/Reward/Growth

A positive-thinking, results-oriented, and team-spirited athletic coach with a sound, verifiable record of success in building winning programs and developing values-based students into contributing citizens in their communities.

CORE STRENGTHS

Athletic conditioning and fitness expert
Strategic planning—sound basketball fundamentals
Program marketing and promotions—on/off campus

Nutritional certification
Staff development
Concentration on grades and sport

EMPLOYMENT

Springfield County School System, Springfield, Illinois   1992 to Current
Girls Head Basketball Coach/Math Teacher—McKenner High School

Coaching Highlights:
2001   American Midwest Regional Finals—Top 12 in State
2000   American Midwest Regional Finals—Top 10 in State

1999   NCCA—Runner-up
1998   Northwest Conference Champions
1997   Northwest Conference Champions
1996   Runner-up Northwest Conference Champions

Coaching Record:

	WINS	LOSSES	PERCENTAGE	COMMENT
2001	15	3	83%	First in conference
2000	14	4	77%	Second in conference
1999	16	2	88%	First in conference
1998	12	6	66%	Third in conference
1997	13	5	72%	Third in conference
1996	13	5	72%	Third in conference
1995	9	9	50%	Sixth in conference
1994	10	8	55%	Fifth in conference
1993	9	9	50%	Sixth in conference
1992	6	12	33%	Last in conference

EDUCATION & TRAINING

Providence College
Rhode Island

Master in Athletic Coaching
Bachelor of Science: Sports Science: Providence College   1991
Bachelor of Arts: Education: Mathematics and Statistics   1988 (Dual)
    1988 (Dual)

AFFILIATIONS

National Coaches Federation—Member/Former Board Member, Springfield County Chapter
American Heart Association—Board Member—Springfield County Chapter

References upon Request

deborah lorenz .... data warehouse manager

101 W. 10th Avenue, Denver, CO 80201...e-mail@e-mailaddress.com...303.555.1010

core competencies ....

- Data Warehouse Manager offering 10 years of experience and in-depth knowledge of the functional and data needs of e-businesses.

- Data warehouse development experience incorporates skills in programming, analysis, architecture, and project management. Expertise in high-level and detailed system design, requirements gathering, logical and physical data modeling, development, and implementation. Expert knowledge of data modeling in ERP and other major application areas.

- Well-versed in Oracle (Oracle Express, Oracle Reporter, Oracle Financial), Oracle tools, and Erwin products. Data migration experience using Informatica, C++, Java, Corba, multidimensional database, JavaScript, Oracle Web server, and Java. Exceptional use of CASE tools as part of an overall development effort.

- Extensive knowledge of DBMS: Oracle RDBMS, SQL, PL/SQL, STAR Schema Modeling. Experienced in UNIX operating system, Microsoft PC operating systems including NT, desktop productivity software, and client/server system architecture.

- Proven ability to assemble and mobilize project teams, building consensus among multidisciplinary technical and functional teams in the rapid development and implementation of data warehousing solutions. Recognized by managers and colleagues as a strong, positive leader and a sharp strategic thinker.

experience ....

amazon.com, Denver, CO
Data Warehouse Manager, 1995–Present

- Drive the strategic vision and realization in the evolution from centralized data warehouse to distributed data marts. Report to divisional IT management with accountability for global processes. Manage a budget of $5.6 million.

- Provide guidance to software development teams on the use and purpose of data warehouses. Direct a team of seven data warehouse developers/analysts in the daily operations of the corporate data warehouse. Oversee all aspects of the warehouses, including data sourcing, data migration, data quality, data warehouse design, and implementation.

- Scope, plan, and prioritize multiple project deliverables, based on data warehousing dependencies and changing business needs. Develop project plans, identify and fill project resource needs, and manage projects to on-time, on-budget completion.

- Influence toolset and business needs assessment. Lead the selection of third-party software; manage vendor relationships. Successfully manage multiple projects in the design and implementation of warehouse functionality and interfaces.

Colorado Department of Revenue, Denver, CO
Data Warehouse Architect, 1990–1996

- Translated an enterprise data model, created dimension and fact tables to support budgeting, financial planning, analysis and data ware systems, in collaboration with the DBA and Data Steward.

- Determined database/data mart business requirements. Created the logical and physical database/data mart design for Relational and OLAP Data Warehouse environment.

education..

Master of Science, Data Warehouse Management, University of Denver, Denver, CO

Bachelor of Science, Computer Information Systems, University of Colorado, Boulder, CO

Melanie Olsen, CRNA

1555 Main Street • Charleston, WV 25302 • (304) 555-8443 • e-mail@e-mail.com

> "... exhibits high degree of intelligence and readily grasps new concepts ... has an affable charm ... interacts well with patients, colleagues ... even in the most stressful of situations."
>
> James McCroskey, MD
> General Anesthesia Services
> Charleston, WV

> "... reliable and responsible team player ... willingly shares the workload ... level-headed and competent in an emergency ... proficient and knowledgeable in anesthetic skills and techniques."
>
> Barb Schmitt, CRNA
> CAMC-Memorial Division
> Charleston, WV

Professional Profile

- **Certified Registered Nurse Anesthetist**
- Bachelor's degree and four years CRNA experience
- Clinical instructor with over 1,000 hours experience
- Outstanding clinical expertise and proficiency
- Attend weekly continuing education meetings
- Excellent problem solver who works well under pressure
- Reputation as a team player with superb people skills
- Upbeat, personable, and highly energetic

Licensure & Professional Affiliations

- Certified Registered Nurse Anesthetist, Certificate #22250
- Registered Professional Nurse, License #0556500
- Member, American Association of Nurse Anesthetists
- Member, West Virginia Association of Nurse Anesthetists
- Professionally involved with local Women's Health Center

Professional Experience

CHARLESTON AREA MEDICAL CENTER MEMORIAL DIVISION   1984-Present
Charleston, West Virginia

☐ **CRNA - Cardiovascular Center** - 1993-Present
Surgeries include arterial bypasses, hearts, amputations, gallbladders, mastectomies, biopsies, major orthopedics

☐ **RN - Medical Surgical** - 1984-1993
RN and charge nurse duties on a 40-bed med/surg unit, included adolescent ward and peritoneal dialysis

Education

- **Certificate of Anesthesia,** Charleston Area Medical Center School of Anesthesia, Charleston, WV, 1989
  ☐ Received Josephine A. Reier Memorial Scholarship Award
- **Associate Degree in Nursing,** University of Charleston School of Health Sciences, Charleston, WV, 1983
  ☐ Received Nursing Student Achievement Award
- **Bachelor of Fine Arts Degree,** *magna cum laude,* Arizona State University, Tempe, Arizona, 1977

" ... an excellent anesthetist who remains calm under pressure ... highest integrity ... exhibits excellent leadership ... has been a tremendous asset to our organization."

Lee Ann Smith, CRNA, BA
Instructor, CAMC School of
Nurse Anesthesia
Charleston, WV

" ... a very responsible employee ... always volunteering for additional assignments ... prompt and punctual ... has a positive attitude ... a valuable asset to our staff."

Tamy L. Smith, Charge CRNA
CAMC-Memorial Division
Charleston, WV

GREG MYERSON

555 Morgan Avenue South ✉ Richfield, MN 55555 ☎ (612) 555-3106 ✉ gmyerson@e-mail.e-mail

PROPERTY MANAGEMENT PROFESSIONAL

- 10 years of experience managing multiple rental properties, complemented by impeccable credentials.
- Relate warmly to diverse individuals at all levels by using a friendly yet confident communication style.

Asset Management & Valuation	Mixed-Use Property Occupancy	Commercial & Residential
Renovation & Turnkey Operations	Capital Improvement	Site Remediation
Tenant Relations & Retention	Collections	Legal Processes

CREDENTIALS & LEADERSHIP

Certified Property Manager (CPM®)
Certified Commercial Investment Member (CCIM®)
Registered Professional Adjuster (RPA®)
Institute of Real Estate Management (IREM®) Minnesota Chapter 45 Secretary

CAREER CONTRIBUTIONS

- Planned and directed the purchase, development and disposition of real estate on behalf of business and investors for Minnesota's largest privately owned multifamily housing manager.

- Recruited as temporary Marketing Director for a distressed, 360-unit market rate housing project with 150 units down, including vacate notices. Spearheaded and led a marketing campaign, reducing a 25% vacancy to 5% in 4 months.

- Managed receivable activities for 1,600 units. Successfully reduced large outstanding (1-2 months) debt accounts to 25% above acceptable industry levels; maintained these long term.

- Turned the occupancy rate of a 7-building distressed student housing project from 40% to 95% in 3 months.

- Consistently achieved a satisfactory (or better) return on owners' investments.

- Analyzed property management companies' computer needs and implemented updated systems integrating construction and property management software with word processing and spreadsheet applications.

CAREER HISTORY

Property Manager / Marketing Director ▪ HART MANAGEMENT, INC. ▪ St. Paul, MN 1998 – present
34 buildings comprising 440 residential and retail units, plus 346 mini storage units.

Real Estate Asset Manager ▪ STEVEN BYRON PROPERTY MANAGEMENT ▪ Edina, MN 1996 – 1998
Largest privately owned multifamily housing manager in Minnesota.

Property Manager ▪ BLD PROPERTY MANAGEMENT ▪ St. Cloud, MN 1993 – 1996
15 buildings comprising 300+ residential units.

EDUCATION

ST. CLOUD STATE UNIVERSITY – St. Cloud, MN Degree: 1996

Ariel S. Conroy

e-mail@e-mail.com

212 · 555 · 5555

10 West 25th Street, Apt. B · New York, NY 10001

Event Planning · Public Relations · Media

High-energy, background in fast-paced corporate event planning, promotion, and media relations / production. Possess outstanding cross-industry skills, superior presentation abilities, a passion for excellence, and a contagious enthusiasm. Tenacious and resourceful; will work any hours necessary and will always find a way to get project done on-time / on-budget.

Summary of Qualifications

- Blend creative and administrative abilities to coordinate unique corporate affairs, and media meeting planning for Dun & Bradstreet, Canadian Imperial Bank (CIB), and Jump-Start Productions.

- Manage budgets; select event venues; handle bookings, travel planning, entertainment, and gift selection. Team with design groups to create event ads and collateral materials.

- Function as associate producer on commercials and as media marketer for Jump-Start Productions, a television/cable commercial production firm. Maintain excellent rapport with producers, clients, and high-profile talent.

- Highly experienced in PC word processing, database / spreadsheet design, and presentation development. Familiar with Mac programs.

Areas of Expertise

corporate representation

PR strategies

press releases

presentations

conflict mediation

investor relations

consumer relations

event coordination

budget development

travel planning

meeting planning

venue selection

cocktail receptions

luncheons / dinners

entertainment selection

golf outings

theme design

invitations

corporate gift selection

collateral materials

vendor payment

Career Highlights

- Helped plan and deliver Dun & Bradstreet's largest and most luxurious special event, a $1 million golf/spa outing at Pebble Beach, CA, that was attended by nearly three hundred top clients, executives, and their guests.

- Coordinated cocktail receptions, luncheons, company tours, and interviewing rounds for D&B's recruiting events. Created sophisticated spreadsheets to organize hundreds of participants into six $100 thousand events.

- Planned high-profile golf and entertainment excursions and closing dinners for CIB. Coordinated cocktails, dinner menus and locations, transportation, executive suite at Madonna concert, and other entertainment. Purchased amenity gifts, inspected sites and paid invoices.

Professional Development

PUBLIC RELATIONS AND EVENTS COORDINATOR   1996 to present
Dun & Bradstreet, New York, NY

MEDIA MARKETING REPRESENTATIVE (freelance)   1994 to present
Jump-Start Productions, Inc., New York, NY

SPECIAL EVENTS COORDINATOR / PROJECT ASSISTANT   1991 to 1994
Canadian Imperial Bank, New York, NY

Education

Bachelor of Arts in Communications, Queens College, Flushing, NY, 1990

GRACE MATHERLY

578 Frisco Road ◇ Plano, TX 45237 ◇ H(214) 555-0254 C (214) 555-3604

- 10 years experience in professional sales within Fortune 500 arena
- Specialty in high-tech industries, including computer software, telecommunications and consumer electronics
- Specialty within sales is "hunting" -- new sales acquisition and relationship development
- Excellent presentation skills, good rapport builder with sales support (internal) and generally self-sufficient

- 2002–2003: Took new sales region with $0 in customer base and in 2 years grew that to over $7MM
- Acquired 2 new "logo" Fortune 100 companies in 2003. Developed the account relationship where no previous existed; designed customized solution for client and closed order within 14 months
- President's Club winner in 2003, 1999 and 1997
- Consistently ranked in top 10% of all sales professionals
- Top salesperson in 1997

AT&T, Denver, Colorado   2001 to Present
Global Account Manager, Mountain Region

- Target Fortune 250 companies in Rocky Mountain region that have no current use with AT&T. Developing customized voice and data solutions for all verticals.
- Won business with third largest corporation in Colorado, representing $4MM in revenue annually for AT&T
- Grew total revenue base of five target accounts from $0 to $7MM in two years.
- President's Club winner in 2003
- Achieved some level of sales penetration in three of five global accounts within 18 months
- 187% of sales plan for 2003; $106% of sales plan in 2002

US West (now Qwest), Denver, Colorado   1994 to 2001
Sales Representative, Denver

- Representing voice and data solutions for medium size businesses in Denver metro area
- Sales Representative of the Year in 1997
- Specialty was hunting – developing new business where there was previously none.
- Achieved following sales performance:
  - 2000: 163% of sales plan
  - 1999: 112% of sales plan
  - 1998: 210% of sales plan
  - 1997: 230% of sales plan

Patti Coury

555 North 555 Place • Tulsa, Oklahoma 74155 • Residence: 918-555-5555 • Cell: 913-555-5551 • E-mail: pcoury@e-mail.net

Executive Sales

President's Club winning sales professional with 15 years sales experience. Specialty is developing account strategy, sales execution and account management for leading uniform supply company. Verifiable sales performance record with expertise in:

- ☐ Hunting and new account acquisition
- ☐ Account planning
- ☐ Networking with referrals
- ☐ Sales account renewals

Patti is an excellent sales professional. She was aggressive, yet smooth through the sales process. She kept on us, but never turned us off. She developed a solution to meet our needs, and we ended up awarding her 80% of our total share of business for uniform service.

— Emma Thompson, ABC Company

PROFESSIONAL EXPERIENCE

Regional Manager   ARAMARK Industries, Atlanta, Georgia   1988 to Present

Promoted through a series of increasingly more responsible customer support and sales executive positions with the leading uniform supply and management company in the U.S. Currently specialize in custom uniform and apparel design for large multinational firms in Atlanta area. Have been in direct sales since 1995 and have always been ranked in top quarter of country each year.

As a customer service and later sales executive, many challenges have been overcome. This is a vital attribute of a successful salesperson. Below are four examples of volatile situations faced and the associated resolution:

Situation ᕲ	Launched new market segment selling corporate signature apparel to a new and unestablished market with no base from which to grow.
Result ᕲ	Developed strict account plan and executed it through first year. Achieved 23% above sales objective in new market place.
Situation ᕲ	Increased sales objective in 1999 to reflect need for increased business in response to increased competition.
Result ᕲ	With sales quota increase over 35%, continued to meet challenge and exceed quota; ranked number one in sales in 1999.
Situation ᕲ	Customer churn increased in 2001 due to increased competition.
Result ᕲ	Increased customer visits, proactively reviewed contracts, focused on renewals and generally showed more customer interest. Churn decreased in base from 16% in 2000 to 7% in 2001.
Situation ᕲ	Promoted to Regional Manager in 2002 while still responsible for revenue acquisition in abbreviated sales territory.
Result ᕲ	Exceeded personal sales objective while also achieving as manager: 0 employee turnover, 100% participation in sales plan and maintaining low customer churn.
Situation ᕲ	Employee churn and sales rep participation identified as major impediment to successful sales management.
Result ᕲ	Selectively hired sales reps and focused on their success through training, account management, team-building activities and employee development. Achieved 0 employee turnover and leading sales performance in SE Region.

EDUCATION   Georgia Tech University, Bachelor of Arts, History   1988

Pete Weldon

50 New England Drive   Garden Grove, New York 10576 (516) 555- 7645

NATIONAL ACCOUNTS SALES PROFESSIONAL

Verifiable track record of exceeding sales objectives and winning "logo" national accounts

2003	2002	2001	2000	1999
186 %	132%	240%	148%	155%

Strengths

- Developing strategic plans based on identifying customer functional needs
- Relationship building at the CXO level
- Working effectively internally with support staff
- Exceeding sales objectives and leading sales organization – winning President's Club!

PROFESSIONAL EXPERIENCE

National Accounts Manager, D'ITALIA, INC., New York, New York (1996 to Present)

Senior Account Manager with this $1 billion global clothing manufacturer. Challenged to plan and orchestrate an aggressive market expansion into key leading retailers nationwide. Scope of responsibility includes strategic planning, competitive assessment, market positioning, customer acquisition and retention.

- Led the successful national market launch of three product lines.
- Target Fortune 250 retail companies nationwide to distribute specialty clothing line.
- Won business with second largest retailer in Northeast, representing $4MM in revenue annually.
- Grew total revenue base of five target accounts from $0 to $7MM in two years.
- President's Club winner in 2001 and 2003.

Retail Manager, SAKINAS, INC. (1988 to 1995)

Recruited to this upscale national retail chain to manage daily operations for start-up and high-growth retail sites throughout the Midwest. Scope of responsibility was diverse and included daily operations management, recruitment, training, scheduling, inventory control, administration and the entire sales, marketing and customer service function. Led a staff of up to 65.

- Led the Chicago store to ranking as the highest-volume operation nationwide.
- Managed the start-up of Detroit store. Recruited 45 personnel, created merchandising displays and coordinated grand opening activities. Built operation to solid first year revenues.

EDUCATION

B.S., Marketing, Syracuse University, New York, 1988

MARIA CRUDO

11935 West 9th Street • Sun Valley, Idaho 83404 • (208) 555-1212 •
e-mail@e-mail.com

SPECIAL EDUCATION TEACHER

Highly dedicated, compassionate, patient, and positive professional with
numerous accomplishments working with the handicapped.

SUMMARY OF QUALIFICATIONS

- Current teaching certificate for Elementary Education—endorsement in Special Education.
- **Quickly develops rapport with students, employees, and staff.**
- Three years' experience (summers) working with handicapped individuals in a Developmental Disabilities Agency and writing programs for handicapped individuals.
- **Manages and promotes self-directed work teams and coordination for three employees.**
- Experienced with licensure surveys for Developmental Disabilities Agencies.
- **Strong leadership, management, and organizational skills; exceptional work ethic.**
- **Self-motivated, creative, dependable, and patient.**

EDUCATION

Current Teaching Certificate valid in Idaho and Washington. 2001.

Bachelor of Science Degree in Special Education, Idaho State University, Pocatello, Idaho. 1997.

Developing Capable People Seminar, Temple Elementary, Presented by Stacie Smith. 1997.

Managing People with Handicaps Seminar, Temple Elementary, Presented by Stacie Smith. 1996.

EMPLOYMENT

AIDE. DEVELOPMENT WORKSHOP, INC., Idaho Falls, Idaho. 1994 to 1996.

- Traveled to clients' homes to teach cooking, cleaning, shopping, and budgeting.
- Assisted in writing, developing, and implementing program procedures.
- Taught life skills to clients; ensured the safety of the clients.
- Monitored facility maintenance and security.
- Special project: worked with young boy, age five, who would not speak. After nine months of intense therapy, patience, and special equipment, he began speaking broken words. He is still in therapy and doing very well considering the circumstances.

LAYAWAY/SERVICE DESK CLERK. K MART, Nampa, Idaho. 1991 to 1994 (Part-Time).

CASHIER/COOK. SCOT'S DRIVE-IN, Idaho Falls, Idaho. 1988 to 1991 (Part-Time).

Have lived with and cared for a sister and a brother with handicaps.

Tom Anika

123 Arlington Court, Denver, CO 80239
e-mail@e-mailaddress.com
303-555-5451

Summary

- **Voice & Data Communications Engineer** with 10+ years of experience seeking continued project leadership role, integrating emergent technologies into comprehensive communications solutions.

- In-depth knowledge of communications network operations. Proven ability to build proficiency in new technologies and collaborate with multidisciplinary project teams to ensure successful project integration.

- Strong skills in coordinating all facets of multiple complex projects, ensuring on-time, on-budget, on-target results.

- Articulate, flexible, and personable communicator, with excellent skills in client and vendor relations. Frequently selected to serve as a project consultant and task force contributor on critical corporate initiatives.

Experience

Internet Fiber, Inc., Denver, CO   1998–Present
FTTH Project Manager

- Design and build Neighborhood Networks™ (customer-owned Internet Fiber networks) using a high-speed fiber to the home (FTTH) architecture for Internet, telephony, and video.

TECHNICAL PROFICIENCIES

Network/Operating Environments:

- Solaris, AIX, Linux, Novell Netware, VMS/CMS Mainframe, DOS, Windows 95/98/NT, Xwindows, Banyan Vines, SunNet Manager

Network Equipment:

- Cisco (1000, 2500, 4000, 7000 series Routers)

- Bay Networks (Contivity 4000 Extranet Switch, BCN and BLN series Routers, 28000, 58000, and 350T series Ethernet Switching Hubs)

- Synoptics (2813, 3000, 3030, and 5000 series hubs/concentrators)

- 3com (3100 series Terminal Servers, Netbuilder II Routers, Lanplex 2500 series, Linkswitch 3000 series)

- Perform feasibility studies, determine network requirements and specifications.
- Maintain strong partnerships with top-rated residential homebuilders. Coordinate construction schedules from rough electrical to interior finishing phases.
- Hire and manage telecommunications and network technicians and subcontractors to meet all implementation deadlines.

AT&T/Lucent Technologies, Westminster, CO   1990-1998
Telecommunications Engineer, IP-based Network Services

- Supported implementation of multiple projects, including Interspan Network, IP network services (the AT&T Worldnet backbone), frame relay, ATM, AT&T Broadband services, APS (a PC-based, Unix O/S Voice Recognition Call Processing System), and 900 MHz Spectralink phone systems.
- Determined location of hardware and schedule installations to minimize impact to customers.
- Coordinated all unit and system testing, ensuring 100% turn-up of equipment prior to cut-over.

Education

BS, Telecommunications Engineering, Cum Laude
University of Colorado at Boulder

- Cyberguard (Firewall), Sniffer, OneTouch.

Programming/Scripting Languages:

- C, C++, Assembly (370,8086,8031,8051), HTML, FORTRAN, BASIC, Visual Basic, Java, Perl, CGI, SQL, Shell Scripting

Protocols/Services:

- IPsec, PPTP, SNMP, TCP/IP, RADIUS, PAP, MSCHAP, DHCP, DNS, FTP, Telnet, RMON, x.509, DES, Triple-DES, FTTH

Applications:

- Microsoft Outlook, Word, PowerPoint, Excel, Project, Access, Bay Networks Optivity, Harris Network Management, Exceed, Lotus ccMail, Ecoscope, Netscape, Internet Explorer, Visio, Informix, Oracle

Résumé and Job Search Tips

You would be shocked how many typos still exist in résumés today. Sometimes I will review résumés of very experienced professionals and think, "You have got to be kidding me," as I see so many typos. If I were to guide you to avoid typos, it may not mean the same thing to you that it does to me. Here are some specific things to watch that I see all the time:

- Randomly capitalized words in sentences or phrases. If it is not a proper noun or the beginning of a sentence, it doesn't get capitalized. You should not use capitalization because you want to add punch.
- Spaces after commas and periods. You need to have them.
- Long, run-on sentences. Look, I am no Stephen King when it comes to creative or effective writing, but I do know short sentences are more powerful than long ones. In long sentences the point gets lost. Tip: If it runs over 1 1/2 lines, it's probably too long. Break it up.
- Use bullets to get your point across. Bullets make it easier to read and get to your point. Is it easier to read *USA Today* or *Don Quixote*?

Internet Tips

- When typing your résumé out with the intent of e-mailing it, make sure it is in an ASCII format.

- When you paste your résumé in the field provided on careerbuilder.com or monster.com, proof it and reconstruct the bullets and formatting lost, at least with spaces and dashes. Make it easier to read!

- When sending your résumé via e-mail in an ASCII format, attach (if you can) a nicely formatted one in case it does go through and the reader would like to see your creativity and preferred layout. If you do attach it, use a common program such as Microsoft Word.

- Before you e-mail your résumé, try sending it to yourself and to a friend as a test drive.

- Include your e-mail address on your résumé and cover letter.

- Don't e-mail from your current employer's IP network.

- Don't circulate your work e-mail address for job search purposes.

- In the "subject" of your e-mail (just below the "address to" part), put something more creative than "Résumé Enclosed." Try, for example: "Résumé showing eight years in telecommunications industry" (if that is your chosen industry).

- Be careful of your spelling on the Internet. You will notice more spelling errors in e-mail exchanges than you will ever see in mailed letter exchanges.

Networking Tips

- Remember, networking is a numbers game. Once you have a network of people in place, prioritize the listing so that you have separated top-priority contacts from lower-priority ones.

- Sometimes you may have to pay for advice and information. Paying consultants or professionals or investing in Internet services is part of the job search process today as long as it's legal and ethical.

- Know what you want from your contacts. If you don't know what you want, neither will your network of people. Specific questions will get specific answers.

- Ask for advice, not for a job. You should not contact someone and ask if that person knows of any job openings. The answer will invariably be no, especially at higher levels. You need to ask for things like industry advice and advice on geographic areas. The job insights will follow but will be almost incidental. This positioning will build value for you and make the contact person more comfortable about helping you.

- Watch your attitude and demeanor at all times. Everyone you come in contact with is a potential member of your network. Demonstrate enthusiasm and professionalism at all times.

- Get comfortable on the telephone. Good telephone communication skills are critical.

- Be well-prepared for your conversation, whether in person or over the phone. You should have a script in your mind of how to answer questions, what to ask, and what you're trying to accomplish.

- Flatter the people in your network. It's been said that the only two types of people who can be flattered are men and women. Use tact, courtesy, and flattery.

- If a person in your network cannot personally help, advise, or direct you, ask for referrals.

- Remember, out of sight, out of mind.
- Don't abuse the process. Networking is a two-way street. Be honest and brief and offer your contacts something in return for their time, advice, and information. This can be as simple as a lunch or an offer of your professional services in return for their cooperation.
- Show an interest in your contacts. Cavette Robert, one of the founders of the National Speakers Association, said, "People don't care how much you know until they know how much you care." Show how much you care. It will get you anywhere.
- Send thank-you notes after each networking contact.

Interviewing Tips

- Relax. The employment interview is just a meeting. Although you should not treat this meeting lightly, don't forget that the organization interviewing you is in need of your services as much as, or perhaps more than, you are of theirs.
- Be quiet and poised. Don't talk too much or too fast.
- The key to successful interviewing is building rapport. Most people spend their time preparing for interviews by memorizing canned responses to anticipated questions. Successful interviewers spend most of their time practicing the art of building rapport through the use of powerfully effective communicating techniques.
- Prepare a manila folder that you will bring to the interview. Include the following in the folder:
  - Company information (annual reports, sales material, etc.)

- Extra résumés (six to 12) and your letters of reference
- 15 questions you've prepared based on your research and analysis of the company
- A blank legal pad, a pen, and anything else you consider helpful (e.g., college transcripts)

- Dress appropriately. Determine the dress code and meet it. If their dress is business casual, you still need to be dressed business professional. Practice proper grooming and hygiene.
- Before meeting the receptionist, check your appearance. Check your hair, clothing, and general image. Test your smile.
- Secretaries, administrative assistants, and receptionists often have a say in the hiring process. Make a strong first impression on them.
- Your handshake should be firm, made with a wide-open hand, fingers stretched wide apart. Women should feel comfortable offering their hands for firm and friendly handshakes. A power handshake and a great smile will get you off to a great start. Just don't overdo the power handshake.
- Eye contact is one of the most powerful forms of communication. It demonstrates confidence, trust, and power.
- During the interview, lean toward the interviewer. Show enthusiasm and sincere interest.
- Take notes. You may want to refer to them later in the interview. If you are uncomfortable with this, ask permission first.

- Communicate your skills, qualifications, and credentials to the hiring manager. Describe your market value and the benefits you offer. Demonstrate how you will contribute to the bottom line. Show how you can (1) improve sales, (2) reduce costs, (3) improve productivity, and/or (4) solve organizational problems.

- Key in on specific accomplishments. Accomplishments determine hire ability.

- Let the interviewer bring up salary first. The purpose of an interview is to determine whether there is a match. Once that is determined, salary should be negotiated.

- There is no substitute for planning and preparation, practice and rehearsing—absolutely none.

- Practice interviewing techniques by using video technology. A minimum of five hours of video practice, preferably more, guarantees a stellar performance.

- Close the sale. If you find that you want the position, ask for it. Ask directly, "Is there anything that would prevent you from offering me this position now?" or "Do you have any reservations or concerns?" (if you sense that). At the very least, this should flush out any objections and give you the opportunity to turn them into positives.

- Always send a thank-you note within 24 hours of every employment meeting.

Salary Negotiating Tips

- Delay all discussions of salary until there is an offer on the table.

- You are in the strongest negotiating position right after the offer is made.

- Know your value. You must know how you can contribute to the organization.
- Before going into employment negotiations, you must know the average salary paid for similar positions with other organizations in your geographic area.
- Before going into employment negotiations you must know, as best you can, the salary range that the company you're interviewing with will pay or what former employees were earning.
- Remember, fringes and perks such as vacation time, flex time, health benefits, and pension plans have value. Consider the "total" salary package.
- Listen carefully and pay close attention. Your goals most likely will be different from the goals of the employer. For instance, the firm's main focus might be "base salary." Yours might be "total earning potential." A win-win solution might be to negotiate a lower base salary but a higher commission or bonus structure.
- Anticipate objections and prepare effective answers to them.
- Try to understand the employer's point of view. Then plan a strategy to meet both the employer's concerns and your needs.
- Don't be afraid to negotiate because of fear of losing the offer. Most employers expect you to negotiate as long as you negotiate in a fair and reasonable manner.
- Always negotiate in a way that reflects your personality, character, and work ethic. Remain within your comfort zone.
- Play hardball only if you're willing to walk away from or lose the deal.

- What you lose in the negotiations most likely will never be recouped. Don't be careless in preparing for or conducting the negotiation.
- Be sure to get the offer and final agreement in writing.
- Never link salary to personal needs or problems. Compensation should always be linked to your value.

Part II

Perfect Phrases by Professional Habit

Introduction

The following phrases may help with your statements. When choosing the phrase that best describes the situation, read it over once or twice in the context of the sentence to be certain that your selection is correct and that the sentence reads well.

Proven track record of/in …

During employment with …, successfully …

Specific responsibilities/functions/duties included …

Total/Complete responsibility for …

Experience involved/included …

Within ___ year/month period, …

In addition to …, responsible for …

Total accountability/Totally accountable for …

Successful in/at …

In order to …, …

Contracted/Subcontracted by … to …

Temporarily assigned to/Temporary assignment(s) included …

___ years' extensive and diverse experience in …

In support of …, …

In support of …, provided …

Specifically concerned with all phases/aspects of …

Expertise and demonstrated skills in …

Due to/Because of/As a result of/By …

Acted/Functioned as …

Sales volume/Profit/Sales quota accountability for …

Extensive and involved academic background in …

By exploiting/using …

… on an individual and group basis/level.

Direct operations accountability involving …

Extensive and diverse practical experience in …

Selected as/Elected to…

… includes the following functional responsibilities …

Reported to/Reported directly to …

… on an ongoing/regular basis.

All of the above resulted in …

Experienced in all facets/phases/aspects of …

Personally responsible for …

… to ensure maximum/optimum/minimum …

Instrumental in …

… included the following management functions …

Direct/Indirect control over …

Provided valuable/invaluable …

Recipient of …

Knowledge of/Experience as/in …

Prior to relocation/promotion …

Constant/Heavy interaction with …

Honored as …

Extensive training in …

In the capacity of/As …

Promoted from … to …

Consistently …
Proficient/Competent at …
Dual/Multiple responsibilities included …
Provided liaison for/between …
Remained as …
Company provides/supplies …
Regularly undertook …
… nationally and predetermined territory.
Won …
Company specializes in …
Concerned directly with …
… from inception to operational profitability.
… ensuring/assuring …
Extensive involvement in …
Served/Operated as …
… from outset/inception to profitable operation.
… allowing/enabling the …
Newly established company/entity engaged in …
Now involved in …
Assigned territory consisting of …
… representing a …
Initially employed to/joined organization to …
Company is one of …
Project(s) involved …
… facilitating a …
Specialized in …
In charge of …
Promoted to …
Innovation resulted in …
Company engaged in …

Familiar with …

Function to …

… amounting to a total savings of …

During association/affiliation with company …

Employed by …

Accountable to …

… saving the company an average of …

Ongoing concern with/responsibility for …

Assigned to …

… for the purpose of …

Recommendations accepted by …

Department/Division consists of/responsible for …

Primarily responsible for/Primary responsibilities included …

… according to …

Cost Reduction

It's no coincidence that the most effective cost-cutters are companies like Wal-Mart or Dell Computer, which use technology to keep processes like inventory management at the cutting edge. Cost reduction in general is a big part of business. It has always had its place, but more since the economic climate softened in 2000. Events since then have compounded the economic stability, and countless companies have taken drastic measures to reduce costs to remain viable. In the telecom industry in particular, cost reduction, not limited to but impacted by workforce reduction, has been paramount for survival.

Here is what you need to be aware of: Cost reduction always has value. You need to position the cost-reduction measures in your discipline to be associated with improved performance of some kind, and not just eliminating a workforce or particular product or function. Associate reduction of costs with improved performance and you'll really have something to talk about.

The phrases below are to be used as a template for a more substantive description of how you drove reduction in costs. You won't be able to use all these exact phrases because some are specific to the given candidate's accomplishments. Use them as a guideline to be more specific rather than general. Don't be vague!

Perfect Phrases

- Led team that accomplished a successful turnaround from $1.5 million loss to $.5 million profit in one year; reduced breakeven cost by more than 30 percent, and delivered a 50 percent quality improvement.

➡

- Developed and executed corporate development and growth plan for equity investment and refinancing.
- Implemented key operational changes to drive profitability improvements.
- Met or exceeded cost reduction goals by more than 245 percent, delivering over $100,000 in savings in the first year.

Try to be specific so your message does not appear fake or made up. Even this could be more specific.

- Rewrote and implemented new safety handbook, resulting in an immediate 25 percent reduction in workers' compensation claims.
- Reduced costs by redesigning front and back office call center processes for a $100 million-plus annual inbound operation, which led to a cost reduction of 18 percent per member in FY05.
- Developed business case for an inbound telemarketing acquisition vehicle, leading to a significant reduction in acquisition costs (14 percent) and to an incremental 2 million annual registrations.
- Supervised production of printing plant and performed efficiency studies of equipment and operations that resulted in waste reduction from 8 to 3.5 percent, and production increases of 15 percent. Customer complaints reduced to zero.
- Led cost reduction and efficiency activities during revenue downturn, improving bottom line 5 percent, despite 13 percent revenue reduction.
- Implemented cost containment strategies for medical and workers' compensation programs.

- Chief Negotiator, as well as assisted in negotiations with UAW and URW. Major achievements in latest UAW contract (6/03) include COLA savings of $1 million and 30 percent reduction in medical absenteeism, saving $2 million.
- Developed and delivered training to employees and customers, increasing knowledge and awareness of quality care and cost containment.
- While balancing the requirements to have a cost-effective marketing and distribution system with a progressive organization capable of generating explosive growth, identified cost containment and restructuring opportunities that led to a total 75-basis-point decrease in sales acquisition cost, a 32 percent reduction while increasing sales $2.3 billion, almost a 50 percent increase. Cost reductions have allowed for additional promotional opportunities, increased price competitiveness, and a self-financed expansion into new distribution channels.
- Cost of Goods Sold reductions of 7.5 percent while improving customer-perceived quality of finished products.
- Reduced direct labor costs by $2.5 million on annual budget of $12 million. Implemented employee incentive programs, which cost-reduced operation by $1 million.
- Reduction of inventory by $500,000 through sell-back and product rationalization program.
- Accomplished the reduction of inventory by 24 percent, utilizing MRP [Management Resource Planning], JIT [Just In Time], and Value Managed Partnerships with suppliers.
- Directed Corporate Inventory Reduction program, achieving 15 percent reduction in inventories.

- Assigned as Project Manager for the PRI, working with "Global Shared Services," to reduce total cost of ownership of digital output devices (printers/copiers/faxes), establishing processes, standards, and enabling Web access and usage monitoring for cost containment and reduction of nonbusiness activities by minimizing unauthorized use. A 10 to 15 percent cost reduction was projected after a complete cost/benefit analysis and equipment inventory was completed.

- Pharmaceutical Development and Program Management processes ensuring successful implementation and cost reductions of 3 to 5 percent.

- Key member of an executive team responsible for the reduction of over $65 million in annual expenses prior to the purchase of Ameritech by SBC.

- Introduced several procedural and methods changes resulting in a 34 percent cost reduction on a specific product line.

Employee Satisfaction

High employee satisfaction is essential for the acquisition and retention of a quality workforce. Tracking the attitudes and opinions of employees can identify problem areas and solutions related to management and leadership, corporate policy, recruitment, benefits, diversity, training, and professional development. A comprehensive employee satisfaction study can be the key to a more motivated and loyal workforce.

Good managers and good companies realize a happy employee is a productive employee. Poor managers might lead by intimidation, fear, or be too far the other way and appear lackadaisical. A good sports coach knows that to squeeze that extra level of performance, the athlete must be motivated and driven.

Driven and motivated employees will be more creative and work harder to solve problems because they care about their career and about the company or organization for whom they work.

For your part in this, you want to be the manager or employee who creates this drive for excellence, who is able to get the team to perform at a high level by being highly satisfied.

Consider the following phrases for articulating that you have and can create high employee satisfaction.

Perfect Phrases

- Implemented a performance management process that created a strong overachieving team with high employee satisfaction and a less than 5 percent turnover rate.
- Recipient of Award of Excellence in recognition of exceptional employee relations for six consecutive years, as

voted on by management. Exemplifies the important characteristics of high integrity, loyalty, and dedication.

- Focused on building supportive employee relationships with demonstrated responsiveness and confidentiality.

- Resolved employee/employer issues fairly and effectively, which contributed to high employee satisfaction.

- Improved call center productivity at least 40 percent and achieved a high employee satisfaction rating as evidenced by an independent study by planning, managing, and monitoring personnel, labor relations, and training.

- Managed a $1 million project that increased office morale, customer service, and diversity ratings, according to T.D. Finley Rating Survey, by 50 percent.

- Increased productivity 25 percent overall with reduced staff turnover and high employee satisfaction by creating a positive, teamwork environment, setting goals, and sharing the vision.

- Consistently achieved high employee satisfaction, resulting in minimal employee attrition numbers. Maintained a 90 percent or better rate of retention for the senior seasonal staff team, and zero percent turnover for full-time staff for two consecutive years.

- Introduced employee financial/award incentives that improved productivity, reduced absenteeism, and resulted in a 15 percent increase in gross profits. Achieved the highest percentage of employee advancement in the organization. Maintained high employee satisfaction during tough economic times.

- The Southern Region flagship operation was one of the fastest growing and most profitable in the entire company, and held the highest employee satisfaction rating of all companies in the plastics sector.

- In order to improve employee loyalty and satisfaction, worked with management to create program offering free, in-house leading industry certifications. This program offered employees optional classes in the evenings within our shop for courses leading to certifications such as MCSE and CNE. Visible improvements within employee satisfaction, and had a less than 2 percent turnover during program's two years.

- Provided face-to-face contact needed to resolve sensitive employee issues, including terminations, violence in the workplace issues, harassment/discrimination investigations, and labor relations issues. Partnered with senior/executive business leaders to deploy business initiatives and improve employee satisfaction.

- Responsible for department- and centerwide employee satisfaction results. Achieved improvement in employee satisfaction through implementation of employee-focused initiatives.

- Organized and participated as a lead in task forces set up by management to improve employee satisfaction.

- Facilitated employee growth through a culture of openness, continuous feedback, and a practice of prompt decision making (most employee concerns addressed within one working day).

- Lowered employee turnover rate from 35 to 5 percent. Started employee involvement groups to improve morale and safety. Only one recorded injury and no loss time injuries in past year. CEO stated that morale had never been higher.

- Led an organization effectiveness program that improved employee satisfaction by 40 percent in first year.
- Exceeded service delivery goals for quality, quantity, response time, employee and client satisfaction for a 1.2 million member/190-plus employee division; reduced attrition from 50 to 4 percent within one year; directed development of soft skills training program; developed and implemented client relationship management strategies; directed HR activities within the division to improve employee satisfaction and service delivery outcomes; developed and delivered leadership and management training; achieved 120 percent of operational and professional development goals; collaboratively developed divisional budget and delivered all results within budget.

Initiative

The word "initiative" is both a noun and an adjective, and both are valued in business. As an adjective, employees who have initiative are always in demand. Over the long run, they create innovations that create new products, better customer acquisition and retention, and reduce costs.

As a noun, a "business initiative" describes a new innovation, program, or direction. It can be a new sales channel, cost reduction program, or anything new designed to add value. For example, when GE announced an aggressive e-business campaign in 2001, it was designed to increase Internet-based commerce from about 5 to 30 percent. We have new initiatives in business, politics, and sports, everywhere. The important thing for you is to position yourself as someone who may drive or support new initiatives as a means to evolve to remain current and competitive.

Perfect Phrases

- Provided employee training on hazard communication program, ergonomic computer use, and other health and safety initiatives.
- Took initiative to devise a system of referral documents to provide employers with information regarding programs such as respiration protection, hazard communication, and blood-borne pathogen exposure.
- Managed and directed all facets of business development initiatives for Eastern Region; played an integral role in revamping sales philosophies and marketing strategies to successfully lead division to the first profitable year in two years.

- Instituted comprehensive, corporatewide performance metrics initiative with the slogan, "You can't manage what you can't measure," resulting in a proactive—instead of reactive—management of the company.

- Developed and managed sourcing strategies for high-volume initiative to include virtual job fairs, proactive research, and on-site job fairs in multiple locations.

- Primary responsibility is for worldwide field engagement, specifically, aligning Account Managers with Client Business Managers in AT&T's most strategic accounts.

- Developed and implemented a Proactive Teaming Initiative with sponsorship from both sales and marketing. This initiative required active facilitation of joint account planning meetings between the Account Managers and the Client Business Managers to identify pockets of opportunity in those accounts in which both sides would benefit. Also responsible for developing additional incentive and promotional programs that lifted sales results 23 percent over previous year.

- Collaborated with Finance to reduce Accounts Receivables collection cycle by implementing a proactive discrepancy resolution initiative. Revised procedure increased available cash by $1 million annually.

- Developed proactive marketing initiative to maintain company's leverage and protect future interests while meeting market expectations for standardization and integration.

Listening Skills

Many people say they are good listeners. In fact, I've never met a candidate who said he or she was a poor listener. No one ever writes "poor listening skills" on their résumé. Some should, if they were honest or knew themselves! However, so many are in fact weak in listening skills. I can recall many interviews where I've asked questions and gotten a response that is a 50 percent hit and the rest is babble that clutters the original point and renders them too wordy. You've heard that silence is golden? The interview is where you demonstrate just how good your listening skills may be.

The résumé is where you may try to describe in writing that you do in fact have good listening skills. Generally speaking, I am not a fan of even using "good listening skills" on your résumé or attempting to go in that direction. It's too vague, too hard to validate.

Consider these phrases if you must use this trait; for example, if you are in sales, social work, or health care, where listening skills are vital to success.

Perfect Phrases

- Possess strong analytical and assessment skills. Keen listening and negotiating abilities facilitate understanding of all facets in decision-making process; this results in reputation for writing solid packages and good business for all parties. Proven ability to cultivate new accounts, establish strong business relationships, and immediately contribute to operations.
- Led resolution of employee inquiries concerning policies, procedures, programs, or personal problems through active listening and standard coaching methods.

- Good empathetic and listening skills; ability to use knowledge to systematically solve problems. Facilitation and team development skills; strong interpersonal and influencing skills.

- Exercised listening skills and patience toward adolescents and adults struggling with substance abuse. Empathetic listening is a critical part of social work to gain trust and belief in working toward improvement in behavior.

- Furthered corporate identity and sales with effective presentations, established rapport based on well-developed listening skills and ability to match desires with product. Profitably directed key account management and distributor management programs. Was recognized every year for outstanding distributor development. Increased direct sales by 100 percent and increased distributor sales 135 percent during nationally difficult economic times.

- Fostered consultative relationships with customers to attain 20 percent annual increase in new business production. Skills exercised included leading, listening to customer needs, connecting solutions to those needs, and effective follow-through.

- Presented parenting skills workshops emphasizing play and motor skills, active listening, problem solving, behavior modification, positive self-image, and single parenting.

- Excellent listening skills, and ability to pay particular attention to detail. Was able to consistently uncover new sales opportunities by keying in on client trends, where other sales managers might have overlooked them. Able to listen and respond to all functions within an organization, from Finance to Sales and Marketing to Production.

Managing Conflict

Certain types of conflict—over a new product idea, for example—are potentially creative and can be enormously beneficial to the organization. This sort of conflict should be encouraged, although it may still need handling with care.

When conflict becomes personal, however, it is often negative and destructive. This type of conflict may arise from a range of causes. They can include poor communication, misunderstanding, problematic working conditions, unrealistic work expectations, discriminatory behavior, skill deficits, lack of resources, selfishness, stress, or depression. This destructive form of conflict can also result from a difference in personal opinion, the causes of which may lie outside work altogether.

You need to position yourself as one who manages conflict well, that you grow teams, keep morale high, and drive your team or projects to "strive, stretch, and reach."

Perfect Phrases

- Resolved conflicts between departments to ensure personnel were available for flights, conducted team leader meetings, and resolved all customer problems.
- Developed and led Conflict Resolution program in K–6 schools, linking leadership program with life skills awareness within a Baldrige in Education framework.
- Acted as liaison between executives, tenants, brokers, and corporation, managing conflict and ensuring shared understanding, accountable for coordination of final agreements.
- Responsible for driving change and managing new staffing model utilizing "workout" change model by leading a team of 30 cross-functional managers.

- Reviewed annual culture survey results and consulted with management teams on potential suggestions to enhance/improve culture.
- Facilitated several conflict resolution sessions between operations and functional groups.
- Facilitated new manager assimilation sessions.
- Facilitated change management workout sessions.
- Demonstrated strengths in managing diverse job processes, building and maintaining relationships throughout an organization, motivating staff and colleagues, assessing and developing high potential talent, and managing corporate objectives through major change.
- Managing Conflict—AT&T School of Business, Course MS6431, completed.
- Managing People and Performance—AT&T School of Business, Course MD7601, completed October 1993.
- Certifications: Numerous technical and managerial courses: Managing People and Performance, Managing Conflict, Communications Workshop, Leadership for the Future, Achieving Communication Effectiveness, and Labor Relations (AT&T School of Business & Technology).
- Contracted Trainer for specialized workshop programs.
- Programs topics include: Stress Management, Interpersonal Communication Skills, Career Management, Customer Service Skills, Conflict Resolution, Understanding and Managing Change, "Who Moved My Cheese?" Team Building, and Assertiveness and Self-Esteem.
- Prepared training materials and instructed workshops on Stress Management, Understanding and Managing Change (incorporating "Who Moved My Cheese?" materials), Career Development and Advancement.

- Selected local facilitator for the nationwide training broadcasts Coaching Skills for Managers, Planning and Organizing, Oral Communications and Listening Skills, Training Aids, and Training Technology Update.
- Certified facilitator for group feedback sessions for managerial and support staff that completed the training assessment instrument for the "Performance Development System."
- Contracted Instructor for school's two- and three-day training courses.
- Programs include: Conflict Across Cultures, Assertiveness Skills, Constructive Conflict Resolution, Negotiating Techniques, Dealing with Workplace Negativity, Effective Customer Service, Interpersonal Communication, and Creative Problem Solving.

Oral Presentation Skills

Oral communication skills are critical to the success of individuals and their organizations. This is equally true whether you are communicating one-to-one, or one-to-250. A good presentation has the power to deliver your message and the emotional force to move your audience to new ways of thinking and/or behaving.

Delivering oral presentations or having excellent oral presentation skills is important to any position, but perhaps more vital to those in training, sales, marketing, consulting, and in senior management positions in general. In almost every résumé I read the candidate writes "excellent oral [or presentation] skills." Okay. So what? Everything you write should answer the question: "So what?"

Consider modeling your phrases the way the following, which are more specific, are written.

Perfect Phrases

- Excellent oral skills: presentations that excite and inform, speeches—prepared and extemporaneous. Training skills include developing and delivering training curriculum, including the presentations and workbooks.

- Presentations: engaging speaker and seminar leader, sales presenter, and technical management liaison. Enjoy a natural ability to work with others, influence C-level decision making, and promote company products and services to a wide range of targeted prospects, alliance partners, and vendor leaders. Create and present executive-level seminars and workshops, create goodwill and future interest at corporate trade shows, and author specialized articles and procedural documentation. Establish quick rapport with coworkers, professionals, and staff. Exercise diplomacy and tact; enjoy a reputation of excellence in relationships.

- Promote company products through oral presentations in a variety of venues, including trade shows and conferences to create exciting buzz. Regularly requested to speak at industry trade conferences [you might be specific here] and global billing and trade shows.

- Communicate compliance results to corporate management through oral presentations and written reports.

- Conduct corporate staff presentations and creative employee training seminars.

- Responsible for new product presentations and sales techniques throughout California.

- Gave over a thousand lectures, primarily for Ford Motor Company, Fidelity, and Anderson Consulting. Recognized by *Marketing and Sales* magazine as one of the top 10 speakers in the United States. Recognized by the WTC in Dallas as "America's number one motivational technology speaker." Featured in many magazines, and have written three books published by McGraw-Hill.

- Wrote keynote speech for a motivational speaker. Doubled the original content through extensive research and interview. Made countless revisions to make the tone and texture of the language sound consistent with the speaker's personal style. Received excellent audience feedback and a repeat invitation to be the speaker.

- Motivational speaker (current): as a speaker, contract out with various organizations to bring exciting and

➡

educational presentations to schools and businesses. Speak to audiences that range from 100 to 2,500 people. Speak to an average of 15,000 people a year.

- Marketing/motivational speaker: participated in training classes through the delivery of entertaining and informative lectures to middle and high school students. Topics include those that encourage and support self-confidence, social skills, etc. Audience number ranges from 30 to somewhat more than 300.

- Prepare and deliver exciting and informative lectures/workshops on a variety of topics, with emphasis on positive thinking and personal empowerment. Some topics of discussion include interviewing techniques, clarifying goals, personal life mission statement, believing in yourself, and living your full potential.

- Communication: communicate well when speaking and writing; excellent public speaker; conducted training seminars for candidates, volunteers, and party activists; able to act as a liaison between different personality types; comfortable and effective communicating with both superiors and staff.

- Leadership: able to motivate a project team; background provides wide range of interpersonal skills to encourage and lead others.

- Management: known for a contagious passion for excellence, a talent for resourceful business solutions and motivational leadership. Effectively use an empowering, participatory management style that encourages accountability, teamwork, and the continuous improvement of desired results.

➡

Organizational Skills

I interviewed a candidate named Steve some time ago and hired him based on his ability to manage multiple projects simultaneously. His résumé said: "Excellent organizational skills." Then I worked with him, and within 90 days it proved to not only be untrue, but just the opposite. Steve could not plan or manage multiple projects or issues simultaneously. Sometimes I wondered how I missed it in the interview. I was faked out. I now discount that phrase "excellent organizational skills" as a hiring manager unless it is supported.

That's the key: to support the skill with some backup so it seems credible and not résumé fluff. Consider the following phrases and how they are supported. Notice that the actual phrase "organizational skills" is not always present; it is implied, and therefore perhaps more powerful.

Perfect Phrases

- Achieves win-win outcomes; strong communication and organizational skills with an acute attention to detail; ability to manage multiple projects; efficient, organized, detail-oriented, self-starter; good analytical, follow-through, and decision-making skills.
- Consistently brings projects to a successful finish on time, on budget.
- Successfully manages multiple projects simultaneously, using effective time and priority management skills.
- Promoted to lead the Project Management Team. Responsibilities included managing all aspects of the division's business and systems projects by preparing and managing project plans, scheduling, and facilitating status meetings; also, evaluating and analyzing cost-

➡

benefit relationships, documenting, and communicating issues.

- Responsible for marketing, coordinating, and managing vendor services for large corporate accounts. Represented multiple regional vendor services specializing in workers' compensation, auto, medical malpractice, and disability insurance, which required excellent organizational skills and project planning.

- Brought on to provide risk, logistics, inventory, facility, and warehouse operations management, including personnel supervision for a leading remanufacturer of consumer electronic products. Possess excellent organizational skills required to manage all functional areas properly. Responsibilities included coordinating international logistics between multiple manufacturing and refurbishment centers, and establishing and managing the reverse logistics department, handling over 15,000 units per year.

- Efficient in managing multiple projects simultaneously while utilizing excellent organizational/critical thinking skills and good judgment; consistently able to provide high-level, systematic standards of performance.

- Fifteen years experience in managing multiple projects simultaneously, including the ability to work under pressure, meet tight deadlines, and utilize problem-solving skills to ensure projects met stated goals and objectives.

- Highly successful project manager of lead and revenue generation programs, with particular skill in managing multiple projects simultaneously from concept to completion.

- Partner Program support: managed the production and distribution of Electronic Partner Packages, multiple collateral projects (data sheets and Division Overview brochure), trade show collateral, and signage requirements.

- Effectively managed integrated marketing programs on limited resources from development and implementation to program reporting and analysis.

- Experienced at consulting with teams, to understand their needs, uncover opportunities, and recommend creative ideas and solutions.

- Proven skills in organizing, prioritizing, and managing multiple projects simultaneously on time and budget. Effective working independently or leading a team with minimal direction toward broadly defined objectives.

- Interfaced with three regional sales centers and field marketing to develop projects targeting installed customers to increase customer loyalty. Developed and managed integrated marcom projects from concept to completion.

- Managed the creative development of sales literature, including product software specification sheets, brochures, reference guides, and case studies. Ensured completion of projects on time and within budget guidelines. Worked with various agencies regarding copywriting, design, and print production, managing multiple projects simultaneously.

- Recruited for coordinating, analyzing, and developing a communication strategy to ensure that group goals were being tracked and met project deadlines. Developed streamlined project tracking processes, which resulted in acquisitions of over $53 million, while managing multiple projects simultaneously with outside vendors.

- Increased production efficiency by managing multiple projects simultaneously, including client relations, schedules, and deadlines.

➡

- Adept in designing brochures, collateral, annual reports, and flyers, as well as conference, exhibit, and presentation materials, advertising, campaign materials, Web sites, and many other design projects.
- Expert at Project Management and CRM Direct Mail projects using in-house databases. Experienced in all areas of targeted marketing, retail management, and ad production and printing, and at managing multiple projects simultaneously.
- Developed a strategic marketing plan for the company, researched and evaluated new safety software, provided detailed case research and accident reconstruction support for ongoing litigation, and published press releases.
- Managed multiple projects simultaneously in a consulting firm atmosphere; broadened background and enhanced skills and knowledge in the field of safety through design.

Problem Solving

A manager's primary function is to solve problems. Understanding his or her own approach to problems and the problem-solving style most often used is an essential early step to becoming a more effective creative problem solver.

Managers tend to deal with problems in one of three ways:

1. Avoid them—refuse to recognize that a problem exists. Not quite the strongest managers, but I have had the pleasure of knowing some of these folks. Some people just don't understand that most problems do not self-correct.
2. Solve them as necessary—deal with the urgent. Better, but still not senior management material.
3. Seek them out—anticipate, to avoid them becoming urgent. Ah, here you go. This is where you need to position yourself and represent your skills on your résumé and on the interview.

Articulate in your résumé and interview that you are the latter.

Perfect Phrases

- Recognized abilities in problem solving, with a strong background in Methods and Time Studies for setting Production Standards. Managed the startup of a new state-of-art distribution center. Particularly effective in assessing and resolving employee conflicts and organizational problems, allowing for increased productivity.
- Developed strategic relationships with various department heads and suppliers, which significantly facilitated

communication and problem resolution capabilities within the organization.

- Implemented the following structured programs and methods into the engineering department: Advanced Quality Planning, Dimensional Control Plan Plus, Failure Mode and Effects Analysis, Design of Experiments, Quality Operating System, 8-D Problem Solving, Continuous Improvement Plan, process potential studies, preventative maintenance, packaging engineering, flow charts.

- Applied strong interpersonal and communication capabilities in working with a wide range of personnel at all levels to gain valuable insight, avoid potential problems, and facilitate the timely completion of projects.

- Successfully implemented customer deductions program for Claims Department, which identified problem areas within the corporation and reported results; made recommendations to upper management on a daily basis.

- Veteran production manager experienced with quality assurance, problem solving, streamlining processes, and optimizing production work flow. Extensive experience in project management, creating intuitive business collateral, Internet promotion, and developing proactive marketing strategies. Creative experience in the following:

  - Strengths in problem-solving ability, analyzing the symptoms, identifying what is wrong, and finding the solution. Also, strong in conceptual intellect.

  - Creative problem solver. Ability to move beyond limiting questions and to nurture problem-solving ideas through each of four phases of creative problem solving.

➡

- Strategic thinker, 10 years solving design, communication, and process problems.

- Management/problem solving/communication skills: managed all print and presentation projects with over a 95 percent on-time rate. Handled project tracking, system/file management, estimating, budget/billing, vendor billing, and liaisons with all vendors.

- Administration, Planning, and Problem Solving:

  - Oversee multiple tasks with varying priorities, work with many departments within an organization to ensure smooth operation, productivity, and marketing; identify areas of improvement; research, develop, and implement improved procedures.

Reengineering

The only thing that doesn't change is "change" itself. In a world increasingly driven by the three Cs—Customer, Competition, and Change—companies are on the lookout for new solutions for their business problems. Recent headlines in the mainstream press that reflect these changes include, "Wal-Mart reduces restocking time from six weeks to thirty-six hours," and, "Hewlett Packard's assembly time for server computers touches new low—four minutes," and, "Taco Bell's sales soar from $500 million to $3 billion." The reason behind these success stories is reengineering.

Reengineering is the fundamental rethinking and radical redesign of business processes to achieve improvements in measures of performance such as cost, quality, service, and speed. Since the softening of the economy in 2000, reengineering has redesigned many corporations. In the late 1990s AT&T was a powerful force in telecommunications. In 2005, AT&T has exited its consumer business and is a mere shadow of its former self.

Reengineering is not always a reduction in the size of the workforce. The workforce reduction that may accompany can instead be a by-product of a company changing itself.

In terms of your résumé and interview, you should think about noting whatever experience you've had in affecting these reengineering changes in the past.

Perfect Phrases

- Initiated turnaround with a complete restaffing of entire marketing organization. Recruited qualified personnel, introduced internal training programs, redesigned core processes, enhanced technologies, and created a ➡

sophisticated and responsive organization. Provided executive team and senior operating management with meaningful financial data.

- Redesigned organizational structures and business plans for the corporation. Introduced series of personnel and executive incentive plans that enhanced performance and accountability.

- Relocated corporate offices, field organization structure, and associated equipment for 9,300 employees in less than 120 days.

- Facilitated several successful turnarounds, introduced standardized financial and accounting processes, upgraded technologies that improved financial condition from flat line growth to net income increases from 2 percent first year to 14 percent in year three, highest in industry.

- Expert in the use of Business Process Reengineering to optimize work flows prior to developing or introducing new technology.

- Directed national cost study and methods reengineering program that achieved more than 10 percent savings per review.

- Senior Lead Management Consultant to Citibank's Business Division, directing work in reengineering design, development, testing, business analysis, and implementation of Citibank's enterprise migration and conversion. Provided senior management direction in gap analysis, data architectural design and functionality, vendor relationship decisions and implementation guidance.

- Process reengineering, commercial markets:

  - Responsible for building an infrastructure to support new marketing initiatives, integrating traditional long distance into bundled offerings for the prospect segment directorate.

- Led a major reengineering project to automate the marketing program release processes, including an intranet marketing program offer and message template generation system, an automated data feed to all downstream processes, and a redesigned database algorithm to optimize table size and vendor performance. This project dramatically reduced marketing program cycle time and recycle errors.

- Specific areas of expertise include Risk Management, Operations, Manufacturing, Project Management, Product Management, ERP, Business Process Reengineering, Change Management, Client and Customer Value Management, as well as the integration, customization, and implementation of Distribution, Supply Chain Management, Purchasing, AP, AR, GL, Billing, PeopleSoft, and SAP applications for small to large corporations.

- Served as the team lead for the redesign of member customer service processes for a major state health maintenance organization (HMO). Led the creation of conceptual design models, business procedures and rules, decision trees, and templates to support customer service process and tool implementation.

- Facilitated an organizationwide reengineering effort to reduce costs, improve efficiency, and increase resources. Established and enhanced relationships with vendors, partners, and subcontracting companies to ensure on-time implementation of systems.

- Credited with reengineering IT operations and establishing new enterprise computing environment within nine months.

- Created and implemented IT processes, procedures, and standards:

    - Planned and designed network and topology architecture. Directed teams in reengineering network infrastructures and migrating company from Token Ring to Ethernet topology. Managed the implementation of WAN to ensure appropriate data access and integration throughout all locations, including firewall and security strategies.

- Promoted renewed commitment across the IT division to change management process and practices, doubling the level of regular participation in weekly change management meetings, greatly improving interdepartmental coordination with regard to middle to high visibility changes.

- Refocused, realigned, and sized sales force territories based upon detailed customer segmentation, opportunity fit analysis, and change management.

- Developed a process for production test, implementation, and change management, as well as security policy, systems performance process and reporting, migration process, and redundant facilities environments.

- Responsible for the quality of service delivery to multiple business units and trading operations, project management, problem escalation, crisis management, change management, and service level standards across multiple platforms and network systems. Key member of change management panel.

- Evaluated help desk functions, focusing on structure and strategy, perception and performance, methodologies and procedures, staffing and education, systems, and ➥

technology and management reporting. Managed all change management initiatives to improve these functions.

- Consulted with customers and managed multiple projects such as information security and access control, enterprise change management, disaster recovery and business continuity planning, and new core network build-out support.

- Engaged in the instructional design, courseware development, and deployment of end-user training. Developed business process procedures, functional scripts, and change management deliverables.

- Directed a cross-functional team to custom-build an intranet-based application that enabled time management, team collaboration, and project management. Integrated the solution with Hyperion and PeopleSoft and facilitated a nationwide rollout of the application.

Time Management

Time management is a giant skill for a successful person, in any discipline. No question. So many people think they have it, and so few do. I had a vice president several years ago who used to say, "Give me someone smart, passionate, and who knows how to use their time, and we can give them the experience." Same with time management for me. It's vital to success. If you can convey that you effectively manage multiple projects simultaneously, you will be much more valuable to your prospective employer. Then call me because I want you working with me!

Don't let anyone steal your time. It is priceless and should be guarded with care. Benjamin Franklin once said, "Dost thou love life? Then do not squander time, for that is the stuff life is made of." More recently, former Secretary of State Henry Kissinger said, "There cannot be a crisis next week. My schedule is already full." Needless to say, the most valuable commodity in the world is time. It is easily wasted and can never be replaced; therefore, time management is essential.

Consider the following phrases candidates might use to convince employers that they use their time effectively.

Perfect Phrases

- Expertise in finding out how much time is worth, concentrating on the right things, deciding work priorities, planning to solve a problem, tackling the right tasks first through prioritized "to do" lists, and executing the plan in a timely fashion.
- Extensive project coordination, prioritization, and details/time management techniques.

➡

- Employed outstanding time management and resource allocation skills to coordinate multiple tasks while maintaining strong quality focus.
- Organized, detail-oriented, and self-motivated, with excellent time management, prioritization, and multiple task/project coordination skills. Strong work ethic and professional attitude emphasizing reliability, integrity, teamwork, and the willingness to work as necessary to get the job done.
- Certified in Time Management, Franklin Time Management course.
- Proven ability to prioritize tasks, organize and coordinate activities, manage time, set and achieve goals, meet deadlines, develop relationships, and establish procedures.
- Sponsor of 80:20 program at Toyota, which argues that typically 80 percent of unfocused effort generates only 20 percent of results. The remaining 80 percent of results are achieved with only 20 percent of the effort. Led initiative to improve time management skills of 670-plus employees.
- Assisted the production coordinator by leading the floor, training the staff, and pulling statistics. Skills used: Time Management, ability to meet strict deadlines, and ability to work under pressure.
- Business Analyst MPS/FI Project SAP Time Management:

    - Assisted in the implementation of SAP R/3 as the time management deployment lead. Directed the implementation of the time management module at each mill site. Lead the site payroll and HR personnel with data mapping and conversion. Instructed site power users and end users in time management training classes.

➡

- Effective use of time management, understanding the key principles of time management to become more effective and efficient. The essence of time management can be expressed in five major points:

  - Know the big picture.

  - Understand the difference between urgent and important.

  - Learn to think and act in a proactive way.

  - Use weekly planning as your major tool.

  - Avoid time wasters.

- Employed outstanding time management and resource allocation skills to coordinate multiple tasks while maintaining strong quality focus.

- Certifications: Active Listening Course; Decker Communication Course; Franklin Time Management.

- Time Management: able to manage multiple assignments and maintain quality of service under fast-paced conditions.

- Two full life cycle implementation of Payroll with ADP, time management, and organizational management, personnel administration. Attention to detail and ability to prioritize multi-upgrades activities along with excellent communication skills. Experience with working in a team-oriented environment, and an outstanding problem solver.

- Time Management: work schedules and time recording—substitutions, absences, absence counting, absence quotas, leave entitlement, FMLA (Family Medical Leave Act) workbench, overtime, availability—as well as time evaluation.

- Involved in training the clients' project team and determining global template functionality for the global project team in the USA. Duties included project plan preparation, progress reporting, training of local project team, determining local requirements, identification and specification of system interfaces, final configuration of the system, system and acceptance testing. Modules configured and implemented were PA, PD, Training and Events, Recruitment, and Time Management.
- Project planning experience to list out tasks, prioritize them, and map out execution. Does not procrastinate, uses time wisely, plans exceptionally, employs use of Covey planning system.
- Provide relevant and timely sales and time management training:
  - Conducted training needs assessments to determine training shortfalls and needs.
  - Attended several sales and time management courses (i.e., Covey, Franklin, Career Path), developed and conducted specific training courses that addressed the needs of the business.
  - Provided consultation services in time management training to two corporations.

Written Skills

Having written a dozen books on topics like the one in this book, I am biased about the importance of writing in business. I majored in accounting and never thought about writing early in my career. In fact, pride had more to do with my attention to detail in writing than anything: I never wanted to be caught with a typo or incorrect grammar and have the reader think I was less professional or not queued to be promoted.

Then e-mail entered the workforce in the mid-90s and poor writing skills were exposed more than Pete Sampras's fast court game on red clay. Sometimes my managers get irritated because I will take the time to rewrite poorly written e-mails or those with typos. I bet some even snicker behind my back, and were I not published, it would be even worse. But not most of my colleagues—only the ones who are lazy and lack the drive to excel.

Still, good writing skills are an absolute reflection on your professional skills. Much of it is in proofreading and some attention to detail. I'll tell you this: When you write poorly, people think less of you professionally.

Demonstrating excellent writing skills begins with your résumé. Here are some phrases to consider in order to validate that you do in fact have excellent writing skills. Note how detailed and specific some of the descriptions are. As a hiring manager, I would not doubt the writing skills of candidates like these.

Perfect Phrases

■ Wrote preview briefs for two clients for the upcoming CES Show in January 2005.

- Built briefing books for clients utilizing information obtained from various sources.
- Took the initiative to sort out the magazine lists and ed cal lists—giving them the chance to refocus their top tier, thus giving their clients a better service level.
- Validation of other consultants' plans, thoughts, and presentations for their clients.
- Provided consulting, business plan, and market plan assistance; prepared multiple presentations, marketing brochures, and mailing programs for a diversity of companies.
- Worked with Creative Directors, training manager(s) to develop, implement, create, and design staff instruction manuals, newsletters, Web pages, policy and procedure manuals, and announcements to publicize various training programs using Excel, PowerPoint, Word, and Lotus Notes.
- Assisted in layout design and production of printed materials, including newsletters, brochures, slides, graphs, and other visual PowerPoint presentation materials. Created Excel/Access spreadsheets, database, word processing, and graphics computer software programs. Conceptualized and designed layouts and formats for brochures, annual reports, direct mail, newsletters, advertisements, and corporate imaging.
- Highly resourceful, possesses strong merchandising and visual presentation skills. Strong attention to detail and keen sense of color, balance, and scale. Ability to expand on creative ideas and concepts.
- Additional duties include:
  - Proposal writing
  - Presentations

- Technology auditing
- Contract writing (including Statement of Work)

- Client communications, product branding, product rollouts (creative and tactical implementation), communication templates, proposal style guides, process documentation, ad campaign development.

- Collateral development: writes copy for marketing pieces, including but not limited to product sheets, press releases, brochures and flyers, ad copy, board reports, client communications.

- Proposal writing for various business lines, effective content with high-impact responses, high-quality proposal packaging, strategic messaging and targeting.

- Media and public relations: development of strategies to heighten awareness and visibility in the industry, speech-writing, media collateral, and kits.

- Online communications/Web writing: concept and copywriting for Web site and multimedia demos.

- Web design using HTML, Basic Management program, and several advanced writing and communications courses including Effective Writing for Business and the Professions, University of Chicago.

- Senior technical writer under contract to Sprint. Developed the Sprint Proposal Library, which included writing and editing proposal materials, proposal boilerplate, forms, templates, technical manuals, technical requirements, and design reports. Also developed the following: an organized proposal library system, proposal sections for all offerings, sales presentations with product managers and marketing to place in the proposal library, white papers on core offerings, proposal boilerplate,

➡

capability statements, corporate overview boilerplate, and project plans.

- Editor and Writer for the Presentations Department: edited and wrote test reports, schedules, proposals (cost, logistics, technical, and executive volumes), promotional pieces, management and technical volumes.

- Strategized and wrote client newsletter, e-brochures, sales presentations, Webinars, project descriptions, qualification statements, and other external communications.

- Copywrote a series of trade magazine ads discussing technology issues of "electronic post office" for collections industry.

- Developed communications strategies and marketing plans.

- Authored business proposals.

- Managed advertising, award submittals, and client relations program.

- Contributed monthly newsletter column on marketing and communication.

- Served as Web editor responsible for writing and maintaining content, including service offering descriptions, value propositions, FAQs, news items, and seed content for online community.

- Managed content administration for Web site, including updates, revisions, and posting of new material (ATG/Interwoven content management system).

- Redevelopment of Web sites, including page design, site structure, and navigation.

- Researched, developed, and wrote Web-based, interactive business training (included instructional story and material, quizzes and tutoring, expert interviews and audio, ➡

glossary and FAQs), conceptualized and worked with tech staff to develop multimedia component that reinforced instructional material.

■ Developed informational resource articles on work/life issues. Identified new areas and ideas for development, including resources, tools, and potential alliance partners.

Writing/Editing

■ Research, drafting, and editing for book, *Understanding Financial Statements: A Journalist's Guide,* published by Marion Street Press.

■ Former teacher of writing seminars at Newberry Library and Latin School Adult Programs.

■ Author of nine articles that have appeared in national trade magazines, including the interviewing of subject matter experts.

■ Editor of employee newsletters.

■ Research, writing, and editing of public communications (policy statements, speeches, correspondence, and ceremonial messages).

■ Writing and editing reports (a client deliverable) covering investigative findings, conclusions, and recommendations.

Grant/Proposal Writing

■ Routinely researched, edited, and wrote a range of materials for corporations and not-for-profits, including:

   ■ Requests for Proposals (RFP), Requests for Information (RFI), and Requests for Qualifications (RFQ) for projects varying from $25,000 to $2 billion, with a 33 percent win ratio.

- Responded to, prepared, and solicited documents above, analyzing and using sound judgment practices to select or identify opportunities, accuracy, appropriate capabilities, and content.

- Identified and developed proposals, which resulted in three years of backlog (booked revenue stream) for URS Consultants.

Presentations and Graphic Design

- Designed presentations based upon determination of best response to client's needs, often working in a team environment.
- Led presentations to clients and trained marketing and project staff in making presentations.
- Developed multimedia presentations utilizing advanced software for use in large seminars and trade shows.
- Improved the response rate of sales and marketing materials by:

  - Dramatically increasing the quality of PowerPoint presentations and Word documents through creative writing, formatting, and use of design elements, including tables and graphics (Excel charts, Visio diagrams, organization charts, logos, and images).

  - Researching prospect business interests and creating material targeted to those interests.

Part III

Perfect Phrases by Industry and Discipline

Advertising Director

Career Summaries

Creative, Web-savvy Marketing and Advertising Executive with unparalleled ability to build advertising revenues in the Internet publishing market.

Exceptional skills in business development, including market definition, campaign design and implementation, and development of online services.

Key strengths in identifying and managing opportunities for strategic alliances, spotting trends in consumer markets, and anticipating emerging technologies.

Dynamic, inspirational leadership style, eliciting the best from creative contributors and sales support teams while meeting publication standards and deadlines.

Credited by executive management team for outstanding results in forecasting, budgeting, executive reporting, and project management.

Dynamic and proven professional with over 12 years marketing and advertising experience with demonstrated success in agency, consulting, and Fortune 1000 environments.

Acumen for developing solutions using the full complement of the marketing and promotional mix, inclusive of database, PR, sales promotion, events, and online channels.

Able to organize complex variables, build partnerships, then orchestrate internal and external resources toward shared objectives while maintaining clear communication and positive relationships. Possess self-initiative, an attention to detail, and a standard of excellence. ➡

Reputation for completing projects on time and in-budget with solutions focused on meeting marketing and promotional metrics, articulating strategic communications objectives, and maximizing production efficiencies.

Polished interpersonal and communications skills, with public speaking and presentation abilities. Wide range of computer systems and software knowledge and experience.

Manage an advertising operations support team of eight with a sales budget of $58 million.

Perfect Phrases

- Media Marketing Executive with 15 years of success in development and execution of strategies to position targeted cable network as "best in class" in reaching and influencing a niche market. Skilled at translating market intelligence into profitable business solutions. Extensive knowledge of the advertising sales and stewardship process.

- Areas of Expertise: Strategic Planning, Competitive Analysis and Positioning, Brand Management, Consumer Insights, Project Management, Media Planning, Staff Development and Training, and Profit Center Development.

- Create and continually improve a market-sensitive menu of strategic advertising options serving the diverse needs of e-commerce businesses across multiple industries.

- Foster strong business relationships with Fortune 250 clients. Act as advertising consultant to up-and-coming Web and technology companies.

- Facilitate innovative, interactive territory meetings on a weekly basis. Set and measured progress toward team and individual objectives.

- Ranked number one among RCA's six global regions, 2003, 2004, and 2005. Grew key account base by 72 percent in first year, representing new revenues of $48 million.

- Promotion was recognized by executive leadership in a press release:"Samantha has consistently achieved major gains in advertising revenues by positioning iWORLD as the number one Internet news destination for executives."
  —Kevin Talon, VP of Marketing for RCA

- Fashion and entertainment industry Advertising Production Specialist. Extensive credentials in key account sales, marketing, and management.

- Produce, cast, negotiate, and budget photo shoots for multimillion-dollar domestic and international accounts. Coordinate and execute worldwide photo shoots. Direct 20 to 40 international production teams. Engineer and maintain high-profile fashion photographers. Cast, book, and schedule leading models and performers.

- Open and retain million-dollar accounts, including Verizon, NBC, KKR, and Acushnet (Titleist Golf). Supervise departmental staff of 15.

- Supervise 25 employees in the page layout and printing of syndicated comics, newspaper articles, and puzzles for national newspapers. Oversee weekly page makeup and client contact for personal ads in 15 nationwide publications. Manage electronic pre-press section. Schedule and quality-check four-color promotional ads for licensing, sales, and comic art departments. Set prep quality standards. Design and quality-check covers for syndicated newspaper TV guides.

- Department is nationally recognized as leader in in-house printing.

➡

- Developed concepts and designs for clients in the film, theater, nonprofit, and fashion industries. Designed special promotional material, direct-mail brochures, press kits, and corporate identities. Produced exceptional quality work for clients on a tight budget and a tight deadline.
- Designed newspaper ads for real estate companies, stores, restaurants, and politicians.

Attorney

Note: Look at the tone of the phrases used, the type of subject matter. Of particular interest is the phrase below that objectively describes the attorney's compensation plan, hours worked, and his or her contribution to the firm.

Career Summaries

Fifteen-year partner in busy corporate and consumer bankruptcy and commercial litigation practice. Representation of various businesses in collections, contract drafting and negotiation, SEC issues, financing, leasing, commercial loan drafting and review, loan workouts, asset-based financing, master-factoring agreements, liquidations, receiverships, and assignment for the benefit of creditors

Representation of corporations in successful Chapter 11 reorganizations, including contentious in-court legal proceedings, complex negotiations with secured creditors and creditors' committees, as well as regular briefings with senior officials/executives of the involved entities. Drafting of intricate legal and business documents and ability to communicate said documents clearly in court under litigious situations.

Manage client relationships and develop and implement business strategies to promote the financial development of the firm. Oversee associate development and work-product as well as all matters related to staffing, budgeting, resource utilization, and office administration. Daily utilization and enhancement of managerial and organization skills, in addition to the ability to handle ongoing multiple projects while maintaining a sharp attention to detail.

Twenty-one years experience in U.S. and international business development and technology commercialization efforts relating to space exploration by integrating fully and applying the following experiences:

- Eighteen years of patent and other intellectual property, legal, and business experience in a broad array of complex technologies.

- Ten years of combined civil service and Navy Reserve experience in defense systems development and acquisition.

- Six years of active duty Navy Submarine Force service as a nuclear trained line officer focusing on the new construction of a fast attack nuclear submarine.

Perfect Phrases

- Annual Salary: $350,000. Hours worked per week: 75. Supervisor: Victor Hinojosa, Intellectual Property Section Lead Attorney (Columbus, OH). Recruited to serve as Partner in Intellectual Property Law tasked with assisting in establishing firm's Dayton, Ohio, office. Firm size: 525 attorneys.

- Initiated and managed expansion of office file for national law firm.

- Increased business for office expansion by 300 percent.

- Progressive expertise in trial law involving catastrophic injuries and complex commercial issues.

- Oversaw billing on regular basis, utilizing innovative software word processing program.

- Managed trials of commercial and personal injury claims with 100 percent success.

➡

- Point person in associate development for multimillion-dollar billings.
- Oversaw establishment and provided management of associate training program.
- Provided consultation to products manufacturers regarding proposed safety changes.
- Experienced in alternative dispute resolution.
- Representation of various banks/businesses in security agreements, commercial loan workouts, contract negotiation, UCC issues, loan drafting and review, regulatory matters, asset-based financing, master-factoring agreements, liquidations, receiverships, and assignments for the benefit of creditors.
- Detailed experience in corporate reorganizations, creditors' rights, and commercial litigation. Representation of secured and unsecured creditors, creditors' committees, debtors, equity holders, and trustees in all phases of proceedings under the United States Bankruptcy Code.
- Drafted and successfully confirmed debtor's plan of reorganization for multimillion-dollar company in Chapter 11 proceeding. Settled client's claim against large trading card company, which included complex negotiations with Major League Baseball, the National Football League, and the National Hockey League.
- Solo practitioner with a diversified caseload of real estate transactions and litigation, business transactions and litigation, corporate and partnership matters, estate planning, probate, bankruptcy, and mortgage foreclosures.
- Real estate transactions and litigation, business transactions and litigation, corporate and partnership

matters, estate planning, bankruptcy, mortgage foreclosures, and homeowner associations.

- Worked closely with CEO and COO to define new organizational structure and drive standardization throughout the organization.
- Developed policies and procedures, job descriptions, pay scales, and produced first Employee Handbook.
- Credited for taking little-known health-care company and making it employer of choice by formalizing corporate culture and leading internal/external branding/communications campaigns. Established HR and Legal Services as strategic partner with corporate leaders and Facility Administrators.
- Standardized hiring and training program and spearheaded strategy to attract medical personnel in extremely competitive market.
- Challenged in last 12 months to drive employee morale in the face of management reorganization from six partners to one. Collaborated with executive and field management to support downsizing, including nearly 50 percent of corporate staff and roughly $1million in combined field staff reductions. Led communications program to employees and ensured compliance with HR policies to avoid legal issues and complaints.
- Counseled management and used legal expertise to thwart lawsuits and threats, defeating all employment-related complaints with zero dollars used for settlements or legal fees. Maintained strict oversight of outside legal counsel, closely monitoring strategy and cost.

Banking

Career Summaries

Devise and implement innovative marketing principles and promotional sales events for commercial and consumer projects to further support financial growth.

Counsel high-net-worth individuals and corporate clients with regard to investment opportunities, risk analysis, and monetary returns.

Cross-sell banking services and products to clientele.

Participate in community events to position the bank as a leader within the territory.

Senior Operating Executive in the banking industry with proven leadership skills and expertise in refining credit quality, returns on investment and capital, cross-marketing, asset growth, and analysis of risk-adjusted returns on mortgage lending. Successfully orchestrated the centralization of lending, collections, underwriting, and loan-processing procedures to maximize asset performance. Early background includes regional operations and training management for a St. Louis–based investment company, supervising offices in 12 midwestern states.

Recruited to bolster the lending operation for community bank established in 1956, now serving 25,000 customers with $170 million in total deposits.

Centralized the Collection and Secondary Mortgage departments. Sold real estate loans in the Secondary Market totaling more than $20 million from 1993 to 1995. Collection of recovery accounts exceeded charge-offs for the last three years.

Increased loan outstanding from $63 to $106 million.

Decreased classified loans from $10 to $3 million.

➡

Implemented an indirect lending department now serving more than 3,000 loan customers.

Perfect Phrases

- Reduced retail delinquency from 4.45 percent in 2003 to 1.79 percent in 2005.
- Assumed additional responsibility of servicing all commercial collections deemed a Workout Status. Accepted the responsibility of managing the bank's Other Retail Estate Owned (ORE). Reduced ORE from $1.1 million to $700,000.
- Centralized the Indirect Lending area into a single location servicing 46 auto dealers in the Metro-East area. With two underwriters and a clerical staff of four, processed more than 1,000 applications each month. Purchased $11 million in auto loan paper in the first three months of 1993 for a net gain in outstanding of $3 million.
- With the centralization of the collection department, reduced the amount of charge-offs from 1.67 percent in 1991 to 0.85 percent in 1992.
- Centralized all Direct Lending into a single department processing approximately 200 direct loan applications per month. Provided a centralized approval process for Central Bank's 11 locations.
- Successfully organized and set up a Secondary Mortgage Department for Central Bank in 1989. Originally started this effort as the sole underwriter for FNMA. Formulated a staff that grew the department to $12 million in FNMA loans and serviced direct real estate loans totaling $60 million. FNMA delinquency was zero when I left Central Bank.
- Generated over $100,000 in revenue and fee income within a four-month period.

- Branch Manager with 17 years of progressively responsible positions in the financial industry. Strong managerial, administrative, interpersonal, and problem-solving skills, with proven leadership ability. Directed daily operations for retail bank, including branch sales, business development, customer service, and credit analysis. Managed staff of 15 Customer Service Representatives and Tellers.
- Manage operations, personnel, budget, profit planning, and audit and compliance for branch with assets up to $19 million. Proven ability to achieve success given difficult situations. Turned around Mason branch within three months, bringing branch within audit compliance. Maintained excellent audit ratings. Effectively managed branch throughout merger process. Able to plan, organize, delegate, administer, and direct in order to meet branch goals and corporate mission.
- Sales Team Leader; strong customer service orientation. Of 79 offices, Mason Branch was number one in Cross-Sell Ratio for 1990. As individual, placed second in Cross-Sell for that same year. Outstanding achievement in Cross-Sell Ratio for 1992. Increased branch average monthly deposit balance by $1.5 million from 1992 to 1993.
- Strong leadership skills with the ability to generate enthusiasm among staff. Supervised, developed, and directed staff of seven. Determined staffing levels and reorganized job responsibilities to effectively utilize resources during merger. Implemented a Retail Sales Performance System to train employees to be part of sales culture.
- Named "Rookie of the Year," for most productive new teller, 2005.

- Recognized for highest level of accuracy of all 18 tellers, 2006.
- Significantly expanded bank's community development efforts through increased involvement with local, state, and federal programs (SBA). This resulted in new inroads to more complex, nontraditional business opportunities, which yielded profitability as well as greater market penetration and share for United Bank & Trust.
- Increased 2005 commercial loan closings over 2004 through aggressive promotion and marketing; personally responsible for developing and managing capital investment programs for approximately 45 Cincinnati businesses.
- Effectively promoted visibility of United Bank & Trust through planning and presentation of seminars for clients and through participation at conferences and trade shows.
- Managed promotion and sales of complete breadth of financial products and services to portfolio of 60 clients characterized by high net worth. Responsibilities included origination, underwriting, and closing of commercial/consumer loans.
- Successfully restructured entire $3.2 million portfolio in noncompliance with bank loan policy.
- Managed $8 million loan portfolio for savings bank with assets of $7 billion. Oversaw new business development, financial data collection, and analysis.
- Elected to bank officer's position to assist in formation and establishment of commercial bank.
- Managed consumer/mortgage lending department, generating $12 million in consumer loans and $6 million in commercial loans for fiscal year 2005.

Biotechnology

Career Summaries

Management professional attuned to the ever-changing needs of business. Extremely service-oriented, with a unique combination of intuitive and analytical abilities. Astute in identifying market plan needs, creating actionable programs, and effectively interacting with the sales field.

Robust analytical and problem-solving skills.

Methodical, investigative, and creative.

Specialized in the physicochemical and mechanical characterization of solids.

Knowledgeable in formulation science, physical pharmacy, and analytical chemistry.

Well-acquainted with most of the instruments and techniques used today, such as UV, FT-IR, HPLC, DSC/TGA, powder X-ray diffractometry, scanning electron microscopy, light microscopy, VTI water sorption analyzer, GMP dissolution, BET surface analyzer, and helium pycnometer, among others.

Experienced in solid dosage form design and development.

Perfect Phrases

■ Carried out preformulation studies for new drug applicants. Conducted formulation studies of various dosage forms.
■ Performed HPLC assay method development, prevalidation, and validation studies, and prepared the corresponding reports.
■ Carried out stability and excipient compatibility studies and completed the related reports.

➡

- Analyzed in-process samples, cleaning equipment samples, and finished pharmaceuticals to ensure quality, uniformity, and safety of products.
- Experienced lab data and record keeping, lab logs maintenance, purchase orders, equipment maintenance/calibration, and hazardous waste management.
- Practiced current Good Manufacturing Practices and Good Laboratory Procedures (cGMP and cGLP) to execute projects and to report the same.
- Updated the master batch records for most of the pharmaceutical products and elaborated SOPs.
- Supervised packaging processes and experienced managing personnel.
- Poster Presentations/Honors/Awards:

    - Pharmacy Graduate Program Excellence Award, Michigan State University (2003–2004).

    - Graduate Student Travel Award, Michigan State University (2004).

    - Graduate Student Travel Award, Michigan State University (2003).

    - Graduate Student Travel Award, Michigan State University (2002).

    - John Lach Fellowship, Michigan State University (2000).

- As a practicing scientist trained in mammalian biology, molecular cell biology, virology, microbiology, and molecular genetics, led R&D scientists in the support and service of pharmaceuticals discovery. The management and administrative skills gained in industry were further

➡

refined while establishing a state research institute, and then in a start-up biotech company. The process of scientific discovery and promoting practical applications of good science continue to be my interest.

- Managed the design and development of knowledge-based products for modeling complex biological interactions.
- Performed senior management team responsibilities, including business development, marketing, and M&A analyses in the biotechnology and pharmaceuticals sectors.
- Developed strategic plans to promote the adoption of biosimulation products and services within pharmaceuticals discovery and preclinical research.
- Molecular Biology of Inflammatory Mediators.
- Identified human genes responding to anti-inflammatory drugs via differential display.
- Cloned and expressed novel metalloproteinases using unique reporter systems.
- Identified drug targets through SAGE, differential display, and database mining.
- Developed novel gene-family cloning systems, activity (expression) cloning systems, and cell-based assays to find disease-related proteases.
- Management of Biotechnology Research. Simultaneously supervised two groups that combined; formed a 52-person research organization dedicated to produce molecular and cellular reagents as a service:

   Supervised 28 scientists (11 direct reports—eight Ph.D.s) who provided cell and molecular biology support for five drug discovery groups. Technologies: gene acquisition expression cloning, PCR, subtraction

➡

libraries, recombinant protein expression (bacterial, yeast, insect, mammalian), bioinformatics, and protein engineering. Core service facilities: oligonucleotide synthesis, cytometry, and DNA sequencing.

- Biotechnology Resources Group: led 24 scientists (six direct reports—five Ph.D.s) who provided companywide support in scale-up protein purification, protein analysis, fermentation, large-scale cell production, and monoclonal antibody production.
- Duties at Merck & Co. included scale-up and scale-down experiments in fermentation/pilot-plant. Extensive work with HPLC, including Perkin Elmer and TSP models using turbochrom software.
- Worked with fermentation processes in the development of pharmaceuticals.
- Hands-on work with one-liter BioFlo 2000 glass fermentors, as well as 5- and 70-liter Biotech International steel fermentors in preparation for scale-up. Experience with centrifugation, including ultracentrifuge. Provided an intermediate level of analytical support for raw materials and in-process product testing. Familiar with GMP environment.

Chief Executive Officer

Career Summaries

Executive Summary

Telecommunications executive with over 30 years successful industry experience in Executive Leadership, Product/Process Development, Strategic Marketing/Sales, and Operations. Strong leader with extensive knowledge of wireless communications and cutting edge network technologies. Proven record of building revenues, increasing profitability, building strong customer relationships and establishment of solid operations in the wireless communications industry. Visionary leader, able to bring organization, creative thinking, and innovative problem solving to bear on business operations. Inspirational manager of talent teams.

Career Profile

Seven years experience as CEO for Fortune 500 consumer products company.

Twenty-three years in consumer products and packaging.

Over 14 years related business management and marketing experience, with a proven track record in building, supporting, and managing relationships across functional teams and corporate hierarchies.

Experience in leading and managing successful organizations B2B and stewarding new marketing projects and proposals.

Supervised, coordinated, oversaw, and represented complete marketing and advertising initiatives for publication and media for the community at large, and monitored all press-released and printed material for distribution over 200-mile radius.

➡

Entrepreneurial experience in managing and marketing new business development, including finance, start-up operations, and successful turnarounds.

Perfect Phrases

- Built initial sales force, increasing run rate share for Web hosting from 30 percent to over 46 percent.

    - Launched worldwide hosted exchange business through strategic agreement with Verizon.

    - Led strategic agreement with Korea Telecom (KT), leading to $465 million in new revenue.

    - Directed development of and go-to-market partnerships for hosted unified communications solution.

- Managed large organizations with 450 employees internationally, including senior staff of subsidiaries. Managed operating budgets up to $50 million.

- As CEO, contributed vision, strategy, and leadership with full P&L accountability for all aspects of operations. Led a core executive team of 10—CFO, Director of HR, Director of Development, CTO, Director of Product Management, Director of Quality, Support Manager, Director of Marketing, North American Sales Manager, European Sales Manager—and provided indirect oversight to thousands of other employees.

- As Chief Marketing Officer, led all aspects of market research, as well as target market trend sampling. Led Product Planning Specification development, Prototype Alpha/Beta end-user testing, and user documentation. Working with both internal and external resources, led total branding effort, including company and product names, along with all supporting Web presence and sales support tools leading to European and North American market introductions. Led efforts to attract and secure new Growth Phase VC/Private Equity Investors.

- Three years at a top-tier venture capital firm, T. Rowe Growth Funds (TRGF), as a Co-Managing Director of a $457 million fund.
- Helped start a new technology fund: deal flow, business plans, due diligence, investments, portfolio, and boards.
- Two years working with private equity firms when with a consulting firm, PwC: helped with due diligence and structuring deals exceeding $200 million.
- Structured Venture Capital (VC), Leverage Buy-Out (LBO), Initial Public Offering (IPO), and Merger and Acquisition (M&A) deals.
- Helped raise over $600 million in debt and equity for a public company Start-Up and Corporate/Business Development Experience.
- Education Experience:

  - Harvard Business School (HBS) MBA—Alumni Network—for two years.

  - Scored highest in Accounting and Finance at HBS.

  - GE Financial Management Program classes for $2\frac{1}{2}$ years.

  - Michigan State University (MSU): Finance and Accounting B.A. for four years.

  - Taught Strategic Planning course at GE.

➡️

- High technology senior executive experienced in identifying market opportunities, raising capital, building teams, developing new products, forming enterprises/start-ups, and affecting turnarounds.
- Industry experience focused on the Internet, information, communication, entertainment, and transaction services.
- Recent experience with Internet services in the U.S. and Asia Pacific, competitive local exchange carriers, interactive television, cable television, electronic commerce, merger and acquisitions, initial public offerings, data mining, terrestrial navigation systems, and computer-telephony integration.
- Previous experience in electronic banking, electronic brokerage, retail, consumer packaged goods, automotive, airlines, advertising, management information systems, and decision support systems.
- Managed a direct staff of 10 with a total complement of 758 full-time employees and an annual operating budget of $90 million. Approximately 30 percent of the hospital employees are under collective bargaining agreements.
- Responsible for total operations of this 266-bed community general hospital, providing acute care services as well as open heart surgery, OB, NICU, in- and outpatient psychiatry, home care, sleep lab, pain management, wound care, and others. Facilities include an independent outpatient surgery center and a medical office building.
- CEO and President, with a track record of leadership and fast-growth through strategic/tactical execution:
    - Grew four companies from early stages to mid-cap size—two approaching $400 million per annum.

➡

- Career history primarily in Enterprise Software: Licensed Business Process.

- Company Lifecycle/Event exposure includes: start-up, M&A, restructure, turnaround, IPO, and Public.

  - Led pursuit, sales capture, and delivery management of over $3.9 billion in new business since 1985.

  - Directed multiple go-to-market sales and marketing initiatives: direct and indirect channels, alliances, and JVs.

  - Successfully executed seven mergers and acquisitions and four investment solicitations and road shows.

  - Profiled in a 2005 CEO conference as "One of the Best CEOs You May Never Have Heard of": "A rare talent for translating vision into strategic focus with fast-paced tactical execution; a transformational leadership style that empowers organizational effectiveness and high-energy team-building; a hands-on, proactive management style that combines aggressive business momentum with increasing net profits, creating results and rewards for both the employees and shareholders alike."

Database or Data Processing

Career Summaries

Data Warehouse Manager offering 10 years of experience and in-depth knowledge of the functional and data needs of e-businesses.

Data warehouse development experience incorporates skills in programming, analysis, architecture, and project management. Expertise in high-level and detailed system design, requirements gathering, logical and physical data modeling, development, and implementation. Expert knowledge of data modeling in ERP and other major application areas.

Well-versed in Oracle (Oracle Express, Oracle Reporter, Oracle Financial), Oracle tools, and Erwin products. Data migration experience using Informatica, C++, Java, Corba, multidimensional database, JavaScript, Oracle Web server, and Java. Exceptional use of CASE tools as part of an overall development effort.

Extensive knowledge of DBMS: Oracle RDBMS, SQL, PL/SQL, STAR Schema Modeling. Experienced in UNIX operating system, Microsoft PC operating systems including NT, desktop productivity software, and client/server system architecture.

Proven ability to assemble and mobilize project teams, building consensus among multidisciplinary technical and functional teams in the rapid development and implementation of data warehousing solutions. Recognized by managers and colleagues as a strong, positive leader and a sharp strategic thinker.

Data Mining Specialist: Developing Solutions for Online Relationship Marketing.

Specialist in developing customer affinity through the design, implementation, and management of data mining solutions for relationship marketing applications. Full life-cycle experience on enterprise-scale data warehousing/mining projects. Strong team leader and results-focused manager. Capabilities include:

Data Warehousing, Mining, and Reporting	Mass Marketing Communication Tools
Data Analysis and Knowledge Discovery	Systems Design and Development
CRM Technologies and Tools	Web-Enabled Decision Support Applications

Perfect Phrases

- Drive the strategic vision and evolution from centralized data warehouse to distributed data marts. Report to divisional IT management with accountability for global processes. Manage a budget of $5.6 million.
- Provide guidance to software development teams on the use and purpose of data warehouses. Direct a team of seven data warehouse developers/analysts in the daily operations of the corporate data warehouse. Oversee all aspects of the warehouses, including data sourcing, data migration, data quality, data warehouse design, and implementation.
- Scope, plan, and prioritize multiple project deliverables, based on data warehousing dependencies and changing business needs. Develop project plans, identify and fill project resource needs, and manage projects to on-time, on-budget completion.

- Influence tool-set and business needs assessment. Lead the selection of third-party software; manage vendor relationships. Successfully manage multiple projects in the design and implementation of warehouse functionality and interfaces.
- Translated an enterprise data model, created dimension and fact tables to support budgeting, financial planning, analysis, and dataware systems, in collaboration with the DBA and Data Steward.
- Determined database/data mart business requirements. Created the logical and physical database/datamart design for Relational and OLAP Data Warehouse environment.

Computer Technology

Hardware: Main Frames, IBM 360/370, Mini Computers, RISC6000, AS400, PCs, and peripherals

Connectivity: Novel NetWare, LAN, WAN, Windows NT, 95, NT's Workstation

Languages: Assembler, C, C++, COBOL, FORTRAN, PL/I, Visual Basic, Basic

Relational Database: SQL (Relational Database), Informix, SQL Server, FOX Pro

Operating Systems: AIX, UNIX, XENIX, DOS, DOS VS, OS, OS VS, LAN, and WAN

Database Manager and Director of Information Systems of the SW Division. Recruited to assume Director, Information Systems position. Scope of responsibility includes management of all systems. Primary responsibilities involve creating

➡️

new systems based upon client needs. Ancillary duties involve enhancing, servicing, and maintaining existing systems applications for new customers. Oversee daily activities of a Network Administrator and three Systems Administrators, and seven PC Support, Computer Operators, and Data Processing Clerks. Primary duties include identifying specific needs of each department, determining feasibility, and assigning systems administrators to accomplish.

- Achieved $78 million increase in annual sales ($322 to $400 million) by eliminating systems down time, increasing availability of systems time, and increasing customer computers, allowing 24-hour-a-day usage.
- Led focus group that created systems designed to eliminate an average three hours down time. Monitored and modified systems, achieving weekly labor costs savings of $72,000.
- Developed a program that monitors systems every 10 minutes to identify "problems" prior to development and allowing preventive action to eliminate down time.
- Expedited sales orders processing by providing 200-plus laptops to salespersons. Implemented direct order entry systems to expedite sales process.
- Developed and implemented an Electronic Data Input (EDI) ordering system for U.S. Navy within six weeks. Achieved $25 million annual order from Navy by meeting the established deadline.

Review the development, testing, and implementation of data and application security plans, products, and control techniques to ensure the security of clients' personal and sensitive credit card information being transmitted via the Web. Control access to data and change passwords.

➡

Thoroughly investigate and recommend appropriate corrective actions for data and application security incidents. Identify data security risks and report breaches. Lead and direct staff to scan all application and production software environments.

Technically proficient with Firewalls, Virus Detection Software, and Web site checking platforms. Evaluate and test security and virus detection software. Work closely with the administrator to monitor the system for intrusions.

Develop Security Tools

Designed and implemented a highly effective data and computer operations security checklist for daily use by computer operators. The result was a decrease in noted security deficiencies of 11 percent in less than six months.

Designed and incorporated a tiered level of access to databases, creating a "hacker-proof/need to know" security measure environment.

Implement Security Contingency Plans

Drafted an Intrusion Response Plan: implemented the plan during a real-life security crisis—every computer database was infected with a contagious virus that deleted data files. Directed operators to follow protocol, and operations resumed within three hours.

Drafted a Disaster Recovery Plan: wrote and implemented a procedures manual to ensure the security of data through off-site storage measures and theft avoidance, including contingency plans for natural disasters or terrorist attacks.

Technical Qualifications

Extensive experience in design and construction of data warehousing and processing systems.

Oracle Certified Professional—DBA; extensive Oracle PL/SQL qualifications.

In-depth understanding of OLAP, data mining, and ad-hoc query tools.

Experienced in UNIX/Perl scripting; C and C++ software development abilities.

Highly proficient with most popular reporting tools: Actuate, Crystal Reports, and Cognos.

Advanced skills with data analysis applications: SAS and SPSS.

Deep understanding of CRM tools: Epiphany, Broadbase, and Siebel eConfigurator.

Knowledgeable in strategies for linking data to Web content management platforms.

Finance and Accounting

Career Summaries

Certified Public Accountant/Chief Financial Officer with 18 years experience in corporate accounting and 10 years experience in multicorporation accounting operations in the medical field. Areas of expertise include:

> Financial Administration/Reporting
> Operations Management
> Telecommunications Integration
> Multicorporation/Partnership Taxes
> Acquisitions/Joint Ventures
> Credit Lines/Administration
> Accounting Systems Design/Implementation
> Central Accounting Administration
> Financial Planning/Analysis
> Acquisition Negotiations
> Premium Rate Strategies
> Equipment Leasing/Portfolio
> Multisite Retail Purchasing/Negotiations
> Strategic Planning/Budgeting

Corporate Finance/Accounting/Administration/MIS

Sixteen-year professional career directing domestic and international corporate finance for challenging and complex operations. Expert negotiation and transaction management qualifications. Skilled decision maker, problem solver, and team leader. Fluent in French and Scandinavian languages. Conversational German.

> Merger and Acquisition Management
> Corporate Divestiture and Realignment

Strategic Planning and Development
SEC Regulatory Affairs and Documentation
Securities and Investment Banking
Public Relations and Investor Relations
Financial Consolidation and Reporting
Asset and Liability Management
General Accounting Operations
Operations and Financial Analysis
Pension and Benefits Administration
Domestic and International Tax

Perfect Phrases

- Led financial team to orchestrate five major acquisitions in last three years valued at over $325 million each. Entities involved include Cisco Systems, Aramark Services, Cadbury Schweppes, Nokia, and Frito-Lay.

- Prepared comprehensive financial analysis, reviews, and recommendations for acquiring company and subsidiaries.

- Joined early stage company to provide financial and investment leadership to accelerate growth, expansion, and diversification. Focused efforts on developing investor and banking relationships, strengthening corporate business infrastructure, introducing sound financial policies, and implementing advanced information technologies. Supervised organization of 34 people.

- Advised CEO, CFO, and board directors on a wide range of strategic and business planning, finance accounting, and corporate development and acquisition activities.

- Directed all tax work for all 12 corporations and performed all accounting, financial, and tax planning for David Faulk and his family members. Prepared over 400 Federal/State individual and corporate tax returns annually. ➡

- Saved Atlas Transit Inc. over $250,000 in tax accounting fees. Saved the firm over $400,000 by studying and adjusting the depreciation state allocation method.
- Analyzed financial status of London office and recommended its closure. Revenues increased and operational efficiencies improved concurrently with these cost cuts.
- Managed accounting department consisting of A/P, A/R, cost management, and general ledger maintenance.
- Saved the firm over $190,000 by successfully negotiating insurance rates. Also saved the company $100,000 in credit card processing fees. Implemented a 401(k) plan. Streamlined monthly reporting period from 60 to 40 days.
- Managed team with responsibility for all areas of operations and accounting including: budgeting, cash management, monthly financial statements, account controls, year-end accounting/audit preparation, and personnel supervision.
- Instrumental in the research and coordination to integrate voice, data, and fax over data lines that will save $100 to $200,000 in long-distance charges annually.
- Saved $87,000 in annual corporate management salaries through comprehensive management of the financial programs and credit administration of the group.
- Designed, implemented, and managed all centralized accounting, management information systems, and internal control policies and procedures for 11 corporations.
- Instrumental in the negotiation and acquisition of $3 million home-care and retail pharmacy stores; negotiated a $14 million contract for pharmaceuticals resulting in a

savings of 1.5 to 3 percent on cost of goods for each retail store.

- Responsible for the accurate and timely processing of accounts payable/receivable, payroll (48 employees), insurance and union reports, and sales tax/payroll tax reporting for this $2.1 million firm. Performed job costing, account analysis, and general ledger management using Excel.

- Freed up $32,000 by reducing A/R aging from 77 to 38 days.

- Trained and directed six employees in accounting department. Analyzed and interpreted forecasts, capital expenditures, and financial data for $3.2 million manufacturer. Directly involved in budget preparation and cash flow.

- Provided financial data and accounting services in connection with change in ownership, including licensing requirements, conversion from S corp. to C corp., and collaboration with attorney.

- Reduced primary expense category from 50 percent to 34 to 36 percent, saving company approximately $1.2 million through implementation of purchasing controls.

- Instrumental in the implementation of monthly credit reports of each account being forwarded to sales force; enabled comprehension of accounts' creditworthiness and future sales tactics.

- As Director, held full responsibility for directing all accounting operations and monitoring financial performance of each operating division. Defined MIS information requirements to meet operating needs, and established corporatewide accounting policies, procedures, and reporting packages. Led a professional staff of 16 (11 of whom were CPAs with Big Six experience) with dotted line responsibility for 70-plus Division and Group Controllers.

- Established the entire accounting and financial infrastructure for new corporation. Developed policies and procedures for budgeting, financial analysis, financial reporting, tax accounting, and pension accounting. Coordinated with Treasury Department for international cash management.

- Directed complex financial analysis and integration of all accounting and financial operations for 19 acquisitions worldwide ($500,000 to $258 million). Integrated two acquisitions concurrent with company spin-off.

- Developed economic analysis of impact on stock price of share buyback versus acquisition investment with the company's price/earnings ratio as measure.

- Successfully represented Williams in an arbitration of a disputed sales contract. Presented and interpreted financial and contractual documentation for the court, and recovered $20.6 million of disputed $21 million for the corporation.

- Coordinated and implemented all aspects of general bookkeeping. Reconciled bank statements and accounts. Utilized chart of accounts to code vouchers and entered accounts payable invoices. Prepared cash disbursements, applied cash receipts, researched bills, checked batches and day reports for accuracy. Generated computerized end-of-month reports. Utilized trial balance for various schedules.

Fund-Raising

Career Summaries

Started, organized, and managed nonprofit campaigns for 10 years.

Headed national capital initiatives for a national nonprofit for six years, raising more than $20 million.

Executive Director experience at both local and national levels.

Experienced in Economic Development studies and campaigns for Chambers of Commerce, government entities, and Economic Development commissions.

Experienced in self-employment and independent, on-site work.

An individual whose personal philosophy and values have enabled him to succeed and to inspire and lead others.

Perfect Phrases

- As a senior officer, started, organized, and managed multimillion-dollar economic initiatives.
- Experienced as a campaign consultant in: Feasibility Studies, Volunteer Development, seven-figure investment development.
- Managed significant Chamber campaigns all under budget and over goal. Oversaw all systems and operational issues with clients and my team.
- Built on existing Volunteer Development to increase over 50 percent.
- The South Texas program alone raised over $250,000 and gained 5,000 volunteers. Personally volunteered in the program for 15 years, including coaching. Established statewide partnership with the ATP of America and the ➡

First Serve Program. Provided staff support on capital initiatives for handicap accessible parks and buildings.

- Training: for several years, a trainer in development on the executive level. Trained at both the professional and volunteer levels. Extensive public and seminar experience. Presented to groups of 40 to 300. Trained in resource development, planned giving, major gifts, volunteer development, and capital campaigns.

- Responsible for the formation and incorporation of an all-volunteer 501(c)3 charitable organization, including corporate charter, articles of incorporation, IRS status request generation, and internal procedure definitions. Successfully completed state, federal, and local registration for organization with gross income over $100,000 by second year. Successfully negotiated rent-free associations with pet supply businesses for pet-adoption locations.

- Successfully defined volunteer roles and attracted volunteers to grow from three volunteers at our inception to a current status of 50-plus volunteers with a database of over 3,000 supporters with current Volunteer Campaign under way.

- Successfully conceived and oversaw the various fund-raising campaigns that have enabled us to operate in the black since inception. Successfully developed newsletters (current circulation 4,000), database, internal documentation, and externally focused literature.

- Raised over $4.2 million in past five years.

- Five-year consistent record of attaining projected fund-raising targets.

- Reduced volunteer turnover of 38 percent to less than 8 percent annually. Increased donations 123 percent.

Hospitality: Hotel

Career Summaries

General Manager: accomplished Hotel Executive with 20 years experience in food service field; hold distinguished FMP credential.

Consistent track record of successfully turning around faltering operations and creating profitability and excellence; utilize keen assessment and problem-solving abilities, dynamic training techniques, and key motivational strategies that build accountability and enhance staff performance.

Flexible, adaptable style and hands-on approach; a skilled manager who thrives in an atmosphere demanding excellence, autonomy, and strong team-building skills.

Possess highly polished communication and interpersonal skills.

Graduate of several of Europe's premier hotel management/culinary institutions; professional management experience acquired through employment with some of Europe's most prestigious establishments as well as a Boston four-diamond hotel; multilingual fluency includes English, German, and French.

Perfect Phrases

- Responsibilities include management and relationship building of over 60 corporate accounts worth over $1 million in 2002. Liaison between account decision makers and the hotel in negotiating corporate room rates. Solicitation efforts resulting in six new accounts worth over $60,000 in 2002. Averaging 10 outside sales calls and entertainments per week to build and maintain client relationships.

➡

- Responsible for the following markets: Texas, SW Sports, and TX universities. Accountable for approximately $1.4 million in guest-room revenues in last three quarters of 2003, and exceeded yearly goal by $310,000. Maintain aggressive solicitation process to increase new business within the Texas market. Assisted in the preparation of annual forecast and marketing plan. Forecast group room nights and rates for all definite business within territory. Specializing in sports and small corporate meeting negotiations. Built and established relationships through ongoing entertainment, sales calls, site visits, and trade shows.

- Responsible for the following channel markets for the Ritz-Carlton, Atlanta, and the Ritz-Carlton, Buckhead: Small Group Corporate, Sports, and Universities. Accountable for approximately $1.3 million in guest-room revenues in 2004 and exceeded first quarter goal by 10 percent. Maintain aggressive solicitation process to increase new business within the local Atlanta market. Assisted in the preparation of the following: Annual Forecast, Marketing Plan, and conversion to Delphi. Forecast group room nights and rates for all definite business within territory. Specializing in sports and small corporate meeting negotiations. Built and established relationships through ongoing entertainment, sales calls, site visits, and trade shows.

- Responsible for the creation of all service concepts, training, and hiring of all employees prior to the opening of the hotel in 2002. Responsible for overseeing all aspects of the Rooms Division operation. Also in charge of initiating and maintaining vending relations.

➡

- Responsible for writing the entire hotel room club and penthouse unit's integration operating processes. First integration of its type for the Hilton hotel company.
- Created operational room's budget for 2003 and 2004.
- Set up and developed all departmental training programs for all rooms division departments. Instrumental in training all employees on these programs.
- Participation on the weekly new hire orientation "Basic's" presentations.
- In charge of planning, modifying, and disseminating operational logistics on a daily basis and coordinating efforts with all departments to ensure flawless customer service.
- Oversee all hotel operations in the absence of the General Manager.
- Set and refine all seasonal staffing levels to maximize profitability levels.
- Effectively developed a succession planning program for the division, where seven management/supervisory positions were all filled internally, while still maintaining guest satisfaction scores.
- Exceeded 9/10 guest satisfaction score goals in the opening year of business.
- Exceeded 95 percent Rooms Division employee satisfaction in first year of operation. Third highest hotel within the United States.
- Fifteen years experience in hotel management and operations.
- Ability to motivate employees to achieve and exceed individual and group expectations.

- Experienced in the planning and implementation of effective policies, procedures, training, and staff development.

- Increased comment card returns by 20 percent through guest recognition program.

- Operated a Rooms Division payroll at 17 percent to revenue for six months.

- Improved revenue and occupancy 29 percent over previous year.

- Oversee the 617-room full-service convention hotel with 58,000 square feet of meeting space. In the process of reorganizing the management structure. Redeploying the sales effort to increase RevPar and Market Share.

- Managed the operation of a 285-room full-service convention hotel with 31,000 square feet of meeting space. Since arrived, increased market share from 79 to 124 percent, RevPar by 28 percent, and rooms sold by 25 percent.

- Competitive set decreased by 7 percent for the same period. Increased the GOP $1.5 million. Selected "Best Hotel" by *Reader's Choice* for 2002 and 2003.

- Responsible for the financial oversight of this $800-million development project. Revamped all systems and controls for this project. Project consisted of 1,000-room Convention Hotel, 220,000 square feet of meeting space, 60- room Five-Star Country Club, 18-hole golf course, 11 tennis courts, marina, and 50,000-square-foot European Spa.

- Hired as second-in-command for the project. Finalized all budgets and economic modeling for the project. Point person between operations and the asset managers.

- Managed the operation of a 225-suite full-service resort with 10,000 square feet of meeting space. Repositioned the resort within the marketplace, increasing market share by 35 percent and 130 percent of Melia.
- Established working relations with the golf course and spa. Served as management company point person in the sale of the resort. Installed new back office, front office, and payroll systems. Directed all new collateral and marketing direction of the resort.
- Oversaw the operation of this major resort on the island of St. Thomas. Sapphire Beach has 171 condo suites and a 67-slip condo marina. Was named to 50 Tropical Resorts by *Condé-Nast Traveler* in 1993 and 1994.
- Handled all aspects of operation, development, personnel, and government relations. The resort ran 120 percent of its Market Share and RevPar against the competition, which included Ritz-Carlton, Hyatt, Marriott, and Renaissance. Previously served as Vice President/General Manager for Bayside Resorts, responsible for both Sapphire Beach and the 114-condo suite Point Pleasant Resort. Ran both condo associations for both resorts.

Career Summaries

General Manager: accomplished Hotel Executive with 20 years experience in food service field; hold distinguished FMP credential.

Manage all areas of the restaurant, including human resources, operations, and marketing, while ensuring that the company's standards of quality and service are maintained.

Maintain an accurate and up-to-date manpower plan of restaurant staffing needs. Prepare management schedules and ensure that the restaurant is staffed for all shifts.

Staffed, trained, and developed restaurant managers and hourly employees through orientations, ongoing feedback, establishing performance expectations, and by conducting performance reviews.

Directly supervised 125 employees.

Knowledge with both NCR and Micros POS systems. Handled purchasing, receiving, and storing food products, inspection of local suppliers, using correct products and proper PAR levels to minimize food waste and optimize food cost.

Perfect Phrases

- Drove overall in-room dining and honor bar department in Gallup score from number 14 in chain to number five.
- Team leader recipient of Malcolm Baldrige award for quality standards.
- Achievements: Five-Star Employee award winner.
- History of rapid advancement/promotion.
- Raised over $12,000 to benefit local charities by producing and directing musical variety shows.

- First freshman student to be elected Associate Production Director of college television studio.
- Assisted in restructuring and converting the Banquet Department to a self-directed model, assumed managerial duties, and achieved substantial cost savings for the hotel. Reported directly to the Food & Beverage Director.
- Facilitated implementation and continued effectiveness of self-directed work teams.
- Demonstrated proficiency in identifying problem areas, and resolved them in accordance with the Ritz-Carlton nine-step process.
- Participated in a staff compensation task force to benchmark and maximize benefits for the company and employees.
- Managed operational details of various functions, making certain all contractual obligations were fulfilled. Supervised up to 60 employees and ensured that service standards were met. Hired and trained new employees. Assisted with payroll procedures. Produced financial spreadsheets detailing daily revenue for the Banquet Department.
- Highly motivated and results-oriented professional with exceptional leadership and communication skills. Well-rounded restaurant manager with eight years experience in leading and motivating employees and associates in achieving company goals and objectives. Verifiable results of high performance.
- Experienced in positions of Assistant General Manager, Service Manager, Kitchen Manager, and Bar Manager. Dedicated to customer service with a passion to teach and consistently achieve company objectives. Exceptional skills in multitasking and able to identify problems and apply creative solutions for positive outcomes.

- Responsible for managing 100-plus employees in a $4.6 million high-volume, franchised, full-service worldwide leader in the casual themed dining restaurant.
- Main role and responsibility as Service Manager: recruitment and retention, training, scheduling, personnel reviews, customer service, marketing, and overall operations. Directly responsible for controllable costs as well as COGS. Developed and wrote updated training manuals and developed Friday's "Training Coach" program.
- Oversee restaurant operation with annual sales of $1.5 to $2 million.
- Responsible for the management and operation of multibrand restaurant, including the development and growth of people, sales, and profits.
- Manage operations, including scheduling, daily decision making, delegating tasks, staff support, and guest interaction, while upholding standards, product quality, and cleanliness.
- Monthly financial analysis to evaluate the financial position and to clearly communicate expectations and actions to maximize the restaurant's financial performance.
- Responsible for the restaurant's profit and loss centers, including food, supply, and labor costs to meet the annual operating budget.

Human Resources and Training Professional

Career Summaries

Strong HR generalist experience with a proven talent in the development and implementation of training programs for exempt and nonexempt personnel; proven ability to develop material, impart knowledge, and update programs as needed.

Strong research and analytical abilities; notable experience in the management and reduction of costs related to liability and insurance.

Recruiting activities included all aspects of screening, interviewing, hiring, and orientation for union and nonunion staff.

Continuously updated knowledge relevant to workers' compensation, ADA, EEO, Family Medical Leave Act, OSHA, DOT, etc.; developed and implemented new procedures to ensure compliance.

Benefits administration experience includes program development, maintenance of costs through negotiations, and the development/implementation of alternative benefit programs.

Assets in collective bargaining activities; successfully administered benefits to assist in successful negotiation.

Generated ongoing bottom-line savings through the introduction of various cost-cutting programs.

Perfect Phrases

■ Reduced corporate liability insurance costs by one-third; restructured liability insurance management program to facilitate savings. ➥

- Reduced annual costs by $250,000 by establishing an effective self-insured plan for supplemental disability.
- Facilitated a one-third reduction in medical benefit costs by implementing an HMO as an integral part of benefits plan.
- Reduced annual paid claims by 45 percent by developing and implementing aggressive claims-handling procedures.
- Increased parent company revenues by $185,000 in six months by reinstituting billing of subsidiary companies for health-care coverage.
- Played an integral role in 12 different collective bargaining agreements—assisted the Senior V.P. by providing benefit guidance.
- Attained a 50 percent conversion from indemnity to managed health care through the creation and implementation of a successful managed-care program.
- Facilitated 17 focus groups targeting the executive team, nursing managers, new employees, and experienced employees. The purpose of the focus groups was to gather current state/gap analysis from a selected population who touched the talent acquisition, orientation, and assimilation process.
- Conducted three Process Map Workshops that consisted of hiring managers and HR professionals. The purpose of the one-day workshop was to map out the current state of each process, define gaps, and identify desired state.
- Develop report that identifies all the gaps by process, current cycle time, and best practices with desired cycle time. The goal of the workshop was to prioritize the gaps of the current process and develop a project plan for future work.
- Project Manager leading a large-scale recruiting project in the Southeast and Northeast regions. Accountable for

➡

managing the performance of the recruiting and research team, advertising deliverables, and the performance of the technology solution providers. Also responsible for all client communications and for budget review with the stakeholders of the project.

- Conducted an all-day session with HR Directors of Household Consumer Lending Divisions to review the current hiring process, staffing plan, and current metrics.
- Review and evaluation of front-end assessment tools. Developed Web-based front-end prescreening tools to immediately identify qualified applicants.
- Developed and managed sourcing strategies for high-volume initiative to include virtual job fairs, proactive research, and an on-site job fair in multiple locations.
- Conducted weekly review meetings with the Sales Director within each region to review advertising metrics, number of interviews, number of hires, and quality metrics. Developed a final report for the V.P. of Human Resources that outlined a process map of the current recruiting process, current metrics, and future state recommendations.
- Through the optimization of technology and research, we were able to reduce the cycle time by 30 days and increase the candidate's presented/to hire by 80 percent. We also provided a comprehensive report that provided the organization with technology solutions, process redesign recommendations, program design recommendations, recruiting metrics, and a project plan to help them optimize their talent acquisition process.
- Developed current state map and conducted a second meeting with the team to review gaps, metrics, and desired state models.

- Reviewed current sourcing strategies and negotiated contracts with vendors to increase the traffic/awareness of their current openings.
- Developed RFP to review vendors that could automate front-end process (i.e., applicant tracking systems, automated prescreening tools, and relationship tools that automatically contacted qualified applicants).
- Conducted one-on-one meetings with the Executive Team and Hiring Managers to map out the current state of their recruiting processes.
- Developed front-end reports to track metrics, cycle time, and quality of applicants.
- Developed prescreening tools for hiring managers to use to evaluate candidates during the interview process.
- Conducted an organizational assessment to evaluate how to structure and align the newly created Human Resource Effectiveness Practice to deliver services to the customer.
- Developed an operating plan that defined the purpose of the HR business, all the inputs/outputs of each delivery unit.
- Developed role profiles of the key leadership roles within HR, and hired the leadership team for the newly created Human Resource Effectiveness Practice.
- Conducted a review of the current reward systems and staffing plans for this newly created business.
- Hired a total of 45 senior level candidates to include the Chief Knowledge Officer, Products and Services Leaders for the HR Delivery business, and Senior Consultants within the Research, Measurement, and Communication Practice.
- Conducted interviews with the sales management team to define both the current and desired state.

- Conducted a review of the current technology provider to determine if they have the tools to move the sales organization to self-directed recruiting model.
- Evaluated current third-party search firms and selected the top five performers, negotiated contracts, established performance criteria. Conducted a review of their current cost per hire, and worked with Corporate Human Resources to purchase corporate contracts for major posting boards to leverage the cost across the business.
- Created requirements documents for 18 pension plans.
- Conducted and facilitated all meetings to define and develop the event flows for all of the pension plans.
- Developed all the event flow templates, and worked with technology to automate the event flows.
- Worked with technology team to automate all the pension calculations.
- Trained participant services representatives on the plans, event flows, and pension calculations in order for them to effectively service the Chrysler account.
- Managed the tasks and the performance of the project team to ensure that deliverable dates were met in order to outsource all aspects of pension administration within a 12-month period.
- Hired 90 sales professionals in a four-month period in order to launch a new sales initiative.
- Developed all the compensation and benefit programs for this newly created joint venture.
- Managed the benefit liabilities and pension liabilities, and had a dotted line reporting structure directly into the CEO.

Insurance Sales Professional

Career Summaries

BSBA/Financial Planning, insurance, and investment sales. Increased customer base, pioneered efforts in new territories. Innovative in Marketing. Multimillion-dollar producer.

Thirteen-year track record for success in networking and selling: number one Sales Rep consistently. Eight years in insurance, five in retail merchandising/distribution.

Took initiative in self-marketing and self-promotion. Developed promotional materials, grew territories by up to 45 percent, achieved a 100 percent client retention rate, and generated strong referral networks.

Capably positioned the companies represented as a preferred provider through extensive personal contact and a mutual respect for clients' time.

Special knowledge and continuing education in investments, retirement and estate planning, securities, mutual funds, annuities, and life and health insurance.

Five-year entrepreneurial background provides a "whatever it takes" commitment to mutual success. Created winning campaigns that boosted sales an average of 22 percent annually. Controlled expenses, motivated staff, and negotiated competitive terms saving 35 percent.

Perfect Phrases

- Successfully convert new investors into educated clients through persistence, patience, empathetic listening, and establishing trust. Added $17 million in new business.

- Create and secure leads in the most productive, cost-effective means possible.
- Initially acquired clients exclusively through cold-calling. Achieved increased productivity by hiring outside telemarketers. Warm-call qualified individuals, coordinate appointments, and ask for their business.
- Landed 600-plus new accounts throughout the Texas and Oklahoma region over a four-year period, representing more than $12 million in new business.
- Realize a 98 percent client retention rate—by keeping in touch via personal contact and a self-developed newsletter discussing investment tips, generating increased networking opportunities, a more educated clientele, and better quality attention to their priorities.
- Market annuities, securities, mutual funds, estate planning and personal retirement services, and life and health insurance to personal and corporate investors.
- Through interactive conversation, identify clients' long- and short-term needs. Stress alternatives in their best interest—in one instance saved an investor over $110,000 in inheritance taxes.
- Recognized for outstanding performance. Sales Agent of the Month 15 times over a three-year period. Sales Agent of the Year in 1996 and 1997. Won various in-house contests.
- Completing Best Insurance Company's Advanced Life Curriculum Program as well as Part 2, Business Life Insurance, of the Life Underwriting Training Council to receive her LUTCF designation.
- Key Accomplishments:
  - Millionaire Club 1994; 93 paid apps, $25,447 paid premium

- Monthly Activity Average = 65 total apps (30 auto, 15 fire, 10 life, 10 health)

- Took initiative and developed promotional materials, grew territories by up to 45 percent, achieved a 100 percent client retention rate and generated strong referral networks.

- Capably positioned the companies represented as a preferred provider through extensive personal contact and a mutual respect for clients' time.

- Special knowledge and continuing education in investments, retirement and estate planning, securities, mutual funds, annuities, and life and health insurance.

- Five-year entrepreneurial background provides a "whatever it takes" commitment to mutual success. Created winning campaigns that boosted sales an average of 22 percent annually. Controlled expenses, motivated staff, and negotiated competitive terms saving 35 percent.

- Generated $1.5 million in new business within a 22-month period. Prospected new customers via targeted direct mailings. Became involved in local events via memberships with various community organizations.

- Stepped into a nine-county, two-state territory and aggressively pursued leads. Added 200 new accounts, earned membership into "Peak Achiever's Club" in 1991 and 1992.

- Using continued mailings and follow-up surveys, acquired better qualified leads: closed eight out of 10 calls. Number one representative of 24.

IT Professional

Career Summaries

Systems Design /Product Engineer.

Strategic Business Planning/Senior-Level Project Management.

Expert in the design, development, and delivery of cost-effective, high-performance technology solutions to meet challenging business demands for well-recognized international corporations including Motorola and Hewlett Packard. Extensive qualifications in all facets of project lifecycle development—from initial feasibility analysis and conceptual design through documentation, implementation, and user training/enhancement.

Equally effective organizational leadership, team-building, and project management experience—introducing out-of-the-box thinking and problem-solving analysis to improve processes, systems, and methodologies currently in place to exceed business goals and to perpetually delight shareholders and customers.

Areas of Strength:

- National and international marketing
- Business research and analysis skills
- Strategy identification and implementation skills
- Personnel training, team-building, and supervision
- Customer service and retention management
- Supply chain management
- Cost reduction methodologies

- Presentation and public speaking skills

- Finance management/project budgeting

- Quality control management

Computer/Technology

Excel, Word, PowerPoint. Programming languages including Basic, Assembly, C. Use of Unix-Based PC or Macintosh platforms. RF, Wireless, Microcontroller/Microprocessor system skills. Digital and Analog hardware experience. IC design tools: VHDL, Spice, Cadence, Synopsis. Knowledge of technology required to implement small, portable, battery-powered, wireless multimedia, consumer products into the future.

Perfect Phrases

- Identify technology to meet future needs in the areas of wireless communication products for CTSO division (Core Technologies Systems Organization).

- Work closely with market visionaries to identify future product features—especially those needed for future system integration to be used as a driving force for early technology identification.

- Provide strategic insights—marketing, operational, and product development/enhancement—in making recommendations on what business we should do, with whom, for how long, and why to meet business objectives (time to market, features, and related costs).

- Vendor liaison, i.e., seeking out needed technology, reviewing technology road maps, and managing the nondisclosure agreements for the division, projecting base cost of all semiconductor chips to be designed.

- Memory statistics and benchmarking of embedded/external NVM, ROM, and RAM in relative cost die area consumption, relative cost trends over time, and cost trend for various memory sizes.
- Responsible for implementing cost reduction methodologies to reduce direct material cost without adversely affecting manufacturing cost through understanding the supply chain for each technology.
- Perform analysis of different system approaches to meet market needs, i.e., time to market, features, and costs.
- Received professional recognition as an "Intersector and International Resource."
- Changed way of thinking as an option, not previously explored, to meet market needs that are a cost analysis of outsourcing versus traditional in-house methods. This set a precedent that is being used more and more as a strategy to meet business goals and objectives.
- Program management skills including product feasibility study, specification and contract development, scheduling project tasks, managing outsourcing activity (including legal implications), advertising, and customer support.
- Digital and analog design simulation; system level simulation and verification; interfacing with layout design personnel; and evaluation/debugging of integrated circuit.
- Provide technical support to customers to enable the implementation of power management and device driver integrated circuits.
- Provide documentation/transfer design to outsourcing company for continued manufacturing and technical support.

- Motley Rice LLC is one of the largest plaintiffs' law firms in the nation. We currently have more than 100,000 active cases, including clients suffering from asbestos and lead paint exposure, nursing home abuse, complications from use of pharmaceutical drugs, aviation safety, and our representation of the 9/11 families.

- Development and implementation of the firm's first IT strategic plan. Negotiation of new local telephone service, cell phone service, and copy/print maintenance contracts saving the firm nearly $200,000 a year.

- Network and server stabilization with the installation of new Cisco switches and routers.

- Enhanced data storage capacity, reliability, and speed of backup with the installation of a Compaq SAN.

- Improved security through the installation of a Cisco firewall, implementation of network translation table and DMZ for our Web server and Internet e-mail gateway.

- Standardization on Windows 2000 at the server level and on the desktop.

- Migration from GroupWise to Outlook (accomplished without major problem by in-house staff).

- Migration from WordPerfect to MS Word, and the installation of appropriate firewall and DMZ measures to help secure our network from intrusion.

- Development of the software to gather data from thousands of pages of documentation, and integration of that data with an automated link analysis tool to trace the funding of the 9/11 hijackers.

- Design and development of the firm's five Web sites, the firm's intranet, and a secure extranet for collaboration with co-counsel.

- Managed network operations staff responsible for operation of our 40-plus Compaq and HP Blade servers running Windows 2000, MS Exchange, and SQL 2000. We also have a Compaq Storage Area Network (SAN) with a capacity of 12 terabytes; Compaq tape backup tower is used for daily and weekly backups.

- Implementation of a Cisco-based virtual private network (VPN); and conversion of our major system-case management to a Java/SQL 2000–based solution to track and manage the 100,000-plus cases handled by the firm.

- Development of the company's first information technology strategic plan. Paramount in this effort was the identification of the business needs of the company, current problems, or issues associated with using existing automated solutions and joint development (IT staff working with the business areas) of technology solutions to address those problems.

- Procurement of a state-of-the-market telephone system for our Atlanta call center.

- Conversion of existing MS Access–based applications to Webcentric environment using Oracle 8i, ASP, and Active X documents.

- Implementation of Cisco's Secure Virtual Private Network solution to replace long-distance data lines used to provide remote connectivity to the company's servers; and collaboration with the Chief Medical Officer and epidemiologists to develop software used for medical record abstraction and data quality analysis.

- Recruited to provide leadership to and improve the quality of service provided by the 42-member IT group.

- Reduced salary expense 22 percent, data communications 15 percent, and operating costs 20 percent in first 90 days.
- Initiated server consolidation project to reduce server count by 60 percent while reducing cost and improving performance and reliability utilizing virtualization technologies.
- Launched an initiative to reduce the number of software tools in use by development and operations.
- Reorganized department to improve service delivery, customer service, and quality assurance.
- Restructured Project Office (PMO) to improve governance.
- Implemented new help-desk service system and quality assurance tools.
- Documented processes and procedures and implemented staffing and procedural changes to ensure compliance with SOX 404 (Sarbanes-Oxley).

Manufacturing

Career Summaries

At Smith and Woods, achieved a 1,200 percent reduction in line order cuts, exceeded objectives for inventory turns, and reduced total inventory by 15 percent.

Spearheaded production planning, component ordering, and coordination of start-up with co-packers for seven new products.

Minimized scrap losses through disposition of on-hand inventory during formulation and packaging changes, and sales of inventories to contractors.

At TI North America, identified and recovered $1.2 million in supplier overcharges through the development of computer models.

Saved over $500,000 through price renegotiations with vendors.

Devised and maintained cost file spreadsheets by utilizing Bills of Material and costs to determine overall case cost of each product.

Served as team member of Cross-Training Program, Supply Chain Management Team, and numerous task forces.

Perfect Phrases

- Recruited to a high-profile position accountable for master scheduling and production planning for 11 co-packers (subcontractors) at 14 locations nationwide for a major consumer products company.
- Managed $1.5 million monthly projected inventory balances for finished goods inventory; ensured attainment of corporate inventory goals and objectives.

- Accountable for 80-plus SKUs and 20-plus different product types, including powders and liquids. Actively participated in new project management. Utilized AMAPS and MPS II computer systems in daily operations.
- Achieved fast-track promotions in recognition of superior performance. Accountable for the development of contract manufacturing supplier strategies for a company specializing in automotive aftermarket products; managed vendor sourcing, price negotiations, packaging development, and internal coordination.
- Supervised material valued at $80 million; held purchase order signature authority to $20,000 and invoice approval authority to $100,000.
- Procured $6 million annually in products and services. Monitored contractor/supplier performance against strategy plans and implemented corrective action. Controlled raw materials and finished goods inventory at subcontractor locations.
- At Reckitt & Colman, achieved a 1,200 percent reduction in line order cuts, exceeded objectives for inventory turns, and reduced total inventory by 15 percent.
- Spearheaded production planning, component ordering, and coordination of start-up with co-packers for seven new products.
- Minimized scrap losses through disposition of on-hand inventory during formulation and packaging changes, and sales of inventories to contractors.
- At Castrol North America Automotive, identified and recovered $1.2 million in supplier overcharges through the development of computer models.

➡

- Saved over $500,000 through price renegotiations with vendors. Devised and maintained cost file spreadsheets by utilizing Bills of Material and costs to determine overall case cost of each product.
- Served as team member of Cross-Training Program, Supply Chain Management Team, and numerous task forces.
- Change management, lean thinking, strategic and operations planning, and training diverse nonunion and unionized workforces.
- Proficient with several ISO Standards, including the new ISO 9000-2000, MIL-I-45208, ANSI, and ASTM standards.
- Manufacturing experience in a complex plant environment, including sales and customer service leadership roles. Process improvement expertise.
- Complete P&L responsibility for $43 million revenue factory (50-plus nonunion employees).
- Reengineered entire factory of recently acquired division.
- Hired entire new staff following acquisition.
- Reduced force by 50 percent while maintaining same output.
- Established companywide quality policy and SPC requirements.
- Prepared plant for customer audits and ISO 9000 certification.
- Purchased line of CNC equipment for high-speed manufacturing. Implemented lean manufacturing practices.
- Full Profit and Loss responsibility for 244-plus associates.
- Reduced inventory over 47 percent, from $2.65 million to $1.4 million, within first five months.

- Increased on-time shipping to better than 98.5 percent to customer requests.
- Designed new shipping configurations, saving company over $1million annually.
- Diminished headcount over 18 percent, from 244-plus down to 204, saving over $1.4 million per year.
- Consolidated two separate outsourced suppliers and brought production in-house, saving over $3 million.
- Increased productivity over 30 percent, from $16 million sets to over $21 million sets in one year.
- Recruited to turn around 300-employee aluminum wheel manufacturing facility that generates $78 million annually, but has lost $4 million YTD as of August 2005. Hold functional responsibility over human resources, finance, process and manufacturing engineering, new product launch team, operations, safety, quality assurance, materials/purchasing group, and plant engineering/maintenance. Employed lean manufacturing techniques and maintained mandated certifications, including ISO 14001 and Ford Q1.
- Achieved $360,000 in annual savings by eliminating outside contractor inspection operation and instituting upstream quality improvement actions at defect source. Attained 11 percent wheel unit cost improvement within two months as a result, and by optimizing machining bottleneck performance via cycle time, scheduling, and spare parts optimization.
- On target for 22 percent increase in plant capacity through $2.2 million capital program focusing on automating machining operations and robot cell optimization.
- Currently structuring and negotiating $1 million-plus annual contract for machining technical support. New

➡

program will serve as model for wheel plants throughout company.

- Reduced scrap rate 21 percent in October 2004 with changes to paint/clear coat line and deburr process.
- Presently overhauling employee recognition programs to more closely match deliverables and enhance communications.
- Turned around poorly performing plant and improved plant efficiency from 78 to 91 percent. Introduced lean manufacturing techniques and led plantwide implementation of Six Sigma, Five S, Kanban, TPM, Kaizen, and SMED, and replaced MRP II system with SAP software.
- Drove plant cost position from sixteenth to sixth and slashed costs $3.12 million annually through a number of initiatives, including labor reduction, washer/ink/spray usage reduction, efficiency gains, spoilage improvement, PM program, and eliminating spending waste.
- Garnered labor savings of $400,000 annually by reducing both salaried and hourly positions by eliminating duplicate tasks, instituting cross training, and combining positions.
- Improved internal spoilage rate by 28 percent while reducing customer complaints 21 percent over three-year period, leading to $216,000 in annual scrap savings.
- Cut workers' compensation expense by $104,000 annually due to accident-free environment.
- Reduced annual logistics and overtime costs $189,000 and overtime, respectively, by eliminating customer assistance from sister plants.
- Completed advanced management program, focusing on international and domestic business strategy.

Marketing

Career Summaries

Professional Profile

Management professional attuned to the ever-changing needs of business. Extremely service-oriented, with a unique combination of intuitive and analytical abilities. Astute in identifying market plan needs, creating actionable programs, and effectively interacting with the sales field.

Segmentation Targeting	Branding
Financial Forecasting	Advertising
Retail Sales	Sales Promotion
Collateral, Displays and	New Product Rollout
Total Communications Strategist	Strategic Planning

E-Marketing/Online Marketing Director

Award-winning pioneer and expert in Web/Internet/new media marketing.

Career Profile   Web-savvy marketing professional accomplished in creating and leading high-impact marketing campaigns that consistently meet aggressive e-business goals. Initiated groundbreaking programs and delivered large revenue gains. Excel in both start-up and mature corporate environments. Strong leader known for tenacity and positive "can-do" attitude. Fully fluent in interactive and Internet technologies and tools.

Areas of Expertise
- Web, print, and broadcast advertising
- Business development initiatives

➡

292

- Community building and customer loyalty
- E-business strategies and technologies
- Product launch strategy and execution
- Partnership and alliance building
- Online relationship marketing
- Market awareness building
- User acquisition and retention
- Staff development and leadership

Perfect Phrases

- Expert in creating predictive models, customer data mining, consumer pattern recognition, target list segmentation, letter shop and campaign processes, and analytics. Wrote hundreds of proprietary SQL algorithms and targeting models to segment markets and make decisions on what customers will buy and when they will buy it.
- Expert in developing direct marketing plans to meet gross sales and profit targets, including marketing program recommendations, budgeting, unit forecasting, and program ROI analysis. Experienced in modifying marketing plans based on availability of resources and opportunities to maximize ROI on existing marketing programs.
- Strategic and creative marketing and management executive with strong record of contributions in marketing, advertising, and management of people, services, and production. History of effective interaction and relationship management with clients, sales professionals, creative agencies, and multifunctional project teams.
- Expert in driving a cross-functional team (Direct Marketing, Business Management, Sales and Service, Operations and

Fulfillment, Web Commerce Group, etc.) to leverage infrastructure and processes required to successfully execute end-to-end operational implementation of direct marketing programs and retail marketing strategies.

- Areas of Expertise:

    Marketing campaign design
    Brand recognition
    Special event planning
    Creative content development
    Presentations
    Multimedia production
    Public relations
    New business development
    Project management
    Graphic design
    Copywriting
    Business processes
    Contract negotiations
    Budget development
    Live event production

- Creation of marketing materials, including: direct mail, brochures, newsletters, sell sheets, advertising print design, ad copy, radio copy, and press releases. Script writing and producing and directing broadcast television segments. Designing content for corporate Web sites.
- Responsible for developing marketing strategies and creative content production, managing a small staff and outside vendors for this full-service marketing consultancy offering specialized services to corporations, as well as small, home-based, and newly created companies.

- Vertically integrated into large organizations, and acted as outside creative communications resource for small companies and agencies to provide a vast array of advertising, marketing, and event planning services.
- Managed the successful implementation of nationwide branding campaign, conferences, and fund-raising events for the Hispanic Scholarship Fund organization. Developed corporate events for BellSouth, Marriott, Mindspring, Pepsi, and Medtrade.
- Led development and execution of marketing strategies and new business initiatives that drove rapid growth from the ground floor to $8.2 million.
- Pioneered a fully functional marketing department infrastructure, including policies and procedures, streamlined business processes, and a talented marketing and communications team.
- Created and deployed unique advertising campaigns proven successful in positioning the company with a competitive distinction. Won national attention for innovative and edgy ads that piqued interest in the target markets.
- Delivered 54 percent ROI from marketing efforts by employing a shrewd balance of Internet and traditional print and broadcast medias to maximize results.
- Negotiated and structured eight major business partnerships and alliances; built and led successful win-win programs through cost-effective co-marketing initiatives.
- Conducted research and initiated new product line in paper products, including product specification development, segmentation identification, and rollout

plan. New line gained a 32 percent share within six months, nearly the P&G average for toiletry products.

- Identified and developed new distribution channel for P&G paper products line, which included retail recruitment, rollout schedule, inventory management, and training schedule. New channel represented a 7 percent share of distribution mix within two years.

- Recommended shift in brand image to target younger buyers, which was successfully implemented and improved name awareness with that segment by 12 percent. Overall brand awareness for individual product lines reached 93 percent in 1997.

- Dedicated extensive time and energy to improving communications with personnel, accepting full responsibility for scheduling, performance reviews, employee motivation, and boosting morale. ESS feedback for our group was in the top 20 percent in all of P&G.

Career Summaries

Professional Profile

Thirteen years with Independence Blue Cross, 12 years as departmental supervisor of 12 to 21 registered nurses in care management and coordination.

Seventeen years staff nursing at Columbia Hospital, a leading research and teaching hospital.

Seven years as the quality assurance representative for the ambulatory surgery unit.

Two years case management and cost containment analysis with a home health-care provider.

Three years of charge nurse experience at prominent nursing and rehabilitation center.

Perfect Phrases

- Licenses/Certifications:

    - Santa Clara County certified as "5150 Evaluator" (72-hour holds for Psychiatric Evaluation)

    - IV/Central Line/Blood Withdrawal certificates and experience

    - Nationally Registered Emergency Medical Technician (10 years)

    - Certified ICU/CCU monitor and EKG technician

    - American Heart Association and American Red Cross Instructor certifications

    - Certified Patient Care Manager (Hospice)

➡

Direct patient care in HIV/AIDS; end-stage. Services included 24-hour availability and care. Counseling for patients and families, medications and treatments, intervention with Emergency Services to minimize stress on patients and families. Care: direct bedside, hands-on; teaching families and loved ones how to care for patient without exposing themselves, through death care and after care. Care always included both nursing and counseling services.

- Teaching Experience:

  - CPR Instructor for American Heart Association (1988 to 2001).

  - Instructor for American Red Cross (1985 to 1991).

  - Taught CPR (Infant, Child, Adult, Community, and Professional Rescuer), First Aid, Advanced First Aid, and Basic Aid Training. Certified in Advanced Life Saving (Lifeguard) for three years. Received five-year service pin & award.

  - Mission College Teaching Assistant/Tutor (1989 to 1990).

  - Tutoring/Assistant Teaching in Pharmacology, Mathematics for Medications, Anatomy and Physiology, and other science courses for the Mission College Psychiatric Technician Program, under the supervision of Margaret Boone, RN, PHN, MA; approved by the Board(s) of Nursing.

- Nursing professional with over 30 years of experience in Facility Site/Medical Record Audits, Delegation Oversight, Utilization Review, MCQA, NIPAC, Tile XXII, OBRA, OSHA,

➡

and JACHO. Extensive experiences with organizational skills and self-motivation, management skills, director of nursing skills, and 15 years clinical experience (ICU, ER, BURN UNIT, Medical and Ortho).

- Registered Nurse: recent RN grad with recent but intense practical experience in hospital (ICCU/ACCU) and primary care environments. Day-to-day management of high acuity patients on Medication/Surgery. ICCU computer-skilled, managing heavy daily patient volume.

- Proficient in all documentation/record maintenance/paperwork to ensure accuracy and patient confidentiality.

- Exceptional grasp of managed care: excellent mastery of supervisory skills and demonstrated leadership in supervising, training, and auditing Registered Nurses conducting case management and discharge planning at several HCA hospitals. In-depth knowledge of health benefit programs: coverage requirements, medical and departmental policy, procedures, practice, terminology, and pharmaceuticals. An active participant in numerous care management and coordination departmental initiatives.

- Achievements include developing the Independence Blue Cross On-site Review Program and generating and maintaining positive and communicative relations at several challenging health-care facilities.

- Highly proficient in contributing to and reaching team solutions, generating and maintaining positive relations with internal and external clients, maintaining all compliance standards, working well under pressure, and producing error-free work of high quality.

➡

- Credentials:
    - Board Examination 01/2005
    - License, State of Texas 07/2004
    - ICCU/ACCU Staff Nurse, Good Samaritan Hospital, Suffern, New York, Medical Office/ Nurse
- Medical Office Skills: scheduling clients, taking vital signs and initial assessments, scheduling tests, calling in prescriptions, taking phone calls from patients and other physicians, setting up exam rooms, assisting physician with exams, pap smear, flexible sigmoidoscopy, 12-lead EKG, cleaning, and autoclaving equipment.
- Clerical Skills: Answering phones, filing, ordering supplies, daily reports, money handling and scheduling; Microsoft Office, MS Windows, keyboarding, 10-key, e-mail, Internet.
- Customer Service Experience: Customer complaints and problem solving.
- Chief Nurse of a large ambulatory clinic serving over 50,000 clients in a federally funded setting. Oversaw three large clinics with 20 nursing personnel. Responsible for scheduling, recruiting, evaluating, budgeting, ordering, and monitoring all clinic operations with 11 Family Practice physicians.
- Chairman of the Patient Focus Committee, Infection Control Committee, and Performance Improvement Committee. Commended for bringing many clinic improvements.
- Interim Director of Nursing: directed the nursing activities in multispecialty Ambulatory Surgery Center (ASC) consisting of three Operating Rooms, a seven-bed Recovery Room, an Endoscopy Lab, and a Fertility Clinic.

➡

- Managed all nursing activities to include major equipment acquisition worth more than a million dollars, policy development, scheduling, accreditation preparation, quality improvement and utilization management, marketing, budgeting, and supervision of 26 personnel. Commended for problem solving and developing over 230 policies and procedures.
- Current Licenses/Certifications:
    - Registered Nurse
    - Licensed Psychiatric Technician
    - American Heart Association, CPR/BCLS (AED)
    - CPI (Crisis Prevention/Intervention) Certified
    - Certified Director of Staff Development (DSD)

Paralegal

Career Summaries

A results-oriented Legal Assistant experienced in legal administration and paralegal studies involving research, writing, investigation, litigation support, mediation/arbitration techniques, rules of evidence, and dissolution of marriage proceedings. Familiar with word processing, spreadsheet, docket control, and database applications. Key responsibilities included:

- Drafted and filed motions, interrogatories, initial and responsive pleadings.

- Tracked client employment records and other information using various sources.

- Helped clients fill out income, expenses, and property statements.

- Prepared settlement agreements and other closing documents.

Nearly seven years experience in a law firm with general practice cases, including bankruptcy, criminal, family law, civil litigation, business setup, and estate administration.

Successfully settled numerous collection, countersuit, bankruptcy, and preference cases and claims.

Member and chairperson of two (state) creditor committees that assisted in recovery of millions of dollars of unsecured claims for various creditors.

Created database on Microsoft Access of open and closed files with cross-reference of names of principals associated with files.

Recovered over $1 million in bad debt recovery for company.

Perfect Phrases

■ Litigation paralegal/legal secretary: conduct legal research; draft, summarize, and/or transcribe documents and correspondence—pleadings, discovery, trial preparation; calendar; schedule; arrange travel.

■ Insurance claims/legal background: 11 years staff counsel experience; insurance courses completed: risk management, claims, operations, financial/statutory accounting and regulations, business and financial analysis, legal environment, commercial/personal property risk, and liability management.

■ Litigation legal assistant to partner in law firm. Drafted, summarized, and transcribed records, correspondence, pleadings, and discovery (provided legal research and writing of memos, points, and authorities and declarations); managed litigation process, heavy client contact (including investigation and responses to discovery), and coordination of international travel.

■ Responsible for running a staff counsel office separate from the insurance company's Branch and Home Office. Administered, updated, and repaired LAN/WAN (local and wide area network) with telephone help from Home Office. Administered accounts payable/receivable for office, and prepared accountability reports of same to Home Office.

■ Provided litigation support to managing attorney, including document management, legal research, drafting, summarizing or transcribing of documents; heavy client and claims department contact; calendaring coordination.

■ Full-time litigation secretary and legal assistant for an AV-rated law firm.

- Competent in legal writing, scheduling motion calendars, special set hearings, and client interaction etiquette.

  - Diligent in keeping deadlines, scheduling, and billing.

  - Experienced in the procedures of the Circuit Court (civil and family divisions) and the District Court of Appeals.

  - Able to give assistance in preparing for depositions, hearings, vetting witnesses, expert witnesses, and trial preparation.

  - Knowledge of the [state] Rules of Court and the procedures required in civil procedures.

- Substantive legal work in a paralegal/legal assistant position. Responsible for initial meetings with clients for intake of information and case analysis.

  - Manage cases to meet deadlines and provide client support.

  - Draft pleadings and correspondence.

  - Prepare pleadings for filing with the court.

  - Organize discovery responses and prepare for submitting to opposing attorney.

  - Coordinate and monitor attorney's personal calendar and docket schedule.

  - Prepare bankruptcy petitions and file via electronic case filing system.

  - Discuss preliminary and postbankruptcy issues with clients.

  - Experienced with lift stay motions, consent orders, and other bankruptcy court motions.

- Prepare all estate planning documents, and assist clients with funding of Revocable Trust Agreements. Assist attorney with the formation of corporations and limited liability companies, also assist in filing domestic and civil complaints. Administrative duties include preparing daily deposit for general operating account, posting client payments, and paying the bills for the firm.

Career Summaries

Career Profile

National Board for Certification in Occupational Therapy No. 004127.

Texas Board of Occupational Therapy, License No. 019243. Analysis for all clients in the industrial rehab program.

Identified the Physical, Environmental, Psychophysical, and Psychosocial risk factors for clients employed in industrial and office settings.

Recommended controls for process flow, safety equipment, and ergonomically designed workstations/seating used to reduce risk hazards in industrial and office settings.

Perfect Phrases

- On call for very exclusive, high-profile, 150 member-only center for preventative medicine.
- Partnered with staff nutritionists, psychologists, physical therapists, massage therapists, and exercise therapists to provide customized, one-on-one care for clients.
- Able to perform Swedish, deep tissue, sports, and medical massage as well as reflexology and Table Shiatsu.
- Trained in a variety of spa treatments and body wraps.
- Responsible for Work Conditioning, Job Simulation, Job Coaching, and Job Performed VDT Ergonomic Analysis, and facilitated training sessions on Injury Prevention, Posture, Body Mechanics, Joint Protection, and Energy Conservation Techniques to improve Work Efficiency/Productivity and injury reduction.

- Educated clients on the Abnormal Illness Behavior Cycle and its correlation to Pain Management. Collaborated with Engineering, Safety, and Management to integrate workplace operations, processes, and conditions to reduce the number of low back strain and musculoskeletal injuries with Nursing Staff and Material Handlers.

- Supervises Physical Therapy interns in performing routine activities, and conducts training needs regularly to upgrade the skills required to meet company's quality standard. Motivates and supports the care team; anticipates and overcomes problems that may affect residents' care or care staff.

- Delegates staff to train interns and Junior Physical Therapist for clinical experience and/or observation in their respective areas. Instructs and delegates Physical Therapy interns to formulate home program for patients and their families to continue treatment at home.

- Administers diagnostic tests and physiotherapeutic treatment, such as:

  - Assigns and monitors Physical Therapy interns in performing patients' activities of Daily Living, such as ambulation, maintaining personal hygiene, and proper nourishment. Teaches functional employment skills, including proper lifting techniques and functional strength testing.

  - Monitors therapeutic exercise to increase endurance, strength, and coordination for specific muscle groups or entire body. Evaluates and trains sitting and standing balance, transfer, and mobility. Progressive gait training, with or without ambulatory aids offered, including instruction in negotiating ➡

> barriers and obstacles such as rough grounds, ramps, and chairs.

> - Offers various Physical Therapy modalities such as superficial/deep heat/cold, as well as other hydrotherapy techniques and electrotherapy techniques and massage.

- Managed busy rehabilitation with patients by treating according to the rehab standard.
- Successfully working in all areas of the rehabilitation as required, and treating patient at the highest possible level at all times.
- Advocated and linked chronic mentally ill consumers with needed services.
- Independently provided services in the community. Set independent schedule, including productivity that was consistently 10 to 15 percent above productivity requirement.
- Provided individual and group therapy to chronic mentally ill consumers.
- Monitored medication of mentally ill consumers. Supervised care of chronic mentally ill consumers (psychiatric, medical, and activities of daily living). Minor case management duties as required, paperwork included: daily vouchers, monthly treatment plans, authorization requests, quarterly. Developed therapeutic groups for individuals with varying needs.

Product Management

Career Summaries

Professional Profile

Seven years experience in product management for Fortune 75 consumer products company with high brand awareness, and winner of numerous consumer product awards.

Segmentation Targeting	Offer Development
Financial Forecasting	Advertising
Channel Development	Sales Promotion
Collateral, Displays, and Marcom	New Product Rollout
Total Communications Strategist	Strategic Planning

Perfect Phrases

■ Led strategic development for new health/beauty property launch, developing market launch plan, aligning multifunctional team to changes in pricing and packaging, and coordinating copy development with advertising agency.

■ Won alignment of senior management to pricing changes for new product launch. Proficiency in financial modeling, analysis of consumer preferences, and an open, collaborative approach contributed to a strategic and financially optimal choice.

■ Synthesized health and beauty segment data from numerous sources, developing competitive profiles on key competitors. Extensively employed data from IRI, industry analyses and literature, and feedback from sales force and consumer focus groups, among others. Knowledge was employed to inform new product selection, guide market research, and refine product launch plans. ➡

- Extensively engaged key functional stakeholders throughout the planning process—sales, market research, finance, packaging, operations, marketing services, legal, and external vendors—to ensure optimal product launch.
- Analyze market requirements, in-house technical strengths, and competitive threats, to develop a strategic product road map of product features for current and future product releases.
- Produce business case, cost, pricing, and competitive analysis reports to upper management to win approval for product development.
- Manage beta tests at selected customer sites to provide support and get feedback on early product versions to improve products and increase customer satisfaction.
- Develop product strategy and supervise product direction from concept through obsolescence to produce three new product releases.
- Gather and analyze product requirements and manage development with engineering to meet product release schedules.
- Produce white papers, data sheets, sales training, order forms, and provide sales support for all product releases to enable sales process.
- Develop test plan to determine if all business case requirements had been met, and track user issues through to resolution with engineering.
- Manage cross-functional teams of developers, tech writers, and network engineers to produce fully integrated products.
- Achieved strong and sustainable revenue for the company through demonstrated knowledge of financial

➡

and product management practices. Expertly determined long-range objectives and managed projects within or below established budgets.

- Gather technical requirements, prepare proposals, and manage the implementation of product features with corporate operations, marketing, and sales efforts. Create and monitor business metrics. Analyze revenue streams; establish and manage costs, draft schedules, and product delivery. Keen insight for reviewing processes and advising production and operations.

- Planned and drafted a formal, master production schedule for annual and five-year product manufacturing plans based on current and projected trends.

- Made sales presentations to 40 of the Fortune 100 list of companies, explaining converged network services and how ION represented a new approach to voice and data networking.

- Developed product implementation process for new platform, including training, support of the sales staff, and resolution of issues related to implementation.

- Evaluated key retail clients' product segment strengths and weaknesses; cooperated with key retail clients to develop strategies and guidelines to modify and complement in-process product lineup.

- Negotiated and implemented private label/branded consumer product agreements, guidelines, and contracts with both retail clients and suppliers.

- Developed key channel strategies with major retail clients and formally presented various proposals to both internal and retail clients' decision makers.

- Built cross-functional teams between the marketing, purchasing, material control, and engineering department to quickly resolve product issues, develop new products, reduce procurement costs and efficiency, and provide the quickest production turnaround and shipping time possible for key retail clients.

Career Summaries

Areas of Expertise

Multiunit manager for best-in-class retailer with premium brand awareness and reputation.

Recruiting, training, and developing staff to high performance levels.

Scheduling employees in accordance to customer traffic and demand.

Displaying eye-catching merchandise and planograms to increase impulse purchasing and impact sales.

Reducing costs and shrink to ensure optimum profitability.

Overseeing all functions pertaining to operations, including sales, adherence to company policy, controlling shrinkage, maintaining inventory levels, customer service, and strategic planning.

Career Highlights:

Lowest turnover in region of 11 districts and 145 stores.

Achieved 123 percent of revenue objectives.

Instrumental in the success of seven new store launches.

Slashed budget expenditures by 11.7 percent while gaining enhanced productivity.

Invited as Key Speaker at company's conference in recognition of outstanding performance.

Perfect Phrases

- A multiunit retail sales and operations manager skilled in driving high sales performance, P&L management, strategic planning, and business development in start-up, growth, and contract-managed environments.

- P&L responsibility for a 210,000 square foot design center selling design and remodeling services, including 10 specialty showrooms and a trade services office.

- Won the Marcus Award, Home Depot's top award for volunteerism and community involvement.

- Increased project sales penetration to a chain-leading 24 percent and improved service recovery by developing a new customer service matrix.

- As one of 30 managers representing 1,700 store managers to senior management, nominated for and joined the prestigious Home Depot Store Manager Council.

- P&L responsibility for 36 Borders stores in the Southeast. With sales of $219 million, led field management team of District Managers, Area Marketing Managers, Regional Human Resources Manager, and Recruiters.

- Increased market share from 18 to 23 percent and controlled costs during industrywide sales downtrend.

- Increased customer service scores through a focus on a selling culture and implementation of new customer service standards.

- Built and strengthened celebrity relationships and product placement opportunities, creating brand awareness via award shows, movie premieres, press junkets, and movie wardrobing opportunities.

➥

- Opened 10 domestic freestanding stores. Responsible for the daily store press activities, including the Madison Avenue flagship store opened in summer 2005.
- Responsible for all product, marketing, licensing, and strategic planning activities of private label brands for the Internet, stores, catalog, and new businesses. Merchandise areas include: Toys, Juvenile Home Furnishings, and Accessories.
- Directed the development and implementation of the private label branding strategy on Toysrus.com, which increased sales by 150 percent and improved margin by 30 points.
- Developed Hispanic product and marketing strategy for private label brands. Sales increased 30 percent in Hispanic market areas.
- Expanded the merchandise assortment and circulation of a direct mail Toy Guide for Kids. Sales increased 60 percent.
- Initiated new premium and promotional business for the company to create additional brand exposure, licensing opportunities, and a new revenue stream.
- Achieved annual sales of $600 million.
- Revamped the strategic direction of the catalog media plan, developed new private brand merchandise assortment, and improved return on equity by 20 percent.
- Negotiated and implemented new syndicated media programs to enter totally new merchandise and catalog businesses, which created a multimillion-dollar revenue source.
- Developed Internet programs, which resulted in the three most productive categories in the company.

➡

- Directed all merchandise, marketing, and strategic planning activities in the catalog and Internet merchandising division. Merchandise areas included: Home Furnishings, Electronics, Sporting Goods, Health/Personal Care, and Toys.
- Established catalog returns reduction task force, which reduced customer returns by 12 percent and improved profits by 20 percent.
- Ensures that staff is informed about changing regulations, and communicates changes to impacted areas of the company.
- Ensures that all compliance activities are properly documented and compliance files are maintained.
- Stabilized troubled location by recruiting, training, and motivating an entirely new team of 40 employees. Promoted and coached 10 employees to become successful in supervisory and management positions.
- Participates and provides leadership in activities in the community to promote the image of the company.
- Audits other store locations to ensure compliance with company's policies, and verifies inventory in stock.
- Opened seven new Wal-Mart Discount/Supercenter stores ranging from 95,000 to 230,000 square feet. Units managed ranged from $2.5 to $105 million in sales volume, inventory range from $1.5 to $8 million. Responsible from empty building to Grand Opening Ceremony in four weeks and three days.
- Managed over 630 Store Associates in one location. Regional Trainer of five states, trained over 550 managers in operations, merchandising, and leadership. Certified Franklin Quest time management Facilitator. Walton Institute of Retailing graduate.
- Walton Food Institute graduate; Serve Safe Certified.

Career Summaries

Profile

Enthusiastic sales associate with proven record of achieving challenging goals of the organization. Personable and reliable team player with ability to gain trust and confidence. Improved employee morale by exhibiting cheerful, helpful attitude. Innovative and resourceful, with reputation of adhering to high ethical standards.

Strengths:

Customer Retention	Merchandising
Service Quality	Customer Engagement
Inventory Control	Sales Leadership
Employee Management	Employee Training
Order Processing	

Perfect Phrases

- Number-one ranked salesperson for four straight years.

    - Excellent at engaging customers and achieving high closing rate.

    - Focused on performance management and always conscious of sales targets.

    - Strong product knowledge from five years' experience in the field.

- Promoted from Sales Associate to Key Sales Associate.
- Independently opened and closed store, maintained sales records, and performed banking functions and evening deposits.

- Over four years combined retail-selling experience. Over one year creative design experience (painting, jewelry design, interior design). Strengths include good customer contact skills and multiple single customer sales. Enjoy meeting new people. Considered "hardworker" and "great salesman" by employers.
- Highly motivated, creative, and ambitious customer service representative with over five years of experience in the sales industry. Demonstrated expertise in all areas of retail, including marketing, merchandising, and sales. A convincing and credible communicator with customers, coworkers, and senior management. Ability to prioritize multiple projects and adapt to changing environments while working well under pressure. Able to work resourcefully and independently as well as collectively and creatively within a team structure. Outgoing personality enhances all aspects of customer service.
- Sales expertise in all areas of the store, including cosmetics; women's, men's, children's, and juniors clothing; women's shoes; housewares; jewelry; and accessories.
- Enhanced customer service and increased profits by suggestive selling and extensive knowledge of store's products, primarily in women's shoes, women's clothing, and cosmetics.
- Artistic design and marketing of store products by remodeling projects that enhanced the store's appearance.
- Cash balance and handling with register by sales, returns, exchanges, payments, and opening new accounts.
- Responsible for display and sale of designer jewelry, watches, and fine quality diamonds. Achieved sales of over $350,000 in the first year. Opened and closed daily store

➡

operations, balanced receipts, shipped and received merchandise, and performed inventory for two locations.

- Consistently solved problems to customer satisfaction in this fast-paced sales environment.
- Professionally advised customers on the appropriate merchandise to meet their needs.
- Promoted repeat customers by establishing customer rapport and conducting follow-up as needed.
- Assisted store manager with store displays, merchandising, and sales promotions.
- Assisted with the opening of The Silk Trading Co., new concept store in Costa Mesa, California.
- Worked with the store manager with the daily closing report and daily sales report.
- Assisted in scheduling sales associates and determining goals for counter and sales associates. Assisted with initiating and executing special events. Responsible for achieving personal weekly and monthly goals through sales presentations, product knowledge, and promotional activities.

Career Summaries

Sales/Sales Management Executive

Cutting-edge computer and Internet technologies.

Key Account Management ■ New Business Development ■ Direct Sales and Reseller Partnerships

Consultative and Solution Sales ■ Networking and Relationship Building ■ Contract Negotiations

PROFILE Dynamic 14-year sales career reflecting pioneering experience and record-breaking performance in the computer and Internet industries. Remain on the cutting edge, driving new business through key accounts and establishing strategic partnerships and dealer relationships to increase channel revenue.

- ■ Expert in sophisticated e-commerce sales models, and vast knowledge of both the e-business marketplace and the capabilities and complexities of products.

- ■ Outstanding success in building and maintaining relationships with key corporate decision makers, establishing large-volume, high-profit accounts with excellent levels of retention and loyalty.

- ■ Exceptionally well-organized, with a track record that demonstrates self-motivation, creativity, and initiative to achieve both personal and corporate goals.

"Brad is a dynamic leader and arguably one of the best salespeople who has ever worked on any of the

➥

sales teams I have managed. I highly recommend
Brad for a position within any organization."
—VP of Sales, Millennium Software

Sales/Marketing/Sales Management

INTERNET BANKING AND FINANCIAL SERVICE INDUSTRIES

Senior Sales and Business Development executive with proven ability to drive business growth through aggressive sales initiatives that deliver revenue growth, market share, and market penetration. Conceptual thinker and strategic planner who balances sales production and sales leadership. Experienced in technology/product launch and market expansion. Well-versed in dealing with diverse operational units (Legal, IS/IT, Finance, HR, Investor Relations).

- Cross-Functional Team Building and Leadership
- Consultative Sales
- Internet Business Development and Implementation
- Contract Terms and Negotiation
- Competitive Analysis and Product Positioning
- Relationship Marketing

Strong background in identifying, establishing, and managing strategic relationships to leverage and generate significant business opportunities. Talented motivator with keen business acumen.

Perfect Phrases

- Top-producing Sales Executive with more than 15 years experience in the development, commercialization, and market launch of leading-edge technologies worldwide.

Combined expertise in strategic planning, P&L management, marketing, tactical sales, and client relationship management. Outstanding record of achievement in solutions selling and complex contract negotiations. Diverse industry and multichannel sales experience within the financial services, banking, health-care, retail, and Fortune 500 market sectors.

- Directed global account team responsible for revenue growth, retention, and service of select group of SBC's largest accounts. Built relationships with multiple levels of each customer organization while positioning team members for focus on defined projects and business needs.
- Received promotion to premier level of account support within SBC after two years of successful account management within large business group.
- Currently manage diverse team of product, technical, and sales support resources with direct reporting responsibilities.
- Successful Account Manager with 13 years of experience and a proven record of increasing revenue and complex product sets while providing the highest level of customer service and integrity. Skilled at developing and maintaining longstanding professional relationships within varied functional units of customers and internal groups.
- Demonstrated success in managing individual teams as well as entire organizations, with responsibilities including customer service, revenue growth, technical support, and policy development.
- High-energy sales professional with over 15 years of "business to business" experience dealing with Fortune 1000 business, government, medical, and telecommuni-

➥

322

cations markets. Strong team building and management skills and a passion for helping companies achieve success. Excellent technical background in enterprise-level voice, data, and related IT technologies.

- Leadership for customer satisfaction, business development, and vendor relationships. Managed to a $26 million quota. Focused on voice, convergence, and contact center solutions from Nortel, Siemens, Cisco, and Ericsson. Currently developing our infrastructure and mobility practice for structured cabling and broadband wireless.
- Achieved 133 percent of branch quota in 2004, President's Club award winner, top four of 124 sales reps.
- Achieved 118 percent of branch quota in FY 2004, President's Club award winner.
- Eleven-plus years proven record of accomplishments within the pharmaceutical industry.
  - Ranked first of 94 in the region, first in the district (2005)
  - Ranked second of 94 in the region, second in the district (2003)
  - Ranked third of 86 in the region, first in the district (2001)
  - Six-time President's Club Award Winner (overall); ranked within top 5 percent in overall sales and attainment
  - Continuously exceeding quota and Market Share for products being paid on (Zyrtec, Frova)
  - Member of District of the Year (2002)
  - Exercise initiative and independent judgmen' exceed sales quotas

- Global Sales/Alliance Manager to the Hewlett-Packard Company. Primary responsibility is for worldwide field engagement, aligning i2 Account Managers with HP Client Business Managers in i2s and HP's most strategic accounts. Developed and implemented a Proactive Teaming Initiative that got sponsorship from both i2s EVP WW Sales and HP's EVP WW Strategic Accounts.
- Responsible for facilitating executive-level relationships between HP's and i2's "C-Level" executives, as well as ensuring the "technical integrity" of the alliance. Annual quota of not less than $350 million attained at 125 percent.
- Senior Sales Manager with $125 million global manufacturer of scarves. Scope of responsibility includes strategic planning, competitive assessment, market positioning, business development, new product introductions, and client relationship management. Direct a team of seven.
- Led the successful national market launch of three product lines. Met first year projections, and currently on track to achieve 15 percent increase for 1998.
- Built and managed key account relationships with major retailers, catalog companies, and specialty stores, including Bergdorfs, Bloomingdale's, Macy's, Neiman Marcus, and Saks.
- Worked with home office in Italy to facilitate the design, test marketing, and U.S. introduction of an upscale private label line. Achieved immediate market penetration, with projections for $25 million in first year revenues.
- Developed strategy to leverage D'Italia's position within nontraditional business sectors. Negotiated contracts with the NCAA Collegiate Licensing Committee and several others.

Sales: Consultative

This section of phrases to support consultative selling is a complement to sales phrases in general. Not all sales positions leverage consultative selling to the same degree. A systems integrator with IBM will leverage this approach more than a pharmaceutical salesperson, who in turn will use it more than a retail salesperson.

Perfect Phrases

- Increased customer sales presentations by 50 percent coaching a consultative selling process.
- Reliance on consultative sales approach and process improvement recommendations. Managed territory with $13 million yearly revenue stream. Integration of third-party hardware, software, and services to enable Xerox print solutions. Developed high-level consultative relationship. Managed the channel sales team for Missouri for two years.
- Accomplishments:

    - Increased installed base each year by an average of 28 percent.

    - Consistently placed in top 5 to 10 percent of approximately 250 nationwide sales reps.

    - Top ranking among peers of 98 percent in customer retention over nine years.

    - Achieved President's Club 1991, 1993, 1995, 1996, 1997, and 1999 (160 percent of plan).

- Developed and delivered first formal sales management training program focused on building competencies in

➡

managing a consultative sales force according to group's unique operating model. Completed competency analysis, mapping gaps to drive curriculum.

- Accomplished sales performance expert experienced in marketing and business development. Proven record of success in the design and delivery of training and development programs that drive revenue generation and business results. Skillful strategist with consultative approach. Able to work effectively across organizations to identify needs and build customized training, process, and tool solutions. Valued for ability to identify best practices and integrate them into day-to-day operations. Respected, influential leader known for a company-first approach. Pragmatically focused on value-based selling and business benefit capture.

- Drove integration of consultative selling skills through in-class training that assimilated methodology into sales tools and sales presentations, as well as into sales management curriculum.

Skilled Labor: Trades

Career Summaries

Eleven years experience as crew leader for residential construction, rough carpentry.

Directed a crew of 10 people on the job site in one of largest housing developments in Dallas.

Built loyal client base through personal attention, quality service, and consistency.

Established reputation for excellence within local communities.

Demonstrated ability to work efficiently and effectively in fast-paced environment.

Perfect Phrases

- Successfully completed building project that was behind schedule when first hired, saving the company from liquidated damages.
- Daily management of projects and subcontractors to keep projects on schedule to ensure completion on time.
- Owned small local company and performed project planning, scheduling, and estimating for commercial and residential construction projects. Scope of responsibility included interfacing with subcontractors, obtaining permits, ordering materials, reviewing proposals, and liaising between county officials and owners. Supervised several subcontractors, including electricians, plumbers, air-conditioning installers, framers, and concrete finishers.
- Successfully led reconstruction of home that increased property value by $10,000.

- Managed all construction personnel in new construction of large commercial complexes for this small company that provides road construction services to Florida military bases. Held weekly meetings, ensuring progress of six carpenters, laborers, and concrete finishers in accordance with requirements while maintaining compliance with Occupational Health.
- Energized internal employee efforts that saved company 25 percent in subcontracted labor expenses.
- Expedited storm drain portion of project and reduced labor cost by hiring appropriate skilled subcontractor.
- Tasked with construction of two-story outpatient clinic as on-site supervisor for a large commercial construction company. Communicated with Navy inspectors, resolved job-site problems, reviewed plans and specifications, and ensured timely completion of new construction and renovations of eight floors in hospital.
- Accomplished 35 percent savings by training and leading employees to construct concrete stairways and elevator shafts.
- Led employee completion of all operating rooms, saving 25 percent in potential subcontracted labor expenses.
- Brought on to perform project planning and scheduling for subcontractor crew of framers, plumbers, electricians, and other laborers who completed construction of 262-room student housing building for Michigan State University. Allocated materials and labor as necessary; directed superintendent, assistant superintendent, and field engineer.
- Generated $50,000 revenue savings for company by completing 18, rather than 14, buildings by deadline.

➡

- Reduced labor costs by 25 percent by hiring two Sheetrock companies and instigating competition.
- Chosen by multifamily and student housing construction company to provide project management for three major projects: four four-story buildings at University of Florida, four apartment buildings at apartment complex in Tennessee, and one three-story building at a Hampton Inn in Oklahoma. Led subcontractors, interfaced with owners and city officials, obtained proper permits, and oversaw assistant superintendent and independent consultants.
- Completed university project within critical time constraints through proactive leadership of punch crew.
- Identified and corrected structural problem at Marriott that saved company time and expense.
- Guided several subcontractors on job site for small company, providing framing and construction of exterior walls for various clients, including Shoney's Inns in Pensacola, Florida, and Houston, Texas. Hired and supervised 22 metal framers and Sheetrock employees, ordered materials, and tracked labor costs within budgetary constraints.
- Accurately ordered and delivered materials, finding the best supplier prices, ensuring that no materials were wasted and achieving consistent cost savings.
- Delegated duties to various subcontractors, completed estimations, monitored materials and equipment on daily basis, and managed supply houses. Interfaced with owners and architects.
- Employed creative techniques when repairing old structures with limited original materials; successfully repaired 100-year-old building with 300 damaged bricks, blending new materials with existing structure.

Teaching

Career Summary

Dedicated educator with 20-plus years of teaching experience. Recognized for innovation in program development, instruction, and administration to meet the needs of a broad range of students. Effective communicator, writer, administrator, and student advisor/advocate.

Core Competencies

Curriculum Development and Instruction:

- Assisted in the development, validation, and enhancement of curricula. Introduced hands-on tools (e.g., computer technology, outside classroom activities) to improve classroom interest and retention.

- Taught a full academic curriculum (e.g., reading, writing, communications, mathematics, social science) to children ages seven to 13.

- Designed and implemented customized teaching programs to allow emotionally, physically, and learning disabled students to be mainstreamed into the classroom.

- Launched a highly successful peer tutoring program designed to improve interaction between upper level and younger students while fostering communication and mentoring skills at all levels.

Administration and Special Activities:

- Appointed Vice Principal with responsibility for a diversity of functions, including faculty recruitment and scheduling, curriculum development, discipline, parent/community affairs, and special events planning.

- Prepared documentation for recertification by the National Accreditation of Schools Committee as a member of a cross-functional faculty/administration committee.
- Provided classroom training, performance evaluation, and motivation as a mentor to student teachers completing college requirements for an education degree.

Community and Public Relations:
- Built partnerships with local companies and developed a series of seminars to introduce junior high school students to the business world. Coordinated speaker selection and topics of discussion.
- Participated on cross-functional teams of educators and administrators to design programs to improve the quality of educational curricula, enhance parent and community relations, and increase student participation both inside and outside of the classroom.

Perfect Phrases

- Administered curriculum for fifth and sixth grade Special Education students (emotionally disturbed, learning disabled, and neurologically impaired). Developed lesson plans and instructed all major subject areas, including reading, grammar, science, and social studies. Assessed student abilities and evaluated performance; conducted parent-teacher conferences to provide parents with student development reports. Counseled students and parents to resolve learning and discipline problems. Developed monthly newsletters and participated in IEP meetings for each child.
- Taught fourth grade for three years and full-day kindergarten for four years. Directed the preschool and junior

kindergarten program for one year. Revised curriculum and reading program for kindergarten class. Generated progress reports and evaluated students through report cards. Authored monthly newsletters. Created lesson plans and developed learning centers. Accountable for kindergarten screening and direction/production of annual holiday pageant.

- Established a class of 20 "overload" kindergarten students three weeks after the beginning of the school year. Supported the curriculum by planning and implementing standards-based lessons using visual cues, movement, and music.

- Modified lessons to serve ELL students and students with various learning styles. Created and maintained relationships and communication with the parents. Taught intervention classes to ELL students before school twice a week. Volunteered for PTA and community projects outside of class hours.

- Provided one-on-one and small group tutoring in basic skills of reading, writing, math, science, and social studies.

- Received the Service to Youth Award by a Nonparent.

- Co-taught two regular eighth grade and one honors Earth Science classes. Planned weekly instruction, developed lesson plans, administered exams, supervised students performing lab activities, graded labs and homework assignments, and recorded grades.

- Taught eighth grade English, stressing creative and critical thinking skills, including instruction in grammar, spelling, vocabulary, and creative and technical writing.

- Developed and wrote lesson plans that followed curriculum guidelines. Instructed students in project development through use of the writing process from topic selection to publication or presentation.

- Taught seventh grade public speaking course focusing on the development and oral presentation of individual ideas.
- Currently employed at a child-care facility. Many years of experience in daily teaching as the owner/operator of a home-based day-care facility.
- Experienced volunteer preschool teacher, youth director, and puppet ministry director at church, with additional experience working with children through other varied volunteer activities.
- Home-schooled three children for several years.
- Hosted Fresh Air child/children (seven summers).
- Red Cross First-Aid and CPR certified.
- Collaborated with city officials to petition for rezoning of a residential area; gained approval to further develop a proposed Children's Nature Trail with varied accommodations for children with special needs.
- Experienced in successfully working with Special Education students and developing skills in students at all levels of achievement.
- Utilize creative skills to design and implement well-received lesson plans and program structure.
- Establish learning environments that meet the physical, emotional, intellectual, social, and creative needs of children.
- Create yearly course work, including the selection of teaching materials.
- Effectively counsel students and parents on goals, objectives, and plans.

➡

- Rapidly develop and adjust lesson plans to meet unforeseen classroom situations.
- Significantly increased enrollment and student learning by implementing innovative programs.
- Instrumental in state accreditation.

Section Three

Perfect Phrases for the Perfect Interview

Carole Martin

Acknowledgments

Thank you to Donya Dickerson who is the best editor around. She pushed and pulled and "we" made a great book.

An acknowledgment and thanks to everyone who I have interviewed or coached over the many years of my experience. You are the stories behind my examples and answers.

Thank you to Kathy Sparks, my wonderful Virtual Assistant, who is a "nag" and a wonderful caretaker.

Section Contents

Part III: Perfect Phrases for the Perfect Interview: Specific Types of Jobs   479

Chapter 5: Perfect Phrases for Executive Management   481

Chapter 6: Perfect Phrases for Managers   489

Chapter 7: Perfect Phrases for Supervisors   497

Introduction

Words, words, words. They're everywhere. And using the right words is crucial to your success. Words are extremely important when we are trying to sell someone on an idea or attempting to influence a decision. The most common example of using words to influence is in any type of sales transaction. Regardless of whether you have ever thought of yourself as a "salesperson" or not, when you are in a job search, you are in fact entering into a sales situation in which your words will be used to influence a decision. That decision will be whether the employer thinks you are the best candidate for the job.

Using the right words in the job search begins when you write your résumé. To have a successful résumé you should use the same words that employers use. These are the words that are used in postings and ads. Whether your résumé is read by an electronic résumé system or by a human résumé reader, the process will be the same—scanning for "key words." If the words are not there, you will not get the interview. The point is that it is not only important to use the "right" words and language during your job search—*it is essential!*

This book provides you with the key words and phrases to use during your next interview, regardless of what industry you work in or what position you are interviewing for. These phrases can also be used as you write your résumé. Becoming aware of key words and knowing that the résumé reader will be seeking out these words will result in your being more focused and on track to provide the employers what they are seeking.

In this book, you will receive phrases and words to assist you in expressing yourself in the strongest way possible. You will also learn to determine "key words" for the job you are applying for, as well as the company or industry that you will be working in. By reviewing these phrases and becoming familiar with the words and phrases used to answer questions, you will find yourself expressing yourself with more confidence and will not feel as tongue tied as you may have when such questions were asked in past interviews. The more confident you feel, the stronger the impression you will make during the interview. The stronger the impression you leave, the more likely you will be considered a strong contender for the job.

Part I

Getting Ready for the Interview

Chapter 1

How to Use Perfect Phrases to Land Your Dream Job

The Words You Use Send a Strong Message

You are selling yourself during the entire job search process, beginning with the words you choose to write your résumé and continuing through the interview, salary negotiation, and acceptance of the offer. You are constantly revealing information about yourself and putting together a picture of yourself with words. And the words you use give details and add life and drama to your statements and stories.

Before we look at the specific phrases you can use for success, let's discuss some important ideas about choosing the best words for your interview. For starters, you should be aware of the key words used in your industry, in the companies you want to work for, and in the specific job positions you are applying for. Knowing the vocabulary for these areas is critical to your success as you interview for a specific job.

How will I know which words and phrases are "key" for the position or industry that I am applying for?

There are various sources you can look to if you want to learn words and phrases specific to your industry. You can look at company Web sites, their PR material, and even Web sites of competitors to learn what language they use. You can also look at trade magazines and journals, and even books for that industry as another resource.

Another very accessible source of key words and phrases is actually one that's *free and that can save you valuable time*. Using job boards, you can go online and look at job postings where you will discover the exact words used in the job, company, and industry. One more source to consider is the classified ads in your local newspapers, which also feature the specific job words to use. After all, experienced professionals write these words, and you can use the words to let them know you are on their wavelength and have what they are looking for. Once you become aware of these words, you will discover that there are specific words and phrases that are universal, describing what is required to succeed at specific jobs. The correct usage of these "key words" in your résumé or presentation can make or break your chances of being able to impress the interviewer and sell yourself as the best person for the job.

Some postings or ads are quite descriptive and have lots of details. Other postings will list only the essential facts. Look specifically for descriptive ads, which include a list of qualities and skills that are required in a candidate. This is considered the employer's "wish list." There is no guarantee that the words listed in the posting or description are going to be complete or that the employer won't change some of the requirements, but working with the posting will help you to plan your interview script and be prepared for whatever comes your way during the interview.

During the interview, whenever you are describing your successes and achievements, you will want to use up-to-date terms to describe your experiences and accomplishments. Words, like everything else in our lives have a "shelf life" and become old or dated. An example of using outdated words is to address a cover letter using the phrase: "To whom it may concern." While this is proper as far as grammar and protocol go, it is also very dated. This is true of industry-specific jargon as well.

Exercise

One way to prepare is to start looking at online postings, even if you aren't ready to apply for a position. Begin by visiting one of the major job boards and do an online job search. Enter the title of the job you are interested in pursuing, but at this point leave the geographical preference open. By leaving the location open, you will get a broader look at the industry and the common words and phrases that are used nationwide.

When you find job postings that are of interest to you, print them out and put them aside. After you have seven or eight, read through the postings noticing the words and phrases used. Read through the posting the first time for content. Then, read it again and begin to catch the key words used. Read the posting through one more time, but this time read between the lines.

Become aware of what is *not* written. As you read between the lines, ask yourself, "What would it take to do this job?"

As you answer this question, begin writing down words that come to mind. Words such as "outgoing," "good people skills," "very organized," "good at problem solving," "flexibility" may begin to surface. Even though these words aren't written in the posting, these are the skills and traits that employers are seeking. These traits and skills are considered *transferable,* meaning that they can be taken with you from company to company, no matter the job.

Here is an example of a rather vague ad that required some reading between the lines:

POSTING — Customer Service Representative

Responsibilities include answering customer calls, entering orders, and processing requests. Work in a team environment. Advancement opportunity for a professional individual with outgoing personality, good communication skills, and the ability to resolve problems quickly.

This ad could be for a number of office positions that require customer contact. By reading this posting carefully, you can pick out what is written, but you can also pick up the words that are "not there." Begin to read between the lines. For example,

Answer customer calls—resolve problems quickly (Fast-paced call center)

Good communication skills—outgoing personality (Sales/customer service a plus)

Enter orders and process requests (Computer skills needed here)

Team environment (Work with others doing similar work)

Opportunity for advancement (Supervisor opportunities)

By looking beyond the actual written words and phrases and making some judgments, you can assume that this company is looking for a *very outgoing, high-energy* person to *deal with customers* who have problems—and to *do it quickly*. The person should be *computer-savvy* and have *leadership potential*.

In order to impress your interviewer, you should use the words you glean from the posting. Doing so will prove that you see what it takes to do this job—a certain type of person and you are that person! For our example, you could say:

From the job posting and our conversation during this interview, it sounds like you are seeking a person with high energy to handle customer problems with tact and diplomacy. It also seems that if the person had some computer skills and some leadership potential, you would be impressed.

You have demonstrated your ability to read between the lines and let the interviewer know that you have been listening and that you understand what it will take to do this job.

As you are interviewing, you'll want to use "perfect phrases" to show that you have these desired characteristics and that you are the perfect candidate for this job. Here's an example phrase for each of the desired skills in our example:

Energy

Perfect phrase: "If you were to ask any of my coworkers at my last job, they would tell you they call me 'Mr. Energy.' I am always upbeat with customers or coworkers."

Confidence

Perfect phrase: "I have a successful track record of working with people and solving problems quickly in a very fast-paced environment."

Great communication skills

Perfect phrase: "In my last job my customers called and asked to speak to me directly because they knew that I would take care of them while solving the problem and following through."

Ability to connect with the interviewer

Perfect phrase: "I am very interested in your company and this job. From what I have heard, it sounds like morale and team spirit run high here. That is the atmosphere where I thrive best. I feel I could bring added value to the team and to you as a manager."

Examples of past successes

Perfect phrase: "At my last job I worked in a very busy call center where I had to up-sell customers' original orders. Last quarter I increased sales 25 percent by using my unique ability to connect with customers."

By first identifying the key words and then breaking down what you think it will take to do the job, you will be able to communicate effectively about your abilities and what you can do for your customer (the employer/interviewer). This exercise also provides you with an insider's view of what the employer is looking for in the perfect candidate. The result? You'll be able to sell yourself as the ideal person for the job.

When you can sell yourself as the solution to the interviewer's problem, you will be taken seriously and stand out from the competition. Being able to stand out is especially important in a tight job market where the competition is fierce. In fact, because employers are in the driver's seat in a tight market with many candidates to choose from, they are demanding more for their money. In a normal job market employers are willing to settle for about 80 percent of the requirements they wish for. In a tight job market employers tend to be greedy and look for 100 percent of the requirements, and then some. You'll want to show that you meet their requirements, and you can do this by using the perfect phrases. By using stronger phrases than other job applicants, you'll show the interviewer through your words that you are the best person for the job.

Finding the Key Words and Phrases for Your Position

Once you have collected and printed out several job postings and descriptions—the ones with as much detail as possible— highlight or underline the words that appear more than one time. When you finish, stand back and take a look at what you've done. You will begin to see patterns as the same key words and phrases are repeated over and over. The words in the phrases may vary, but the meaning will be the same.

You will also begin to see sets of words used for specific jobs within an industry. A good way to become knowledgeable about key words and phrases is to write or collect the words that are used repeatedly. As you prepare phrases for your interview, note how often specific words are used as you go through your job search.

Keep a dictionary nearby so that when you find a word and don't understand the meaning, you can look it up before you make it "your" word. It is unwise to use a word without understanding its meaning.

Once you have formulated your list of sample words and phrases, you can review it whenever you have time. One woman conducting a job search wrote the key words and sample phrases in a small notebook and carried it with her wherever she went. When she found herself standing in long lines at places like the post office or bank, she would pull out her notebook and review her list. She was able to improve her industry vocabulary quickly by doing this. You will find that if you continue to practice these words, they will become very familiar to you and become part of your vocabulary.

The following are examples of common words and phrases found in postings for an **Executive Secretary/Admin** position. Even though the words used are not the same, they fall into similar categories. They all came from job postings and were identified as **key** *factors*.

WANTED—Executive Secretary/Admin—Skills Required:

Written and oral communication skills

- "Exceptional **communication** and interpersonal skills…"
- "Strong written **communication**—grammar and composition skills…"
- "Superior oral and **written communication** skills coupled with a professional appearance…"
- "Must have strong **interpersonal and communication** skills, oral and written…"
- "Understand and be willing to work and **communicate** within **cultural protocol**…"
- "Must be **assertive**, adaptable, and able to **communicate with all levels**…"

Confidentiality—judgment

- "Ability to **handle confidential information**…"
- "Use of tact in responding to inquiries within established authority in a **confidential manner**…"
- "Handle complex or **confidential matters** requiring significant discretion and judgment…"
- "Exhibit **high level of moral and ethical behavior**; discreet…"
- "Quality, accuracy, and the ability to work without supervision **using confidentiality**…"

Self-starter

- "The ideal candidate will **work independently**—must be a **self-starter**…"

- "Must be **independent;** handle flow of communication between clients and management…"
- "Ability to work **without supervision,** confidentiality…"
- "Ability to anticipate needs/start projects **without direction** is critical…"
- "A strong sense of responsibility, initiative to problem-solve, and **work independently**…"
- "Team-oriented, flexible, with a **positive, 'can-do' attitude**…"

Prioritizing and multitasking

- "Must be able to **plan,** organize, and **follow-through**…"
- "Expected to **prioritize** and manage **multiple projects,** show initiative…"
- "Ability to handle **multiple projects simultaneously** and be detail-oriented…"
- "MUST have **excellent multitasking and proofreading** ability…"
- "Demonstrated ability **prioritizing** workload—handling **multiple tasks** simultaneously…"
- "Ability to manage **multiple** and/or **time-dependent** activities…"

Organized

- "Must be **well organized** and able to work under pressure, confidentiality required…"
- "Needs to be a quick learner and **highly organized** with excellent follow-up skills…"
- "Ability to take ownership of commitments and **organize/prioritize** workload…"

■ "Sense of **urgency** to understand and **meet the needs** of the team and of the organization…"

You can see by this grouping of phrases that there are certain *key phrases and words* that appear repeatedly in job postings for this position. The words and phrases vary slightly, but they are consistent in the content relating to what is needed to do the job. Note that there is an overlap in the skills desired in some phrases. Certain words appear and are coupled with other skills. For example, *well organized* and able to *work under pressure, confidentiality* required.

Using the job Description to Prepare Your Perfect Phrases

Once you have a firm grasp of the key skills and particular experience that are required for a position, it's time to put together the phrases you will use to wow the interviewer. Let this book be your guide as you assemble the phrases you want to be sure to use in your interview.

To understand how to pick the perfect phrase, let's go back to our example: After conducting a job search for an Executive Secretary/Admin and compiling the key words and phrases, the most common words/phrases were identified as the following:

■ Written and oral communication skills
■ Confidentiality and judgment
■ Self-starter—independent
■ Prioritizing and multitasking
■ Very organized

Using the Executive Secretary/Admin position, you can see how effective it is to summarize what you have found to be the key words for the interview.

Perfect Phrase:

"From what I have read in your job posting, it appears that you want someone who has superior communications skills, both written and oral. It sounds like it would take someone who can work independently and who is a self-starter. That matches with my skills completely."

You have demonstrated an ability to summarize and "cut to the chase" by getting directly to what you believe it would take to do this job. Your use of terms and phrases also shows a grasp of the job requirements and excellent communication skills. Whenever you say, "It sounds like…" you are paraphrasing what you have just heard or read. This is a communication skill that will take you far. It is letting the person with the problem know that you understand his or her problem.

Perfect Phrase:

"I believe my past experiences as an Exec Administrator would make me a perfect fit for this job. One of the qualities I have that I pride myself in is my ability to protect information, particularly confidential information. My last boss would tell you he trusted me with his personal information as well as his top-secret business information."

Since confidentiality is high on the list of requirements for an Executive Secretary/Admin, you have let the interviewer know that this is something you excel in. Using a quote or paraphrasing what your last boss would say is another way of letting the interviewer know something about you without actually saying it yourself. By saying, "My boss would say, …" you are using a third-party endorsement to make your statement strong.

Perfect Phrase:

> "I can see that someone who is organized and able to prioritize and who works well under pressure while multitasking is your ideal candidate. I will remind you that these are my strengths, as proven by my past experiences in similar situations. From what I hear and see, I am the perfect candidate for your job. I am someone who can make your business life easier."

Another opportunity to tell the interviewer that you know what it takes to do this job and that you have "been there and done that." You have also let the interviewer know that you believe in your ability, and you also make an offer that would be tempting to any boss, "I can make your business life easier."

By actually mentioning the skills in your answers, you let the interviewer see that you have an idea of their importance and that you understand what it will take to get this job done. Doing this will improve your chances of both connecting with the interviewer and being remembered as someone who "gets the point." You have also let the interviewer know that you are the "perfect candidate" for the position by relaying your strengths and past experiences. Well done!

Giving the perfect answer in your interview is easier than you think. When you can identify the key skills and speak about the requirements of the job using key words and phrases, you will sound polished and knowledgeable about what the employer/interviewer is seeking. You can also sell yourself with more confidence if you know that you have the required skills necessary to do the job and that you have something to offer. You have what the employer is looking for!

Top Eight Word Mistakes Candidates Make in Job Interviews

1. Use language that is too informal

It is important to remember that you are interviewing for a job, not trying to make a new best friend. Too much familiarity can hurt your chances by making you look unprofessional.

> **Poor Phrase:** "I'm sure **you guys** are aware that the job market is **in the dumps** right now. It's been **one heck of an uphill battle** for me for the past year."

> **Perfect Phrase**: "Unfortunately, as I am sure you are aware, the job market is still tight, and there is a great deal of heavy competition for the same jobs."

2. The use of words that are vague

Words such as "a lot," "various/multiple," and "great deal of" are vague and don't give the interviewer the needed information.

> **Poor Phrase: "**I have had **a lot of experience** with **various lines of multiple** products. I am proud of the results I've had in saving the company a **great deal of money**."

Perfect Phrase: "With over eight years experience working in the paper industry and primarily selling photo paper, I consider myself an expert on the subject and have saved my clients as much as 20 percent on orders over $5,000."

3. Misuse of pronouns

It can be very confusing and words can be misinterpreted when pronouns are misused. Be especially alert to this when you are using the pronouns "we," "I," and "you."

Poor Phrase: "**We** were behind on **our** project, and **we** decided that **we** would stay and finish the job rather than miss **our** deadline. **We** pulled it together, and **we** were able to meet **our** deadline."

Perfect Phrase: "I worked with a team of designers to bring a project in on time. We each took responsibility for a particular area. We worked closely, but at the same time we were completely disconnected from one another. This seemed to work because my four counterparts and I managed to pull the project together on time."

4. Using company-specific words

Each company has certain terms that are indigenous only to that company. Outsiders will not know what you are talking about if you use these terms. This is especially true if you have worked for a public organization or the military. You should use as many specific words as possible in your interview so that the hiring manager knows you are familiar with your industry.

Poor Phrase: "While I was working on **the 767 project**, I discovered an error in the "**Whichamaculit**" used to produce our **656 product line**. This was a really costly mistake."

Perfect Phrase: "At my last company there was a particular marketing project that involved a software conversion. Because of my strong attention to detail, I was able to catch an error that would have cost the company millions of dollars."

5. Assuming everyone knows the acronym you are using

Acronyms are used at every company—shortcuts used internally to eliminate a lot of words. Avoid using these in an interview because the hiring manager may not be familiar with the acronyms used at your current company.

Poor Phrase: "I was considered an **SAR** and supported three **line reps** who were in the **SWSC area**."

Perfect Phrase: "My position title was sales associate representative, and I supported the sales representatives who were responsible for the southwest area of South Carolina."

6. Describing skills by using "weak" words

Beware of small words that can sabotage your credibility—words like "pretty," "most of the time," and "kind of."

Poor Phrase: "I'm **pretty good** with computers—**at least most of the time** I am. I **kind of taught** myself most of the programs."

Perfect Phrase: "I am very knowledgeable about Unix software. When I was unfamiliar with programs in the past, I taught myself in less than two weeks. I am a very quick learner."

7. Use too few words to answer the question

One pet peeve many interviewers have is not getting enough information. When a candidate answers a question with one or two words, it's impossible to make a judgment as to whether this person is the right person for the job.

Poor Phrase: "Yes, I have had experience in that area."

Perfect Phrase: "I have over 10 years working with biotech testing. If you were to ask any of my coworkers, they would tell you that I hold the record for the least number of mistakes when using testing equipment."

8. Talking too much—not getting to the point

When you fail to prepare for the interview, you can easily ramble and go off the subject down some other road. A rule of thumb is, **"Your answers should be no longer than two to three minutes long."**

Poor Phrase: "My last company has developed software to support government enforcement of firearms violators. This nationwide project will be the first of its kind and will allow users to investigate firearms traffickers and purchasers. The software is able to track violent offenders and unscrupulous federal firearms licensees. This product will allow users to investigate and prosecute violators and felons by tracking their activities from remote locations. The product has been developed in cooperation with the U.S. government and will hopefully be purchased and used by all branches of law enforcement agencies that could use this tracking method. The company has invested over two years in developing and perfecting this product and has invested a great percentage of the company's revenue in it, betting that this is going to have a big payoff long term. Short term it has put a considerable squeeze on the finances needed to run everyday work projects. If it is successful, it will be a huge coup for those who have hung in there. If it is not successful, it will be a huge loss to the company and will probably result in massive layoffs. So the whole project is going to make or break the company and it's future."

Perfect Phrase: "At my last company I served as lead in getting a new tracking product launched nationwide. The product will be used to track firearms violators and bring them to conviction through evidence collected. I worked closely with the U.S. government and followed the regulations necessary to develop such a product."

Preparing for Follow-Up Questions

As you put together your phrases, always try to think of any follow-up questions you might be asked. Of course, you would never use a word or say a phrase just to impress your interviewer without knowing the definition behind the word. You should also never use a phrase unless you have an example to back up the word or phrase. When you can communicate to the interviewer a specific example regarding skills you used in the past, you will have a better chance of convincing him or her that you are knowledgeable about the subject you are describing.

Example

A young man might say during an interview, "I have excellent written and oral communication skills." The interviewer could follow up with a question like, "Can you give me an example of a time when you used your written communication skills?" The candidate might look embarrassed if he didn't have an example. He said that he had great written communication skills because he thought it sounded good.

Exercise for Preparing for Follow-Up Questions

Here's a simple exercise that will help you prepare for follow-up questions. It will also help you take a look inside yourself and begin to think about what you want more of, and what you want less of, in your next job. People usually perform at a higher level if they are satisfied with the work they do and are, therefore, motivated to give 100 percent plus.

Start by making a list of the responsibilities and tasks you performed at your last job. These would be the projects or tasks that you were particularly proud of or were energized by. Think about the last time you were so involved in a project or task that you woke up thinking about how you could improve the situation. Write those experiences down and try to determine what the factors were that were satisfying for you.

Let's say you were a project leader. The tasks list would read something like: "Led a team; coordinated and monitored project progress; ensured the flow and completion of work on schedule; monitored expenditures and budget." Now you have solid examples of your skills that you can use for any follow-up question.

After you have written this list for your most current job, try doing the same thinking for previous jobs. If you recently graduated from college, use the classes that were most stimulating and interesting for you or the projects you worked on with teams when you were in school.

By making lists of motivating experiences from your last two or three jobs, you will begin to notice patterns of projects and tasks that stand out. Analyze what those tasks involved. Do you want more or less of this type of responsibility in your next job? The answer will tell you what you want and may suggest some possibilities for fulfillment in future jobs that have similar responsibilities. Knowing what you want will make you feel more confident about finding the right job.

Getting Ready for Success

This book provides you with the phrases you need for success. Use the phrases in this book as building blocks for your own phrases. They will give you the competitive edge.

Perfect Phrases for the Perfect Interview

These perfect phrases are to be used as a guide or template to assist you in using effective wording to express yourself. You may find that seeing examples will give you ideas for your own stories. Forming your own phrases using these guides will make your statements stronger. It would be unwise to use them as "cookie cutter" answers unless the answer matches what you actually did. A good rule is to use these phrases but to never say anything that you don't have an example of a time when you actually had the experience.

Armed with your perfect phrases, you will feel confident going into any interview situation, and you will be sure to wow any interviewer. Now, let's get to the phrases!

Part II

Perfect Phrases for the Perfect Interview: General Questions

Chapter 2

Who You Are and What You Know

The purpose of any interview is to give the interviewer an accurate picture of you. The interviewer wants to know what makes you unique and where you've been on your career path. Using appropriate words and phrases will assist you in getting the necessary information across. This chapter focuses on the topics of you and your knowledge, providing you with words and phrases to help you create an accurate picture for the interviewer.

Breaking the Ice

"Did you find the place okay?"

- "Yes, and I actually had extra time to catch a cup of coffee across the street. Thanks for the great directions. The route that you advised me to take saved me a lot of time and helped me to avoid some heavy traffic."
- "I'm one of those people who plans ahead. I actually took a dry-run drive last week to make sure I knew where I was going. I really dislike the idea of being late—especially for an interview."
- "I took a couple of wrong turns, but I don't ever let mistakes throw me. I just turned around and went back. Luckily I had allowed extra time, so I was not upset when I got lost. Eventually I figured it out and arrived in plenty of time."

"How was your commute?"

- "You know how traffic can be. I used your directions and also listened to the traffic reports on the radio. I was able to avoid a couple of trouble spots."
- "Because I left early, it was very relaxing. I always allow extra time when I have appointments. I learned that lesson when I got a flat tire and hadn't allowed extra time in case of the unexpected. Unfortunately I was late to an important appointment. I've never been late since that incident."
- "I took public transportation in and took the earlier train to allow me time to walk the few blocks to get here. I am an avid walker. I stay in shape by walking whenever I can."

"How was your trip here?"

- "Other than a four-hour delay with my connecting flight, it was fine. I'm sure you have travel experience in today's skies and know the routine. I have learned to always fly with a good book—just in case."

- "Because travel is such a big part of my job as a sales rep, I am used to schlepping and waiting. If you aren't going to be flexible and relaxed about changes and delays, you are going to experience a lot of grief while traveling. I love traveling and experiencing new places."

- "My trip in was great. I took the train instead of flying. I find trains more relaxing. I was able to read a few business magazines on the trip. I read some interesting reports about one of your competitors in today's business section. Did you know that XYZ Company was being bought out by ABC?"

"How is your summer going so far?"

- "Right now my job search is taking up most of my time. I am spending at least six to eight hours a day working on leads and networking. I have been able to get away for a couple of weekends, and that was really relaxing. How about yours?"

- "Summer seems to be flying by. I don't know where the weeks have gone. I took one week at the beginning of the summer to go to visit relatives in California, but since then I have been really busy at work. How about you? Have you been able to take any time off?"

- "It's been going great so far. I have been taking time off from my job search one day a week and going somewhere that I typically don't go during the week. I really find it ➡

delightful because it is less crowded. It would be a real luxury to work four days a week; unfortunately I can't afford that luxury."

"Cold enough for you?"

- "I'm one of those unusual persons who enjoys cold. I guess it brings back good memories of skiing and spending time outdoors in the snow."
- "I have to admit that winter is not my favorite time of the year. But wearing the right clothes makes a big difference. The first year that I moved here I invested in a good, warm topcoat."
- "Weather is not a big deal for me. I just adjust to whatever climate I happen to live in. I moved around a lot as a kid and got used to dealing with whatever was out there."

Getting to Know You

"Tell me about yourself."

- "For the past six years I have been in the electronics industry working on computer systems. I take an analytical view of what is happening and work through the process by trying various solutions. I work well independently or as a member of a team. I have worked in fast-paced environments most of my life and am very goal-oriented and deadline-driven."

- "I have over four years experience as a technician. Two years ago I was promoted to lead technician, and I currently supervise four testers and technicians. My strength is problem solving. I do whatever it takes to get the problem solved as quickly and efficiently as possible."

- "I am a person who enjoys problem solving. For the past six years I have been working on projects and problems involving software design. In my last position I was able to solve a design problem that had been around for a while. As a result, the company was able to sell a product that had been delayed for some time to our biggest customer."

"Are you familiar with our company?"

- "My research has turned up quite a bit of information about your company and its founders. I was very impressed by the background of your two founders. I was also very interested to read several articles in journals about the latest research your company is conducting."

- "I've known of your company for the last couple of years. I happened to see an article in the paper about some funding that you were obtaining from an investment

➡

375

group, and this drew my interest because of my background in the field. I think what your company is working on is very cutting edge and something that I want to be a part of."

- "I went to your Web site and was impressed by all the products and services your company provides. I had no idea that your company had the extensive reach that it has. I also read some articles online that pertained to your latest products."

"How would you describe yourself?"

- "I would say that I am knowledgeable about computer programs and that I have a strong ability to solve problems. Also I stay focused and on track when I am working on a project."
- "I'd describe myself as a person who is upbeat. I try not to let little things in life get to me. I'm known for my positive attitude at work. I'm also looked to for information. People know that they can come to me with their problems and that I will listen and try to do what I can to solve them."
- "Anybody who has ever worked with me would tell you that I am a fun person to be around. I also know when to be serious and when it is important to be focused on what I am doing. I think I am a balanced person who enjoys my work and my surroundings."

"What are three words that describe you?"

- "'Hard working' is the first. Anyone I work with would tell you that I do whatever it takes to get the job done. Second is 'team player' because I thrive in environments that are supportive and collaborative. And last, 'knowledgeable regarding accounting information.' Through my education and my experience I have a strong background in all phases of accounting."

- "'Reliable.' I never miss deadlines. 'Friendly.' I have an upbeat attitude. And 'thorough.' I always try to get it right the first time."

- "The first would be 'expert' on the subject of mainframes. Second would be 'communicator,' because I talk to everyone I come in contact with. Third would be 'organized,' because I am a planner and always have a schedule planned out."

"What experience do you have that qualifies you for this job?"

- "I have a total of ten years experience, with the majority of my experience in teaching. When I read the job posting, I felt confident that I would be qualified and could bring added value to this job, particularly in the area of curriculum development."

- "I provided technical problem resolution and ensured effective coordination of activities in every job that I have held. I have also gained a reputation within the manufacturing industry as a key player when it comes to hard bargaining and negotiations. In my last two jobs I was able to save the companies thousands of dollars by negotiating savvy business deals."

- "First, my excellent communication skills and my ability to work with all types of people. This is important because of the interaction within various departments involved in projects. Next, I am very organized with strong coordination skills. It takes the ability to prioritize and to be adaptable in order to succeed in this type of position. Last are my strong coordinating skills that are necessary to keep on track and on schedule."

"Why do you think you are a good match for this job?"

- "My years of experience in this industry make me feel confident that I can do this job and bring added value. I am extremely knowledgeable about your customer base and your competitors and what it will take to sell your newer products. I am also very well connected in this industry and therefore can be very resourceful."

- "If you asked any of my coworkers at my last job, they would tell you that 'I am good with people, conscientious about my reports, and very organized.' From what I've read about this position, that more than qualifies me as a good match for this job."

- "I'm a person who is passionate about what I do. I am fortunate that I have found work where I can help people have better lives. Nothing gives me more pleasure than to help someone move out of a bad situation and find a new direction."

"What makes you think that you can do this job?"

- "When I compared your requirements with my qualifications, I found that they were a very good match. You are looking for six years experience, and I have over six years of experience selling a comparable product. You are looking for someone with excellent communication skills, and I have a track record of selling to some of the most difficult people in the industry."

- "My six years of experience in sales plus my MBA provide me with the perfect skill set that you are seeking. I have a proven record of being a top performer in my company for the past two years. I know I have what it takes to do this job."

- "I have a strong working relationship with all the manufacturing people as well as the union representatives. As the liaison I can head off problems that might flare before it is too late."

Career Goals

"What are your short-term and long-term goals?"

- "My career path is not set in stone. One thing I have learned is to stay flexible to opportunities. I have read your literature and visited your Web site, and know that there are open opportunities with someone with my background and education. I know that whatever I do, I will continue to take on additional responsibilities and challenges."

- "My short-term goal is to find a job in a company where I can bring value to the team. My longer-term goal is to continue to take classes in the evening in management and eventually manage projects."

- "My last company was my first job out of college, and I've come a long way in experience there. But now my goal is to join a larger company that has career opportunities and programs for development. I have researched such companies, and I know that this company believes in career development for its employees. My longer-term goals are flexible, depending on the career path I establish in the new company."

"What goals have you set for yourself in your career?"

- "I am very goal-oriented and have completed all the goals I have set for myself in past jobs. My long-term goal is to become a specialist in the field of IT management."

- "When I look at goals, I like to remain somewhat flexible. I have found that the world is changing so rapidly that it is not a good idea to lock oneself into specific goals that may not be achievable. I do know that I want to continue to advance and become more and more of an expert in my field. I would eventually like to take on more responsibility as a project or product manager."

- "I am looking beyond what I do at my current company and want to advance when I am ready and someday move into a management position. From what I know about this company and your vision for employees, it is exactly the company that I am looking to join. I know it will take time and hard work, but I am ready and willing to do whatever it takes."

"How do you see our company helping you achieve your goals?"

- "I've done extensive research on the kind of company that I want to be affiliated with so that I can achieve my career goals. Your company is among the top five companies that I have set my sights on. I believe the values of this company are very much in line with the values that I have set for myself."

- "I have been aware of the progress and growth this company has made over the past four years while I have been earning my Bachelor's degree. In fact, I did a case study as one of my assignments in college using your company as a model of steady growth. The career development program your company offers is of special interest to me."

- "I see this company as one that values its employees and the contributions that employees have to make. I have had several friends who have worked here, and they have shared some great employer stories with me. I know this is a company where I could work collaboratively with bright people to achieve my goals."

➡

"What industry experience do you have that qualifies you to do this job?"

- "My knowledge and experience in this industry encompasses a total of 10 years. I see real value in my years of experience with a company that has similar customers and contacts. I have built strong relationships throughout my career that will help me hit the ground running at this company."

- "I consider myself an expert in the field of data mining. As you can see from my résumé, I have worked nationally and internationally as a consultant. I have worked with Fortune 500 companies as well as small start-ups. I have a broad scope of experience and expertise to pull from to analyze and solve problems of a broad scope."

- "I've been interested in working for your company for some time. I have extensive experience in the fashion industry and know that sales are on the soft side right now because of economic conditions. I also know that you have a new product set to launch by the end of the year. I am interested in becoming a key contributor. I want to be part of the team that makes this company a stronger contender in today's challenging market."

"What can you bring to this job from your previous experience?"

- "My extensive experience and educational background qualify me as an expert. My wide range of experiences in both the education system as well as the business sector allow me to have a broader view of how a school system can be run like a business. My past success and accomplishments speak for the value I can bring to this type of position."

- "I have made some long-lasting relationships with customers by building rapport through trust. I pride myself on my customer service skills, including follow-through and experience. I am very thorough, with strong attention to detail. I enjoy thinking 'outside the box' and coming up with new ways to look at old problems—either on my own or as a team member."

- "My successes in customer service have made me one of the top producers in my company. I have customers who ask for me specifically when they have problems because they know that I will listen and do whatever I can to resolve the situation."

"How does this job compare and contrast with what you have done in the past?"

- "This job is very similar in that I would be selling to a similar customer base. The contrast would be the nature of the product and your company's reputation in standing behind the product. I believe that, armed with these additional tools, I can bring very good results to the territory and company."

- "The company is different and the product is new, but I know I have what it takes to do this job. In my last position within two months of being hired I was on the top-performer list."

- "The job I was performing in my last company was almost a perfect match with this job. I really loved that job and was sorry when I was laid off. The company went through many changes, and eventually my job was affected. What I liked most about the job was that I worked in a team environment with some really great people. I know that this job has a similar team environment, and that's why I'm interested in pursuing the opportunity."

Position Savvy

"What experience do you have that matches the requirements of this job?"

- "I have a proven record building strong relationships with key customers that have resulted in increased revenue for the company. From reading through your job posting, I believe that this is exactly the experience and record you are seeking in a job candidate."
- "I have been successful in achieving premium service on a shoestring budget. I received an achievement award last year for producing results in a market that was all but dead."
- "I consider myself an expert in the field of data mining. As you can see from my résumé, I have worked nationally and internationally as a consultant. I have worked with Fortune 500 companies as well as small start-ups. My experience and expertise allow me to analyze and solve problems of a broad scope."

"What would your boss say about your performance in your last position?"

- "My boss would give me the highest praise. He would say that my achievements and my thorough understanding of mergers and acquisitions have made me an invaluable member of the M&A team."
- "She would tell you that I have exceeded all my goals for the past two years. She manages me from an off-site location and depends on me to manage my area independently. We have a very trusting relationship, and she would tell you that I have always been reliable and

385

dependable. She would also tell you that I have built great relationships with internal customers."

- "He would be sure to tell you that I stay current and abreast of the latest changes in the field. That's one of my strengths. I like research and knowledge, and everyone knows that they can come to me for answers to questions on current rules and regulations."

"Tell me about a time when your knowledge of your position made a difference in the outcome of a situation."

- "Because I have such strong planning and coordinating experience, I was able to put together a conference for 500 people that ran very smoothly. I planned the event by starting with a venue that would accommodate that large an audience. I had a committee who I worked with and directed. Each person on the committee was in charge of a segment of the conference—invitations, catering, and entertainment. I used an Excel spreadsheet to track the scheduling and events. We all worked very long and hard, but the results were an extremely successful conference with very positive feedback."

- "During a threatened union strike by our hospital workers, my ability to work with diverse people, plus my negotiating skills, was the key factor in working out a resolution so that the strike never happened. Needless to say, management commended me on my skilled dealings with the workers and my ability to listen to them and work through their issues with the managers."

- "I am very knowledgeable about Unix systems and recently worked on a server for a large facility that had 500-plus employees. I provided Unix support to all divisions, including maintenance of hardware and software on several workstations. I was able to ensure daily backups of software and research data. I also updated the operating systems with the latest upgrades and created accounts for new users. The project was done in record time and continues to run smoothly with minimum maintenance."

Strengths

"What do you consider your strengths?"

- "I have several strengths I can bring to this job. First of all my background—experience and education—are a perfect fit for this position. Second, I have excellent written and oral communication skills. And last, I am very flexible and adaptable to new situations."

- "One of the strongest points is my ability to work with a diversity of people. Regardless of the situation, I have the ability to adapt and work under any circumstances. In my last job I worked in a small room with 13 people all speaking various languages, and still managed to stay focused."

- "My strength is my ability to remain calm in chaotic situations. I have had to keep my cool in every job I have ever held. Fast-paced environments are no longer a challenge to me; they are a way of life. I manage to stay centered no matter what is happening, and as a result the people around me feel calmer."

"What skill has been praised or rewarded in your past jobs?"

- "I have an outstanding record of error-free calculations for my customers. When it comes to money, people don't like mistakes. I pride myself on my ability to be very detail-oriented when it comes to figures."

- "A major strength of mine is my ability to forecast expenditures for budget planning. This has been very important in my success and has kept various managers within their spending limits."

- "I am a proven performer when it comes to connecting with doctors and getting them to recommend my products to patients. As for my appraisals, I have always been a high achiever no matter where I have worked."

"What skills can you bring from your previous jobs?"

- "I have worked effectively in three different industries and have been able to make the transition with minimum downtime. My ability to learn quickly and 'hit the ground running,' has made a huge impact on my career."
- "One of the skills that I take pride in is my ability to listen to people and really hear what they say. I consider this to be key in sales. Before I even think of selling someone something, I find out what the needs are."
- "My key strengths are my strong analytical skills and my ability to use those skills to see all sides of a problem. Problem solving is my strength and greatest asset."

"Give me an example of a time when you used your strength to achieve results."

- "My strength as an employee is my dependability. There was a situation in which I was on call to cover any computer disasters over the weekend. A call came in, and I was not the technician closest to the company involved but I could see that no one else was responding. I had weekend plans but considered my job first. I responded to the call four hours before anyone else and was able to prevent downtime for the company on Monday morning."
- "Working for an executive who was out of town a great deal of time, I often made decisions based on my judgment. There was one incident when I had to make a

decision about calling a meeting off or trying to get someone else to cover the meeting for my boss in his absence. I made a few critical calls and was able to avoid canceling a meeting that would have involved out-of-town executives. Everyone, including my boss, was grateful for my quick thinking and judgment."

- "My knowledge of construction and the laws and regulations—county, state, and federal—saved one company that I worked for a great deal of money. Working as a consultant, I was able to see that one project was in danger of violating several building codes. I was able to make suggestions to bring the project to code and as a result saved the company money in building costs as well as fines."

Uniqueness

"What makes you unique?"

- "Not only am I a successful manager, but I worked my way up from the bottom position in the company to get there."
- "If you were to ask any of my colleagues, they would tell you that I am known for my unique ability to get people to do things for me without asking directly."
- "What makes me unique is that my outside interest is playing the piano and my 'day job' is working on the computer all day long. So I am constantly playing with sets of keys."

"Tell me about a tiỉme when you solved a problem in a unique manner."

- "As a publicist, one of the challenges of my job is to think of unique ideas to promote my client or product. There was one publicity campaign I handled for a product that we called a 'real knock out.' I purchased hundreds of key chains with small boxing gloves attached and sent them as part of the press kit to radio and television studios. It was unique, so it drew attention and got great results for my client."
- "An engineering project I worked on at my last company saved over $1 million in operating costs. I created, published, and implemented a unique plan for underwater storage. I was in charge of implementation, and, because of my planning and coordination of departments, it was a great success."
- "I was given the challenging task of continuing our community educational programs, but with a more limited budget than in previous years. The first thing I did was to

apply for grant money. Then I put together an aggressive volunteer program. Because of my ability to come up with new ideas, we were able to continue our classes, seminars, and workshops in a seamless manner without raising the costs of the classes."

"Give me an example of how your uniqueness has helped you in your work."

- "I'm known for my ability to 'think outside the box.' I came up with an original idea to raise funds for the police children's annual toy drive. I contracted with the local movie theater to give a free movie ticket to every person who brought in a toy over the cost of $5. The results were like none we've ever had before. We had a record contribution, and the donors received a gift in return. It was a very successful year."

- "It was when I was a student. I used a unique way to get around campus and the city; I rollerskate everywhere. I figured I was getting more exercise skating than I would get walking. I didn't have time to exercise, so I kept fit by using this method to commute. I was also able to listen to my class tapes while I skated. It was a great way to get around and study at the same time."

- "The unique part of this example is that I was able to lead a cross-functional team in a company that had never used cross-functional teams before. As the lead engineer I decided to try an experiment, and took people from various functions and cross-trained them. We were able to do twice the design, testing, and production in a shorter period and saved the company money in the process. It was received well and is now a common practice at the company."

Chapter 3

Skills Set

Sometimes when we are asked what our strengths are, we tend to think "knowledge-based skills." These are the skills you've acquired from experience and education. While these skills are important, the next person to be interviewed may be equally qualified in these skills. There are two other categories that are very important when you are trying to establish your uniqueness in interviews. These are your transferable skills and your personal traits.

- **Knowledge-based skills** are skills learned through experience or education, such as computer programs, graphics, languages, and writing
- **Transferable skills** are portable—you can take them with you to almost any job. Examples are communication, listening, decision making, judgment, initiative, planning, and organizing. Chances are that you are probably taking for granted some of the skills that make you unique.
- **Personal traits** are qualities that make you who you are—flexibility, integrity, friendliness, dependability, good attitude. These skills cannot be taught, even though some employers

393

would like to teach them, and they should be valued as important.

When you are trying to establish what makes you unique, think of all three categories and where you want to focus to let the interviewer know that you are the best person for the job and why.

Creativity

"What experience can you bring that involved creativity?"

- "I pride myself on my ability to look at all aspects of a problem. I have come up with some very original solutions to problems that no one else seemed able to solve. I have always been known for my ability to think 'outside the box.'"

- "I have had a full range of experience in the film industry, working with lighting and cameras. I have worked on last-minute deadlines where there were problems to solve, and I solved them using lots of resourcefulness. I not only met the deadlines and goals, but I thrived in those situations. It was when my creative juices were flowing at their best"

- "My design and layout experience runs the full range from producing newsletters to major publications. Every year for the past four years I have received the award for the most creative format for my newsletters."

"Tell me about a time you used creativity in your current (last) position."

- "My latest project involves coordinating an ad campaign for our company. I am working with an agency, but some of the time I have found their ideas to be trite. I have jumped in and offered some 'off-the-wall' ideas to get their juices flowing. It has worked, and we are heading into the home stretch on one of the most creative projects I have ever seen at my company."

- "My job is usually not very creative, since I'm working with systems. But there was a project when I had to solve a problem for a customer that was way out of the ➡

ordinary. The customer wanted to make the system do something that was possible but not the usual way of doing things. I worked with him through numerous phone calls and e-mails, and together we were able to override the system and accomplish what he wanted. He was thrilled with my efforts—above and beyond the norm. He actually called my boss to tell him about my efforts and told him that I had great customer service skills. That was a wonderful experience for me."

- "One of my latest accomplishments was composing and compiling a procedures manual for the biotechnology department in the company I worked for as a consultant. There was no manual in place, and so it entailed interviewing many of the employees from the top-ranking officials to the administrative personnel in order for me to get a sense of what had been used as procedures to that point. I was able to use the general operating practices as a guide for writing the manual so that it wasn't a drastic change from what had been going on. It turned out very well, and the users were satisfied with the results."

"The position requires a lot of outside-the-box thinking. How comfortable are you with thinking creatively on your feet?"

- "I am not only comfortable but very experienced in thinking outside the box. Because I work with so many customers, I have to be highly adaptable to their needs. I remember one customer came into the office and wanted to watch production of her product. This is highly unusual and dangerous. I decided that a way she could view the live production was on camera. I set up a video camera, and she sat in the office next door to production. She could see live work and still be within the safety codes. She was satisfied and felt that we had accommodated her needs."

- "If you were to ask any of my coworkers, they would tell you that I am known for my outside-the-box solutions. In fact, I recently helped one of our workers' son build a racing vehicle for an amateur race he will be competing in. No one else could think of a way to make his vehicle unique. I came up with a design that was unheard of, and he won a prize for most unusual design."

- "My boss accused me of majoring in creativity in college. I have this ability to see a problem from all directions and then to apply some of my unique thinking to come up with outside-the-box solutions. I watched a production line operate one time and could envision a whole new way that the process could be run with fewer people and more efficiently. I sold my idea to the foreman, and he implemented it as soon as he was able. I got an award for thinking uniquely that time."

Communications

"How would you describe your communication style?"

- "I possess superior customer service skills that have allowed me to build a solid reputation as being trustworthy and honest in my dealings."

- "I have the ability to break down very complex technical terms into everyday, simple language for the nontechnical person to understand. This allows me to communicate with a broad range of people to get a task completed."

- "My excellent listening skills allow me to hear much more than most people hear. Using my intense listening skills and then letting the person know that I 'heard' him or her has made a tremendous difference in working with people at all levels within the organization."

"Tell me about a time when your communication style made a difference in a project."

- "I was the key contact during this year's labor negotiations of the new contract. As the liaison between labor and management, I was able to be objective and let each side know that I heard its issues. I was then able to suggest a compromise. Because both sides saw that I was being open and objective, they trusted me and talked to me openly. In the end we were able to satisfy both sides."

- "I am an experienced presenter and often present to groups of major decision makers. There was a particular time that I presented to key decision makers in a multi-million dollar investment firm. By finding out what its expectations and needs were in the beginning and letting people there know that I understood their expectations, I was able to influence them into buying our entire system."

■ "My writing ability has allowed me to present the facts, but it also gives me an opportunity to present ideas within my own framework. I worked with a team of graphic designers to create the Web site for our company. Although the design was very important, the words I wrote blended to make a complete and important message. The site has been recognized as one of the top Web sites in the industry."

"Can you give me an example of a major project you worked on that involved communication and writing?"

■ "Last year I was put in charge of developing a monthly newsletter for the administrative support types in the company. This was my first experience at putting together a publication from start to finish. The first thing I did was consult with people in the company who had written similar publications. From what they told me, I was able to get a sense of what people liked and didn't like. I interviewed everyone from the guys in the mailroom to the CEO and wrote articles about them. I also came up with a clever format that included a writing contest with a prize for the best story. The best part was that people got their story published in the next edition of the newsletter. My idea really sparked a lot of interest and enthusiasm and allowed me to share the writing with others. The newsletter was a big success among the intended audience. I even received an award for the best internal newsletter."

➡

- "A large part of my job as a public relations consultant involves writing media material. There was one project where the company was sponsoring a major spring event as an outreach to the community. I wrote the press releases, public service announcements, radio ads, and even the speeches for key management presentations. The writing project was in addition to coordinating the volunteers as well as the hired vendors such as the caterer and sound technicians. I was really involved in every aspect of the event. It was a huge project that turned out well all around."

- "There was a major project in which I authored seven proposals that secured seven contracts worth over $1 million. I wrote the proposals with tight deadlines that I had to honor. I supervised the field technicians and subcontractors to bring those projects in on time with a 25 percent profit margin. Needless to say, I was rewarded highly for that accomplishment."

Strategic Thinking

"Tell me about using strategic thinking in your current job."

- "I have led the strategic planning team for my company, which has successfully generated $3 million over the last quarter."
- "My responsibilities have encompassed long-range strategic planning and product development. I've worked with a diverse team and have come up with plans that have been extremely successful."
- "I'm a key member of the strategic planning committee. We implemented a state-of-the-art information system to automate core business. This was met with great enthusiasm and support."

"Can you give me an example of a time when strategic thinking made a difference in a project you worked on?"

- "At my last company I developed a strategic plan that reduced payroll costs by 8 percent in the first year. It involved developing and implementing ongoing efficiency training."
- "While working with a strategic planning team, I was the originator of the idea to completely change our Web site sales strategy to be more interactive. The idea was met with great enthusiasm by the team and when it rolled out some months later, I was given credit for the idea."
- "Through strategic planning my team was able to turn around a loss to 20 percent ROI within six months. By

planning and forecasting we were able to control the process that led to the increase."

"Give me an example of your using strategic thinking at work."

- "I worked on a manufacturing project, performing technology programming and support. I developed data models and procedures to convert a training administration system to new software. I also administered data security for the system."

- "I worked on a cost reduction program that entailed developing and implementing a long-range capital improvement purchase plan. I came up with the idea to subcontract and consolidate facilities while increasing machine utilization by 30 percent. Through these cost-saving measures we were able to stay within budgetary restraints and still make a profit."

- "We had a problem with one of our computer systems. The first step I take when solving any problem is to do as much research as possible to define the problem. In this particular case it was a problem with the mainframe. I consulted with the IT department and the systems engineers to tap their resources to help to fix the problem. Based on the research and recommendations of the 'experts,' I put together a plan to attack the problem and then moved into action, and I was able to retrace the breakdown. I kept in constant communication with the IT department until we had the problem solved. We did this with a minimum of downtime."

Assertiveness

"How would you describe your assertiveness?"

- "I have been able to step up to the plate on more than one occasion when no one else would lead a project. I guess you could consider that initiative as well. When I see that there is a problem and that I can solve that problem, I move forward. I am careful to work with the team if that is the situation that I am in."

- "My open communication style has allowed me to be assertive on several occasions when things became tense among employees or when there was a problem between another employee and me. I firmly believe that talking something through in a nonconfrontational style is the best solution most of the time."

- "At my last company I was promoted to lead person because of my ability to speak up when I saw a problem and to suggest a solution whenever I had one. I have learned to speak up when I see a more efficient way of doing things, as long as I am not stepping on someone else's toes."

"Tell me about a time when you had to assert yourself in a difficult situation."

- "There was a woman in my last company who began to be curt to not only me but to the other members of the team. I finally asked her if I could speak with her. At first she denied that she had any issues with anyone, but because I listened and didn't judge her, she eventually opened up and told me that she was having personal problems and that she was sorry that she was imposing her problems ➡

403

on the team. She and I became friends, and she began to be relaxed and friendly around the group after that."

■ "This is an incident that happened while I was in school. There were some students who would abuse the library as a place to hang out and socialize. It was really annoying some days when the other students including me were trying to study. I took it upon myself to seek out a person who I thought was there the most often. I asked her if I could talk with her in private. She complied. I explained the problem of having to use the library as a quiet place where I could concentrate and that there were other students in the same boat. She listened and said she was having such a good time that she wasn't aware that she and her friends were causing anyone a problem She said they would find a new meeting place, and apparently they did because I never saw her or her friends again."

■ "Yes, I actually lost a friend because I had to speak up and be assertive. It was a matter of a man who was coming to work late and leaving early. It wasn't fair to the employees who were coming in on time and working extra, if needed. I talked to our supervisor and explained the problem because I didn't feel it was my place to talk to him directly. The supervisor suggested that the three of us meet. I agreed to attend the meeting. The guy became very angry with me for complaining and as a result never spoke to me again. He did however change his behavior about being late and leaving early."

"Give me an example of a time when you were assertive and took the initiative."

■ "At my last company I was promoted to lead person because of my ability to speak up. I saw a problem and also saw a way to solve the problem. I went to the person in charge to give him my ideas, and he was not only surprised, but he was delighted with the suggestion. I have learned to speak up when I see a more efficient way of doing things."

- "When I saw a need for a new employee orientation program, I spoke to the VP of human resources and was able to initiate a training program for new employees that will allow them to come up to speed on projects much faster than before. I was commended for my idea."

- "I consider myself an assertive person when it comes to internal problems among coworkers. There was an incident among members of our team that was affecting team spirit and our work as well. I spoke directly to the people involved and was able to sit down with them to put the issues on the table. It was a bit touchy for a while. But, because I moderated the discussion and kept everyone in their place, we eventually came to agreement and the misunderstanding was cleared up. Our team was once again functioning as the great team we were."

Negotiations

"Have you been involved in negotiations in your past jobs?"

■ "At my last job I was on the 'best practices' team after we merged two companies. Our team went through extensive negotiating to maintain practices that were important to our department. I was the team leader and managed to keep things under control by being as objective as possible."

■ "As the HR manager, I was in negotiations with candidates regarding salary offers and benefits on a regular basis. The secret to my successful negotiations was to listen first and then talk."

■ "I have strong training in negotiations and was able to negotiate a win/win situation in almost all of the cases I worked on as an arbitrator. Listening and using active listening skills is important when hearing all sides of the problem."

"Tell me about a time when you negotiated a deal at your last job."

■ "The most successful negotiations I have had involved a contract with the shipping dealer who I had to sell over a long period before he agreed to our conditions. But I am happy to report it resulted in a 15 percent reduction in our costs."

■ "Negotiating contracts was a major part of the responsibilities at my last job. In fact, I was given a bonus for saving the company over half a million dollars in a six-month period."

- "I was able to negotiate a pretax ROI on a nonregulated gas storage partnership. It was a deal that made me very popular with upper-level managers. In fact, they gave me a promotion based on the deal I was able to put together."

"In your career, what negotiation are you most proud of?"

- "That would be the time I was involved in analyzing and recommending the purchase of a competitor's company. I was instrumental in the research and preparation of an offer that was eventually accepted and that turned out to be a win/win situation for both companies."

- "As an administrative assistant I normally don't get involved in negotiations, but I was the contact with our coffee vendor and had occasion to discuss our problems with some of the products. He wanted our business and said he would make good on any dissatisfaction. I told him that wasn't good enough. He eventually agreed to reduce his fees to keep us as customers. My boss was very impressed that I had taken the initiative and that I was able to negotiate a better deal."

- "As a buyer, my main focus is to evaluate any purchases for the company and to shop around for better deals. I was able to save the company over $10,000 by discovering an outlet that would supply our technical equipment at almost half of what we were paying. The service was satisfactory, and the products were up to our standards. I got a nice bonus for taking the initiative."

Problem Solving

"How would you describe your problem-solving ability?"

- "I have a process that I go through when solving problems—evaluate, explore, research, prepare, and perform. It has helped me through many a tough problem."

- "If you were to ask my last boss, he would tell you that I thrive on problems and coming up with solutions, particularly problems that involve money. I've always been good with numbers and I am very particular about attention to detail."

- "At work they call me, 'Mr. Problem Solver.' I am the one who everyone comes to when no one else can figure out the problem with his or her computer or a system. I like working with people, so I try to make myself available whenever possible."

"Tell me about a time when you solved a problem at work."

- "On one of my past jobs I was able to detect a pattern of events and could see where the problem was occurring. I immediately worked with the engineering department to solve the problem that turned out to be a leak that was causing irregular test results. Working together, we were able to come up with a solution. No one had thought to look for a pattern, and it would have probably gone on for quite a while before anyone had noticed the problem."

- "I recently had an experience where I analyzed some information that had been used for years and found it to be totally inefficient. By presenting a new format and way of tracking costs, I was able to come up with a way to save significant dollars. Needless to say, the idea was met with much enthusiasm and encouragement. The roll out was a big success."

- "The problem wasn't big enough for anyone to do anything about. But it was big enough so that everyone was complaining about it every day. It had to do with the scheduling of time so that the mail went out that day. I took it upon myself to draw up a schedule and talk to the delivery guy about the time and pickup. The problem was easily solved, but no one had taken the time to deal with it. I received many pats on the back for taking the initiative."

"Tell me about a time when you solved a difficult problem."

- "One of my strengths is my analytical problem-solving ability. I had a recent success when I saw that the numbers were down on the sale of our new product. I worked with a cross-functional team and surveyed the customer only to find out that we had been using the wrong approach for our target audience. I made recommendations to the board of directors and after some discussion and tweaking was able to influence them to approve a whole new approach with the customer. The result was a better product launch, more sales, and very satisfied customers."

- "The toughest problems I have encountered are problems that are the result of an emergency. In my last job I was called in on a Sunday because the power to all the computers in the company had shut down. It was essential that I get in there fast and work on the problem before

➡

employees started arriving in the morning. Two technicians and I worked all day past midnight struggling to get the power back up. We were able to fix the problem so that when employees began arriving on Monday morning, they never knew there had been a significant computer glitch."

- "We had a problem at one of my last jobs with overspending on office supplies. By initiating a process improvement plan, I was able to solve the problem of expensive waste that had been practiced at the company for the previous five years. I was generously rewarded for that solution."

Analysis

"Tell me about an analytical problem that you solved in your last job."

- "I take an analytical approach and see the project from the viewpoint of the user as well as the provider. I can remember a time when a customer needed some facts before she could decide whether to buy our product. The first thing I did was work with her to find out her needs, and then I was able to analyze what was necessary to make the sale. This is an approach I use consistently when working with customers."

- "I was the key lead in the project when we successfully analyzed the company software for Y2K compliance. Because the team I was working with had done such a thorough job of analyzing the data, we were able to ride through the potential catastrophe with ease. It took a lot of proactive analytical work to pull that project together."

- "When working with groups of people who have different agendas, I have found that standing back and analyzing where each group is coming from helps me understand the situation. I did this with a group I was working with at my last job. By staying objective and detached, I was able to lead the team through a project that resulted in a successful campaign and sales effort."

"Are you required to analyze data at your current job?"

- "Yes, in fact just recently I worked on an interesting study done at the hospital I work for. The project involved tracking patients who were taking a certain drug and then

➡

analyzing the data to watch for patterns. My role was to analyze the results and then to enter those results on a spreadsheet that was eventually presented to management. It turned out to be a very successful study."

- "One of the main functions of my job is analyzing costs and then making recommendations. A recent cost analysis resulted in a major change in the way that costs are tracked. This saved the company more that $1,000 a day."

- "I would say that my job is part analyzing and part customer service. Because the focus has shifted to customer service at the present time, I have had to deal more with the customer one on one. However, analysis is still a major part of my job, and there have been occasions when my analytical skills saved a customer time and money, but it is no longer the main focus of my job."

"What has been your biggest analytical challenge?"

- "Believe it or not, it was when I did an internship for a Fortune 500 company. The project I worked on was one of the most difficult of my career. I spent long days—as many as 10 to 12 hours data mining. I had a specific project I was working on for human resources and was able to show a correlation between attendance and performance. I presented my findings to the directors and VPs and received great praise for my intense work."

- "It was while I was working abroad in a marketing department. I could see from the figures I was receiving that there was something wrong with the introduction of a new product. I had the team I worked with go out and interview users to find out why we were missing our mark. It turned out that we were targeting the wrong audience.

➡

My team and I put together a very complete report with facts and figures to support pulling the product and starting over. It was a tough sell to management, but our findings backed our analysis for the change. Managers finally agreed, and the result was very positive."

- "That would be a business development role I had at one of my previous companies. I assumed responsibility for software sales, which entailed collaborating with the implementation team to successfully install document imaging and workflow systems in all 25 locations of the company. After consulting with the team, I developed a cost-benefits and return-on-investment analysis demonstrating the effectiveness of the programs. I gave a presentation to key executives and stakeholders explaining the facts. I won their unanimous approval."

413

Adaptability

"When have you had to adapt in your work?"

- "My military background has prepared me for this part of any job. When you are on call 24/7, as I was in the Army, you learn quickly to move first, think second. Being flexible and being able to adapt quickly was not only necessary in the service, it was mandatory. I have brought that same skill to my work. I do whatever it takes to get the job done—on time!"

- "In the graphic design and print media business, I have learned that whatever the customer wants is important. This has been a recurring situation working with customers who want last-minute changes—and I do mean last minute. I am a very tolerant person who believes in the motto, 'The customer is always right.'"

- "Having had five bosses in three years has been something I've had to adapt to. The problem was that my bosses didn't get to choose me, but they inherited me when they took over the job. As a professional support person I have adapted to my current boss's management and work style. I'm sure if you asked any of my former bosses, they would tell you that I am a professional who knows how to adapt."

"What would you do if you had almost completed a project and the plans changed?"

- "I know this scenario well in the product development area. One particular incident I remember was a project that was within two weeks of completion when the customer called and changed the specs by more than 75 percent. My first thought was, 'Oh, no. This can't be happening.' But then

I got a grip and went to work to get the job done according to the customer's requirements. One thing I've learned in this business is to let go and take the projects as they come."

- "I would do what I do best—adapt. I would see what I could salvage from the project that I had been working on and rework it as needed. Then I would make sure that I understood the new requirements. I would want to talk to the customer and find out why the changes were going to make the project better and what I could do to make improvements on the new plans. I would then put my foot to the pedal and move forward."

- "I can't say that this is my favorite part of the job, but it is a part of the job that I have learned to adapt to. 'Change' is the name of the game in this industry. I keep an open mind about change and would do whatever was needed to make the transition as seamless as possible. I haven't had any problem with adapting to change in my career."

"How have you been able to adapt to new situations in the past?"

- "My experience with new situations has been rich because of the layoffs and changes in the computer industry. I was laid off twice because of reductions in force. In fact, one of the companies closed the doors as we walked out. I've had to accept the fact that not all start-up companies are going to make it. I consider myself a risk taker and have been able to quickly transition into new jobs because of my strong programming skills."

- "Since I have been at one company for over 15 years, I haven't had to deal with new situations as such. But I have had to deal with changes as anyone in business has had to. I think the biggest adaptation for me was to go from paper reports to electronic billing. Fortunately, not only do I have a head for figures but for automation as well. I was able to help many others in the company because I was able to pick up the computer skills quickly."

- "Anyone who knows me would tell you that I thrive on change. I live in the now and believe change and adapting to change are a way of life. I have changed jobs and bosses many times in my career with no problems. I have a natural ability to adjust to the situation and the requirements needed to do the job."

Ability to Work with Others

"How would you describe your ability to work with others?"

- "I know that if you were to ask any of my coworkers, they would tell you that one of my strongest traits is my ability to get along with almost everyone. I even get along with people who others consider difficult to work with."

- "Whenever I start at a new company or job, the first thing I do is find out who the people are whom I will need to know in order to get things done. For example, I made friends with the guy in the mailroom within my first two weeks at my last job, and that relationship really paid off. He was a person who knew a lot about what went on in the company and was able to direct me when I needed a resource."

- "I'm not going to say that I get along with everyone because the truth is that at each company where I've worked there have been one or two people who were difficult to get along with. But I will say that I maintain a professional relationship with all the people I work with regardless of their personality or attitude."

"Tell me about a time when you were required to work with people you had not previously worked with."

- "At my previous job our company was acquired, and I was inherited by a group. There seemed to be a natural hostility toward the new guys from the start. I simply went out of my way to make sure that the people in my group knew that I was a team player and that I would help out in any way I could. Eventually they got the idea that I was on their team and not a threat to them. After a couple of months I was friends with almost everyone on the team."

- "That was when I was in college and had to work with a team for a project management class. At first it seemed that we were each pulling in different directions, but then alliances started forming. What I found worked for me in this situation was to show an interest in the other person's interest. It's amazing how easy it is to make friends when you are willing to listen and put yourself second."

- "In the military you become 'soul brothers and sisters' with everyone very fast. It's a matter of relying on one another. I made fast friends with a woman who came into the group when I did. We were both newcomers and didn't feel welcome at first. We kept a low profile and offered suggestions only when we felt it was appropriate or would save time. She and I continued to be friends the whole time I was stationed at that location, but we both branched out to make other friends as the weeks passed."

"What are the biggest challenges you face when you are required to work with others?"

- "I consider myself a low-key person when it comes to socializing. I can deal with anyone when it is about work, but when it comes to socializing, I tend to pull back until I know the people I'm with better. In this job I want to have a more active role in some of the fund-raising and other events that interest me."

- "The biggest challenge for me is getting to know the personality type of each person I'm dealing with so that I can determine what communication style he or she

➡

418

prefers. By listening and observing I can pretty much figure out the preference of most people. I then try to accommodate that person's needs by adjusting my vocabulary to fit his or her style."

- "I don't see it as a challenge but more of a process I go through in getting to know people and what their role is within the company. I am very observant of others' behavior, and I watch them in action before I judge. This is actually the part of the job that I like best."

Meeting Deadlines

"Tell me about a time you had to meet multiple deadlines in a short period. How were you able to accomplish this?"

- "I can remember one particularly hectic holiday period when there were orders stacked knee deep. There was one woman who kept calling and wanting to know when her package would arrive. I was working on her details when I received another call telling me that the CFO had to be picked up from the airport and driven to her house. The first thing I did was to ask the woman if I could possibly call her in the morning. Because I had been so polite with her from the beginning, she actually agreed to wait. I was then able to focus on the task of picking up the CFO at the airport."

- "I'm one of those people who thrives on deadlines. It's exciting to see how much people can accomplish when they are under time pressure. I was able to get my crew to work overtime and weekends to send out several crucial orders that were on the same deadline. They did it and of course I rewarded them for their efforts."

- "I have worked with some fantastic teams during my career. There was one time at the company before my last job where a team pulled together to get a project completed that had multiple layers. I simply divided up the different tasks and we worked like one big machine. We not only completed the project, but we came in before the deadline. I really enjoy good teamwork."

"Tell me about a time you were unable to meet an important deadline. How did you handle this?"

- "There was one job I had where I was unable to satisfy the customer's request. I had done everything in my power to pull it off, but I had to call and talk to the customer and convince him that I needed two or three more days before I could complete his job. He wasn't happy, but when I told him about the quality that I was striving for, he allowed me three extra days. As it turned out, I only needed a day and a half before I was able to complete the project and send it to the customer."

- "I have never really been unable to meet a deadline, but there was one time in my career when I almost broke my record. The upgrades had not arrived for me to complete the installation of parts in a machine. Even though I had placed numerous calls to try to expedite the shipment, they weren't going to make the deadline. I got on the phone and called every local supplier that I could find. I was able to find a small shop that said that if I were willing to drive across town, they would have the parts ready for me. I did, and I was able to meet my deadline and hold my record of never missing a deadline."

- "This is an unfortunate story that I prefer not to tell, but since you asked, I will tell you about an order that did not get shipped and cost the company several thousands of dollars. I hadn't verified shipment of an order, which I normally did, and it was late getting to us and in turn we didn't get it to the customers when they needed it. The order was cancelled, and the revenue lost. I learned a valuable lesson about follow-through from that experience."

"Deadlines are an important part of this job. How do you feel about this?"

- "I think deadlines are the most important part of any support person's job. If I don't meet my deadline, it will affect everyone up the chain of command. I am very conscientious about deadlines."

- "Two things I pride myself on are my ability to meet deadlines and my punctuality. Both require some forethought and planning. If at all possible I will get whatever project I am working on in by the deadline."

- "I consider myself a responsible, hard worker. Part of getting any job done is meeting obligations expected of you on time. Whether it's getting to work on time or getting information and following up with a customer, I always will do everything I can to observe time demands and deadlines."

Decisiveness

"Tell me about a time when you were required to make a decision that could have had potential negative outcomes. How did you make this decision?"

- "I had to decide what members of the team we could do without. They were to be laid off as a result of my decision. I struggled with the names, but in the end I chose the stronger members of the team to stay."

- "Part of leading a team is making decisions that could have an impact on the outcome of a project. I knew that the costs of a certain project we were working on were going to exceed budget, but I made the decision to move forward anyway. In the end the project was completed, but the rewards promised were not fulfilled. It was a negative experience that I have tried to avoid in all my jobs since that one."

- "I had to make a decision whether to give information to my boss that would change the nature of our project before we even got started. I could have held the information back, and we would have all had several months' work. But in the end I had to share my information with the head of the department. The information had a negative effect on the morale of the group for some time. I feel I did the right thing even though it was a tough decision at the time."

"You may be required to make key decisions when I'm out of the office. How do you feel about that?"

- "I was acting supervisor at my last position a great deal of the time. I had to make decisions about money expenditures and discipline of staff. I think decision making comes with the territory of more responsibility. I know I have what it takes to use sound judgment when it comes to decisions."

- "This was exactly the case in my last job. I was left in charge while my boss did project consulting. I had to learn how to make decisions to survive in that job. I have done the job for more than two years now and feel it has been a great training ground for this job. Decisions are often a matter of knowing whom to consult before taking action."

- "Since an early age, I have had a good head on my shoulders for making decisions. I showed that I could be trusted in my last company. Even though I don't want to stay there anymore, I know I have been highly thought of because of my sound judgment."

"Have you ever made the wrong decision about a project?"

- "I wish I could say that I never made a wrong decision, but I would be lying. I have had to make quick decisions on many projects and have made some without the proper information. In one case it did delay the shipment of an important order, and that subsequently cost the company extra dollars. I can tell you that every time I've ever made a mistake I've also learned a valuable lesson. I have had enough experience to know how to avoid most of the mistakes involved in this line of work."

- "Unfortunately, I made some wrong decisions on predicting investments, especially in the early years of my career. I did not allow for the unexpected and got caught short more than once. Through experience in dealing with

➥

424

the investment market, I have learned to calculate the risk and to factor in the unexpected. I have a formula that I always keep in mind when making decisions. It came from a sign in my Dad's workshop: 'Measure twice, cut once.' That saying has kept me from making hasty decisions more than once."

- "The only way to learn is to make mistakes. I make mistakes from time to time, but I have never made a mistake that jeopardized my reputation or that of the company. Sometimes the orders get mixed up or the prices are misquoted, but overall I have an excellent record. My teammates would tell you that I am fastidious when it comes to attention to detail."

Initiative

"Give me an example of a recent incident where you took the initiative on a project."

- "We were having a problem with our ordering procedure with one particular customer. I went to the Web site and researched it frame-by-frame until I found the problem. I presented the problem to our technical department, and we worked out the problem together. I then went to the customers and trained them on the use of the system. I sat with them and went through the procedure step by step until they were able to get the hang of it. Afterward I continued to follow-up until I knew the problem was resolved."

- "I volunteer as an assistant coach of a basketball team for youths at risk. I observed that the stronger players were playing more than the other players but that they were not necessarily winning. I also observed that the mediocre players had some talent in other ways, like shooting and defending, and they weren't being used. I thought that if we could mix the strengths of all of the players, we would have a stronger chance of winning. I took the idea to the head coach, and he gave me the go-ahead. I held a team meeting and explained my idea that was met with some resistance but was eventually accepted on a trial basis. We practiced and practiced and then began winning games. We ranked second that year, but if I hadn't taken the initiative, we would have ranked in the teens. But more than winning, in the end the players had a real sense of 'team.'"

- "One successful idea I initiated was a way of encouraging people to pay their payments on time during the holidays. I suggested rewarding people who sent on-time payments by contributing a portion of their payments to their favorite charity. Because it was the holiday season, people were more into helping others. Senior managers agreed to the idea because they could write off the contribution. It was implemented with an announcement to card holders and met with a surprising 10 percent increase in on-time payments. Everybody won on that venture."

"When I say the word 'initiative,' what is the first thought that comes into your mind?"

- "The first thought that I have is 'stepping up to the plate.' As both a team player and a sports fan I can relate to the concept of taking a turn at bat. I have stepped up to the bat and even hit a few 'home runs' with successful ideas during my five years as a marketing analyst."
- "'Action' is the first word that comes to mind. In order to take the initiative, you have to be willing to take a risk, and that usually involves doing something. I am the type of person who is a 'doer.' It's one thing to have an idea, but a company has to have an equal number of 'doers' in order to get the job done."
- "I think of 'above and beyond.' Not just doing what is expected but taking whatever actions are necessary to get the job done, and done right. If you were to ask my boss, he would tell you that he is always pleased with my ability to take the initiative and to follow through until the action is completed."

"Would you still take the initiative on a project if you knew you weren't going to be recognized for it?"

- "My rewards are fulfilling my values. One of my top values is job satisfaction and part of satisfaction is doing the job right, whether I'm recognized for it or not."

- "I'm afraid that the type of work that I do is seldom recognized, but I'm expected to perform at the highest level. Because I have such a high work ethic, it is important for me to please myself. I am not saying that I don't mind a pat on the back now and then. I have just learned not to expect them."

- "My self-motivation serves as a reward. I have received many awards for work I have done, and that has been great. But the real rewards are from my knowing that I made a difference in the work or in the fact that I made someone else's life or job easier."

Flexibility

"This job requires a lot of flexibility. How do you do in this type of environment?"

- "I believe 'change' is the name of the game these days. In my last job I had seven different bosses in five years. Because I am self-disciplined and motivated, I have been able to adjust my style to the needs of each boss I have had—and done it with success."

- "Anyone who doesn't realize that the 'job' as we have known it in the past has changed has been living under a rock. I welcome variety and change, and I work hard in whatever environment I am placed. I consider myself a very adaptable and flexible person."

- "I happen to thrive on change and variety. No matter what company I have worked for or what position I have held, I have been able to adapt quickly to change. I have worked for three companies that have gone through mergers or acquisitions, and I was very successful in adapting to the new environments without any problem."

"How comfortable are you with change?"

- "I am comfortable with the changing of procedures, especially when it is communicated in a factual way. If I can see the rationale for the change, then it is easier for me to accept. If I don't understand the change, I will speak up with questions so that I can understand how the change affects me or my work."

- "Experience has been the best teacher for me in accepting change. I have gone through many changes in the start-up company I worked for last. Change is really the nature of a start-up, and if I hadn't accepted that fact, I wouldn't have survived there for over four years. Overall, it was an exciting experience because of all the changes."

■ "I grew up in a military family, and change is a way of life that I know well. I attended five schools before I graduated from high school. It was challenging at times, but I learned to adapt and make friends quickly. That trait has served me well in this fast-paced work environment."

"Our clients frequently ask for projects to be changed mid-process. Tell me how you've dealt with similar clients in the past."

■ "In the printing and publishing business that is an every-day occurrence. There was one woman I worked with who made changes right up until the time we went to press. I eventually began to call her every time we were set to go to make sure that we weren't going to have to do it over because she changed her mind. She told me how much I helped her by accepting her behavior and working with her instead of getting frustrated and angry."

■ "There have been many late nights working in a legal office. Sometimes it seems as though everything is a 'red hot' action item. One time I stayed working with a team of attorneys and paralegals until 2:00 A.M. to assist in the preparation of a brief that had to be done for the next day's court session. I have to admit that we fed off each other's energy, and the team spirit was high. This enabled us to finish in a timely manner. The main thing was that we accomplished the task before the deadline."

■ "There was an incident with a product that was ready to be shipped out when the customer called and wanted a

➡

change made before it shipped. This action required my team and me to work over the weekend to accommodate the change. The company I worked for was a firm believer, as am I, that the customer is always right. We put in the overtime and shipped the product according to the customer's requirements."

Organizational Skills

"Describe your organizational skills."

- "The first thing I do in the morning is check my list of things I want to accomplish that day. I then prioritize them according to urgency. I allow time for the unexpected, and if all goes according to plan and I don't use the extra time, then I have time for the proactive things I like to do. Most days my plan can be followed about 80 percent of the time, but there are days when only 30 percent of the plan gets done. I just prefer to have a plan."

- "I really like technical toys. I have a Palm Pilot and a laptop that serve me well in organizing my day as well as my life. Once in a while I even carry around a 'to do list' as another means of keeping me on track. If the day doesn't go according to the plan, then I reprioritize and do what didn't get done on the following day if possible. I have learned that flexibility is essential to being well organized. I have learned to roll with the punches so to speak."

- "I have been responsible for planning many events that I couldn't have possibly done without being organized. I use a word processing system and Excel spreadsheets to plan my projects and to track the progress day to day. One of my strongest skills is being organized and using the tools necessary to be that way."

"How well do you work with unorganized people?"

- "One of my favorite sayings is that 'I can bring order to chaos,' and I have done just that. I have worked for many bosses who were very disorganized. Once I started showing them how they could track their activities on software, they began to change the way they were doing things. My last boss shared his schedule with me each day, and I was able to jump in when needed. He really praised me for helping him improve his organizational skills."

- "Everybody has his or her own way of working. I am very organized in my work life and have a very organized filing system. Others are more interested in results than they are the details of keeping track. I have been a very valued support person because of my keen organizational ability and my ability to keep the work grounded when there is a problem."

- "One of my strengths is working with all kinds of people. I simply adjust my style to meet their needs. Whether it's planning or doing, I offer my strengths in a way that is very nonthreatening to the people I am working with. I would never want people to feel that I am judging their work because they do not have the same way of organizing that I have. I like to help, not judge."

"Your résumé states that you are organized. How would you describe your organizational style?"

- "My coworkers would tell you that they call me 'Ms. Organized,' because I always have a schedule and a plan. I have to admit that I prefer to plan and not be rushed. I can also adapt quickly and change my plans if I have to, but I like to start out with a plan to begin the day."

- "I have a very organized system that I can access any information that I require to do my job. I've always been a very organized and detail-oriented person. My bosses have rewarded me when my skills have saved them from making the wrong decision because of a lack of

Ability to Learn on the Job

"You'll be required to hit the ground running for this job. How will you be able to handle this?"

- "From what you've been telling me about the requirements of the job, I will have no trouble hitting the ground running. The first thing I do at any job is read whatever information there is about the position or department. Once I have the procedures outlined, I begin to make contacts to locate resources within the working situation. In every job I've held, I have been up and running in a matter of a week or so."

- "This job is very similar to the job that I performed at the bank I worked for. I am sure that the forms are different and maybe some of the procedures, but I am very well trained in handling deposits and customers. I would feel confident that with some time to collect information and observe I would be ready to try my own wings within a matter of days."

- "I pride myself as being one of the fastest people I know to come up to speed on a new job. I will stay and learn whatever I have to by reading and talking to others so that I can move into the position as soon as possible. I've managed this technique in my previous three jobs, and every boss I've had was surprised at my ability to pick up information so quickly."

"How did you go about learning a new skill when it was required for the job?"

- "In my last job, the learning was by trial and error. There was very little training provided and no time to spend training me on the details. I just jumped in, and when I ran into a barrier, I would try to resource the answer either by reading or by conferring with a coworker. If that method didn't work, as a last resort I would take the problem to my supervisor. It didn't take me long before people were coming to me with questions."

- "I am a voracious reader. I read anything and everything. Before I even started my last job, I learned about new trends in the industry and the systems that were being used. When I got on the job, I read through every manual and instruction sheet that I could get my hands on. In a very short time I was as knowledgeable as some of the employees who had been with the company for several years. I was sensitive not to make anyone feel that I had outrun him or her in such a short time. I consider myself a person who works well within a team environment."

- "Because I had taken classes in accounting in college, I had a basic understanding of the fundamentals of finance. When I was given a ledger to work with, I quickly accessed information from the Internet that refreshed what I needed to know. I find the Internet to be the equivalent of having millions of resources at my fingertips. I was up to speed in no time by reviewing the information I had learned in school."

"Tell me about the most recent skill you acquired on the job. How did you acquire this skill?"

- "When we converted from paper to electronic files, the whole department had to learn the new way of filing. I was sent to the corporate office in another state and spent a week there learning the system. I have a natural ability for working with numbers, and I do well with technology. After the training I was able to come back and step into the job with ease. In fact, people would come to me for assistance."

- "I find that most systems are basically the same with a lot of detail to remember. I had to attend classes to learn my current job's data entry system. I learn very quickly, so I took copious notes and really listened to the details of what was being said. Immediately after the class I went back to the office and began to do trial entries before any of the details faded. My notes and my quick learning style allowed me to learn the system so easily that I was able to train my coworkers who started when I did."

- "I recently learned online teaching techniques by taking an online class. It was an interesting experience to go through the assignments and to communicate and partner with people in a virtual manner. I found the techniques of communicating through message boards and discussing views with one another to be very effective. The best part of this approach to learning is that you can do it at your own convenience."

Prioritizing

"What is your process for setting priorities?"

- "I am a multitasker and have no problem with several projects going on at the same time. I am constantly prioritizing and adjusting projects to make sure that the most urgent projects are dealt with first. I also have established a reputation as a person who knows how to get things done, so I can negotiate a deadline if needed and the other person will feel confident that I will honor my commitment."

- "When I worked as a support person for the sales team, this was one of my biggest challenges, keeping everyone satisfied or at least not dissatisfied. I start the day with a list of the tasks I have to accomplish and put them in the order of how each might affect service. If a customer has a problem, I try to deal with that as quickly as possible. I am very customer service–oriented and always make sure the customer comes first. I also consider the internal needs such as executives or managers who need their priorities dealt with. I have worked with great teams, and we have been there for one another when priorities collided."

- "I actually like working in a fast-paced environment where there is a need to prioritize and juggle projects. I usually work with the hottest buttons first and then set a schedule to meet required deadlines. Some of the more 'back burner' projects get worked in as time allows. But I review those projects on a weekly basis so they don't get forgotten. Overall I would rate myself high as a person who can do many things at the same time and still meet deadlines."

"What would you do if your priorities conflict with the priorities of someone you work with on a project?"

- "I consider customers in two categories; external customers and internal customers. When I am working with or for someone on a project and there is a conflict, I take into consideration his or her needs as an internal customer. I have had great success at negotiating timelines and also with delegating to others when pushed to the max. When all else fails, I do whatever it takes to get the job done and will stay late or work on a weekend to meet my customer's needs—whether it's internal or external."

- "The secret to working with anyone on a project is open communications. Although some people are easier to work with than others, I always try to get whatever the issues are on the table so that we can discuss them. I have found that by talking out the conflicts and priorities rationally we have been able to come up with mutually agreeable solutions."

- "My style as a team player has allowed me to have a little slack when it comes to working with others. Because my team members know that I have a high work ethic and that my word is as good as done, they have trusted me when I ask for extra time or have to negotiate some help to meet a deadline."

"What has been your biggest challenge in setting priorities?"

- "My biggest challenge is to try to please everyone. Of course, it is impossible to please everyone, but my experience with supporting groups is that each person thinks his or her work should come first. I try to be reasonable and try to treat everyone as equal no matter what working style I run up against. Working with groups has taught me whom I can ask to give me some extra time and whom I need to move quickly for before he or she explodes."

- "I would say that coping with the unexpected has been the biggest challenge. I plan my day and set my priorities, and then all of a sudden there is an emergency and my plans go out the window. I consider myself to be flexible and adapt quickly to new situations, but some days it is a challenge, and I have had to push through the barriers to succeed at my tasks. The good news is that I have been able to do it with an inner energy that exists deep inside me when I have to respond to whatever the situation calls for."

- "I have worked with every type of boss you can imagine, and every one of them would tell you that I have the ability to rise to whatever challenge is thrown at me. I am a calm person most of the time, but when things get really crazy, I actually get more centered and let the rest of the office whirl around me. Some people refer to me as the 'anchor.'"

Time Management

"How do you approach long-term projects?"

- "Fortunately I was taught early in my education how to outline a project and segment it into parts. This has worked extremely well for me in planning out longer-term projects. I allow myself extra time because I know that the unexpected is sure to be a factor in my plan. I almost always have long-term projects finished weeks before the due date so that I have time to review and rethink the details before I submit them."

- "Because I work well under pressure, I sometimes don't give long-term projects the time that I could. But I get a certain rush from the pressure to succeed. I have never missed a deadline—long term or short term. I am very 'in the moment' when I work. One method that works well for me is to keep a binder for each new project and add ideas whenever I get them. I find this to be very helpful when I do sit down to put it all together. I just piece the ideas together and work full speed ahead."

- "I use software spreadsheets to manage my long-term projects. I break the project into equal segments and then check off the tasks as I move through the schedule. This has been very effective in coordinating projects with others as well."

"How would you describe your ability to manage your time?"

- "I was always taught that 'time is money' and to value time as such. I plan my day so that I know how much time each task will require. If something gets cancelled, I use that time ➡

to do my long-term projects. If something gets added, I move my priorities around so that I can get the things that I have to do that day done on time and move the less urgent things to tomorrow's schedule."

- "I consider my time management skills to be my strongest asset. For as long as I can remember, I have always organized my work every day and plan in reverse to meet my appointments and deadlines. In other words, if I have to be somewhere at 2:00 P.M., I start planning when I will have to leave for that appointment hours before I actually leave. If you asked people who know me, they would tell you I am very reliable when it comes to being on time."

- "When it comes to time management, I am very dependable. In fact as a support person I had to remind my boss when she had to be somewhere and how long it would take her to get there. My last boss was a last-minute person who would have missed many airplanes if I hadn't reminded her to leave hours before the flight. She considered me her 'right-hand man.'"

"If two people give you projects to be completed by the end of the day and you only have time to do one, how do you proceed?"

- "This goes hand in hand with prioritizing. I would look at the deadline and the importance of the impact of that deadline and then make a decision. I will always ask first if there is any leeway in deadlines. If there isn't, I would try to get help or push until I got it done. I have had to work with people when it was impossible to do the two things at once and have found that if I am willing to push and do whatever I can, they have been willing to let go a bit as well."

- "Sometimes I just have to admit that I will do whatever I can but that one of the projects may be late. I find that attitude makes a huge difference when there is a clash in priorities. I am known for my cooperative spirit, and most people will understand that I can do only so much. I have never had a time when I couldn't work out some kind of a compromise."

- "I have had to arrange a conference call with the two people to discuss the priority of the projects. By putting it out on the table and letting them both know the situation, I have found people to be somewhat reasonable in giving and taking. I think the important thing is to talk this type of problem through rather than trying and failing. No one wins in that situation, and everyone is disappointed. I am a big believer in open communications to solve problems."

Chapter 4

The Difficult Questions

This chapter deals with questions that are sensitive and can be uncomfortable to answer. Many of these questions may have a negative undertone and seem to be asking, "Tell us something that is wrong with you." The interviewer is looking to see if past problems are going to follow you to this job. Many of the questions ask for examples of your past behavior—"behavioral questions." You will notice in the example answers that part of the perfect phrase you use takes the focus off of the negative factors and instead accentuates the positive qualities that you bring to the job.

By thinking about and preparing for this type of question before the interview, you will feel more confident about the circumstances of negative situations. You will be able to look the interviewer in the eye as you answer with confidence, talking about those times that you would just as soon forget.

Dealing with Conflict

"Tell me about a time when you had a conflict in your work and how you resolved it."

- "I usually get along very well with everyone, but there was an incident with a person who was not pulling his weight on the team and all the members of the team were getting disgruntled. I took it upon myself to have a talk with the person when the opportunity presented itself. He was defensive at first but eventually confided in me that he had some family problems at home that were affecting his energy and patience. Once we talked, he made a special effort to be more receptive. The key to resolving this was letting him know that I wasn't judging; just caring."

- "A woman at my last job was known to be very difficult to get along with. I figured that this was her problem, and I worked with her as a professional. I gave her the respect I would give any coworker when we work together. She seemed to appreciate that I was treating her as a professional, and as a result we were able to work well together."

- "I volunteer as a basketball coach for disadvantaged kids in my spare time. Last season I had a team that didn't seem to understand the concept of team. I decided that rather than preach at them I would take them out for some fun and bonding. We all went out for pizza one evening and sat around and got to know one another. They seemed to let down their guards when they were away from the court. We ate a lot of pizza that season, but it really made a difference to get them off the court. We became a stronger team and even placed in the finals for the season."

➡

"Have you ever had a conflict at work that you couldn't resolve? What did you do?"

- "It was when I was new at an accounting job. There was a woman there who had been there for four years, and I expected her to take the lead. We had a problem communicating because of a difference in expectations from each other. I approached her and tried to talk to her to see if we could find some common ground. Unfortunately it did not work out. My boss got involved to see what he could do and set the two of us down to see if we could work things out. We just had different personalities and work standards, and we finally agreed to disagree but to treat each other with respect as professionals. We continued to work together on projects, but as professionals and not friends."

- "When I was a volunteer working with a group of scouts, I had an encounter with a parent that didn't get resolved but eventually became a moot issue. One parent did not agree with the way I was organizing things and was very vocal about it. I tried to tell him that all the decisions I make are in the best interest of the troop. But he thought my ideas were holding his child back. We had several exchanges that didn't result in agreement. Eventually his child moved on and graduated to a new level in the program. I felt that I had reason to hold to my position and protect the whole group."

- "I was a student when this happened. I was assigned to work on a group project with five other members of the class. We all met, and each person took a share of the work. After meeting a second time it became apparent that one guy was not participating or doing his part of the project. It began to be a big problem and was affecting team morale. I talked to him one day and found out that he was flunking another class. He ended up withdrawing from the class and program. I felt bad that I couldn't help, but apparently he had just taken on too much. The rest of us had to pull together and complete the project without him, but we managed and received a good grade for our efforts."

"How do you deal with conflicts you have with customers?"

- "I truly believe that 'the customer is always right.' Sometimes I have to bite my tongue and hold back what I would like to say, but I have never insulted a client. I always keep in mind that I represent the company and any action or words that I use reflect on the company—good and bad."

- "When it comes to clients, I know that they are my main customer and that they pay the bills. It is sometimes difficult when the customer is very demanding, but I always try to hear what the problem is and to let the customer know that I heard. If I can't accommodate the request, I try to communicate in as professional a manner as possible."

- "One skill that I am very proud of is my patience. This is the skill that sets me apart from my colleagues when it comes to customer service. It sometimes takes great patience to listen and explain the policy or procedure to the customer. I always treat people the way I want to be treated even when they are nasty to me. I try to put myself in their shoes and address the issue from that point of view as often as I can."

Handling Crises

"Tell me about a time when you had to react quickly to a situation."

- "We often have rush orders, which means that we have to drop everything and run. We had a situation like that last month where the customer wanted a delivery in the evening mail. Fortunately, I know a post office that is open until midnight. I had to work until almost that time to meet this deadline, but I was able to do it. I am known for doing whatever it takes to get the job done."

- "When I was an officer in the military, I had a crew of eight men under me. We were on our way home to a much-needed leave when we received orders to return to the country we had just left. There was a national emergency at the time, and we had no recourse. I had to do some sympathetic talking to try to get morale back up, pointing out that we were doing something that was going to make a difference. Outside we all accepted the assignment and did our job. Inside we were all really feeling down. In the end we did the job we signed on to do."

- "On my way out of the office one night I received a 'panic' call from a key customer. He needed a document sent to him by 8:00 A.M. the next day. There was nothing to do but to back track and start my day over instead of ending it. I worked two extra hours and then drove to a post office to send the document by next day express. I got the job done. The customer was grateful, and that's what matters to me."

➡

"Many of our clients are frequently in crisis mode. How would you work in such an environment?"

- "You might say that I am the 'calm' in the eye of the storm. I have a unique ability to stay level-headed when things get out of control. I find that talking less and listening more is the answer to handling clients in crisis."

- "Have you ever heard of the term 'whirling dervishes'? When customers are whirling, I stay centered and let them whirl around me. When I see that they're running out of steam, I step in and talk in a very calm and quiet voice. I ask questions to make sure that I understand the problem and then deal with the problem. You'd be surprised at how effective this is."

- "When I took my last job, I was able to prove very early in the game that I was the person who could handle escalated problems. First of all I use a voice that shows confidence and authority, and I let the customer know that I am there for him or her. Second, I am very analytical about solving problems, and I make sure that I explore as many options for solution as possible. Last, I make sure that the customer knows that I will do whatever I can to get him or her through this crisis."

"Have you ever had a crisis you couldn't deal with?"

- "We had a fire in our office, and, as you can imagine, it was very scary as smoke began to fill the rooms. I kept calm throughout the ordeal and attempted to get some of the important ledgers and disks to take with me, but the smoke became too thick too fast. I had to leave with everyone else. I felt I had failed in retrieving valuable information, but everything happened so fast that life became more important than documents."

- "I don't know that this would qualify as a crisis, but it was a big deal for me. In my first job I inadvertently sent out the wrong project information to the wrong customer. It was big because there was proprietary information included. I quickly contacted the delivery service as soon as I realized the mistake, and I was able to retrieve one of the two packages before it was opened. The other package unfortunately was opened, and I had to take the responsibility for my mistake. I can tell you that I never made that error again."

- "I can't remember a real crisis, but I have had some unpleasant moments when I've made mistakes. One time I forgot to include some expensive software in a pricing calculation, and the company had to stand behind my quote even though it took a loss. That particular day it felt like the biggest crisis of my career. I learned a valuable lesson about taking my time and checking my figures twice before making commitments."

"Give me an example of a time when you weren't able to deal successfully with a problem."

- "We were having a problem meeting a deadline at my last job. My boss told us that for each day over the deadline, there would be money subtracted from the bonus we were promised. You can imagine how that news went over. But there is nothing like money to motivate a team of workers. I came up with the idea of cross-functional teams to complete our task. Each person paired up with a person who did a different job. By working in tandem, we were able to do twice the steps in half the time. It was a bit confusing for the first couple of days, but it really boosted morale. Everybody was pulling toward a common goal. We came in two days late, but it could have been much worse. In the end we all laughed about working so hard and getting penalized for our efforts. It was the most stressful and fun time I've ever had on a job."

- "This is one of those stories without a happy ending. I usually have a planned schedule for every step of a project. There was a time however when my plan was not as well thought out as usual, and it started to fall apart. I hadn't allowed extra time for problems or emergencies. I had cut it too close to begin with, and of course this is the time my computer chose to crash. It was chaotic for a while until I called and located a computer that wasn't being used for a few days. I was able to retrieve most of my data, and I did complete the job. Unfortunately, my best efforts and resourcefulness didn't kick in quick enough, so I missed the deadline, but I learned a valuable lesson in the process. That hasn't happened to me again."

- "There was one incident when I couldn't deal with a problem in the office, and I was sorry after that I hadn't. We had a customer who was taking advantage of the situation by using our service as a means to get free technical assistance, even when it was not our product she needed help with. I helped her because she was a good customer, and I saw others doing the same thing for this customer. Eventually it was reported that this woman was abusing the services, and she quit the service. I always regretted not taking the initiative and speaking directly to her. I learned a lesson from that incident which has helped me handle similar problems in a more assertive manner."

Past Career Baggage

"I noticed from your résumé that you left your last job after only a year. Was there a specific reason?"

- "Unfortunately, the company I was working for was going through some tough economic times and had a series of layoffs. I survived three rounds, but the last one got me. My whole department was laid off. I really liked the work I was doing there and hope to find a similar job with some of the same type of responsibilities. I applied for this job because it looks like a perfect match for me and the skills that I can bring to the job."

- "My record over the last four years has been excellent, and I would be glad to give any of my bosses as a reference. Unfortunately, I have to admit that I was fired from my last job because of poor judgment. It was a joke that went too far. I'm sorry that it happened and can tell you that I learned a very costly lesson as a result. I can assure you that I won't make that mistake, or one like it, again. I'm ready to start with a clean slate and focus on my strengths as a loyal manager and the value of my experience that I can bring to this company."

- "As a senior manager I was responsible for the people who reported to me. One of my managers made a very serious banking error that should never have happened. But it did. He was called on the carpet for it and was fired. Because I was his manager, I too was fired. I take responsibility for the mistake because it happened on 'my watch.' I will always stand behind any of the people who work with me regardless of what happens. We both learned a difficult lesson and had to pay the price. I know I have the skills and adaptability to avoid such mistakes in the future."

"It looks like you've jumped from job to job for the past five years. Can you explain that?"

- "The job market's instability has kept me jumping. I was laid off for the first time five years ago and was able to get a new position very quickly. Unfortunately the company I went to work for was acquired, and I was laid off again after two years. My last job took longer to obtain because of the great number of people competing for the same jobs. When I finally did get the position I wanted, the company relocated to another state. I'm afraid I have been in the wrong place at the wrong time. I am now looking for a 'home' in my next job with the intention of settling in for a longer duration."

- "If you look closely at my résumé you will see that I've actually been at the same job for the past seven years. It's the company that has changed. The company I originally went to work for was HSF, which merged with another company and became HFP after I was there two years. Then in 2000 HFP was acquired by DWE, and my position was changed. So, actually I have worked in the same building, doing the same work while taking on added responsibility. It's just on paper that I've moved around so much."

- "Yes, unfortunately the last two companies that I worked for have moved some functions to corporate headquarters in other states to consolidate costs. In both cases I was asked to transfer, but for family reasons I have chosen to stay in this area."

"I see from your résumé that you have an 18-month period where you didn't work. What was going on during that time?"

- "I did take time off for personal reasons. I was fortunate that I was able to take a sabbatical from my work. I am now ready to resume my career with a new excitement and energy to give my new job."

- "When I was laid off from my last job, my wife and I made a decision to make an investment in our long-term future. I decided it was in my interest to pursue my MBA. I entered an 18-month program as a full-time student and didn't work during that time. This additional education allows me to view business from a broader perspective and to move more ably toward my career goals."

- "After being laid off twice, I decided to take a time-out from the workplace and to pursue some other interests and deal with some family obligations. For six months I did not seek employment at all. After the beginning of the year I began a very selective search. I have to admit it has taken longer than I had expected, but I would rather find the right company with a viable career path than to jump at the first offer I receive."

Getting Fired

"Have you ever been fired from a position?"

- "Yes, I was fired early in my work career. I can't remember all the details since it was several years back, but I can still remember the horrible feeling attached to being fired. I changed my work ethic and attitude after that experience and have never come close to being fired again."

- "I was fired from the job before my last job. While I don't want to place blame, my boss was known for being demanding and difficult to work for. I lasted longer than any of his other assistants. But one day I made a mistake, and he blew up and fired me. I really should have left before that time, but the economy was tight and I was glad to have a job. It was a bad situation from the beginning."

- "I was fired because of a disagreement between a coworker and me. We were both fired for unprofessional conduct. I think it was a fair call to let us both go rather than to take sides. We were both in the wrong. I learned from that. When there is a disagreement now, I go out of my way to avoid it or go through proper channels to resolve the conflict. It was a difficult way to learn that lesson."

"I know you were fired from your previous job. Can you explain the circumstances?"

- "Being fired is like having a black mark on my record. I am very disappointed in myself, and I can assure you that I would handle the situation differently if I could go back and do it again. It was about a joke that went too far, and there was a claim of sexual harassment by a woman. I am sorry that I was a part of the joke, and I apologized to everyone involved. But I had to accept the consequences of my actions."

- "I wasn't exactly fired, but I was asked to leave. I could blame it on my boss, but that would be unprofessional. Suffice it to say that my boss and I were very different in the way we saw things. Although we operated on a very professional basis at all times, it was agreed that I should move on. It was a very good move, and I regret not doing it earlier."

- "The circumstances around my being fired are still some-what vague, even to me. When the company went through a major reorganization, I got a new boss. She had worked in another department with a support person she had worked with for many years. She wanted that support person with her, and that made me dispensable. If you check the references, they might say I was fired for performance reasons, but the boss I had before that one gave me only the highest performance ratings. It was better to move on than to not be wanted."

"You were recently laid off. How has this affected you?"

- "Being laid off after so many years of loyalty is not easy. I really loved my job and the company and didn't feel good about leaving, but I am mature enough to know that these things happen and I have to move forward. Hopefully I will find a similar job where I can be a loyal employee and key contributor."

- "I have to admit that being laid off after seven months with the company came as a shock. I guess it was a case of being in the wrong job at the wrong time. I'd done my homework and had researched the company before I accepted the offer, but the company being acquired by another company was something I hadn't foreseen."

- "I consider myself lucky to have survived eight previous rounds of layoffs. The company has been going through a difficult time for the last few years, and it is doing whatever it can to keep afloat. I guess bracing myself every time I heard that there was going to be another layoff prepared me for 'my turn.' There is almost a feeling of relief that I am moving forward to new opportunities ahead."

Working for a Problem Company

"I noticed on your application that you have been working with a company that has been in the news lately. Can you tell me about that?"

- "Yes, the company has taken some hits since the news about the CEO being in trouble. I can tell you it sure made a difference in my stock investments. As far as my work in the company goes, I did my job as a marketing person and was not affected in any way by the problem. It's still a good company. It's just time for me to move in another direction."

- "It's been a challenge for me to have that company name on my résumé right now. If I had been involved in some of the decisions made, I might feel responsible, but the truth is that I was hit as hard if not harder than anyone who had invested in the company. I am sorry to see a company that had so many great, hard-working employees and a solid reputation taking such a hit. As for me, I figure it was a 'speed bump' in my career, and the skills and experience that I bring from that company will serve me well in spite of the way it turned out."

- "It's been very difficult for the last couple of years after the problems with the company hit the media. I was really hoping that it would turn around because I believed in the company and enjoyed the work that I was doing there, but it hasn't happened. So I am ready to move forward knowing that even though the company had problems, I had a good work experience where I learned valuable skills such as how to do more with less. I can bring that skill to my next company."

"Give me an example of a time when your integrity was tested."

- "When I was working in the human resources department on a computer project, we knew how to access salary information. My partner on the project printed out the information and gave it to me. I told him I wanted nothing to do with it. He proceeded to take the information and share it with other team members. I was called in by the vice president of human resources a few days later and was questioned about the information. I told him that I never looked at it and had nothing to do with the sharing. I was asked if I knew that my partner had printed out copies, and I said yes. There was a hearing about the incident, and I had to give my input although I didn't like doing it since my partner was in trouble. Unfortunately he was fired. I felt bad for him but knew that I had done the right thing."

- "While doing taxes for one of the companies that I worked for, I was asked to do something that would have saved the company several thousands of dollars. I knew that what they were asking me to do was not legal, and, if we were ever audited, I would be questioned and liable. I refused on the grounds that I could not risk my status and license. My boss was not happy with me, but he realized he was doing something that was very high risk. In the end he decided to bite the bullet and go with the legal way of processing the information."

- "At the bank I worked for, I was asked to process mortgage information for a young couple applying for a loan. I did the calculation and had the figures ready. In the meantime I did some thinking about another way I could do the calculation that would save them percentage points ➡

and a great deal of money. My dilemma was that the bank would make less money on the second calculation. I went to my boss, and he and I looked at the figures together. To my relief, he agreed with me to present the figures saving the couple the money. In the long run the couple returned many times to finance other purchases over the years. We had won their customer loyalty with our honesty."

"Your previous company went bankrupt. How involved were you with the budgeting process?"

- "I worked in the accounting department, so I did see bills that were overdue and late notices and calls from vendors, but that was pretty much the extent that I was aware of what was happening. It was very disappointing to see such a hard-working company have to resort to bankruptcy."

- "As a human resources specialist I was aware of budget problems and plans to restructure the spending, but I had no input into the decisions that were made and the actions taken. I could only do my part with my own department spending and budget. It came as a surprise that the company had to file for bankruptcy."

- "The bankruptcy was inevitable with the amount of spending taking place compared to the amount of money coming in. I didn't have any power in policy matters, but there were several cost-saving measures that could have been taken long before it was necessary to file for bankruptcy."

Problems with a Previous Boss

"Tell me about a boss you didn't get along with."

- "Unfortunately, I did have a problem with my boss and my being assertive in one of my jobs. He was in the habit of talking loudly when he took personal calls, and he sometimes used inappropriate language for the office. Because he was the boss, most of the employees just tried to turn a deaf ear. But one day I happened to be in his office, and we were discussing morale. I took the opportunity to tell him that I had a problem with his personal calls and language. He was really taken aback both that I had brought it up and that anyone was offended by what he was saying. He knew he was in the wrong and changed his behavior after that."

- "My boss and I have very different personalities, and we recognize that. There have been some times when we didn't agree, but agreed to disagree. It wasn't that I challenged him. It was that I sometimes saw an easier solution to a problem. I think we actually enjoyed our 'sparring' times. One thing I can tell you, and he would tell you as well, is that we always treated each other as professionals and respected each other's point of view."

- "There are some problems that just can't get worked out. I always try everything possible, but part of knowing when to give up is a matter of skill and judgment. My current boss and I just don't seem to mesh. He didn't select me as his administrative assistant. He inherited me as the result of a reorganization. I think he would have chosen a less assertive person who wasn't as independent as I am.

➡

462

My independence has allowed me to make sound judgments when I worked for bosses who wanted me to operate that way. I can work with minimal supervision, but I am also a very strong team player and prefer working with supportive teams."

"Have you ever had problems so severe with management that you resigned?"

- "Yes, there were problems at one of the companies that I worked for that caused me to resign. I would prefer not to discuss the details because it is proprietary information that I am talking about, but there were some ethical issues that I had concerns about. I have a high work standard and consider myself a very honest person who chooses not to work with companies that don't have the same values."

- "There was some unprofessional behavior by management at my last company that caused me to resign. I prefer not to say anything against an individual and especially management, but there are labor laws that I feel obliged to uphold, and management felt it could bend the laws slightly. I decided it was in my best interest to resign."

- "I didn't resign, but I also didn't approve of some of the decisions made regarding the payment of overtime in certain situations. I made sure that I was following the law or at least documenting that I had informed the manager of the law so that it was his decision whether he wanted to follow the rules or not. In retrospect, I think I should have resigned when I felt uncomfortable, but I liked the company and the people so I stayed."

"What do you do when you have an irresolvable conflict with your supervisor?"

- "I've never had that happen, but if I did, I would try to talk to the supervisor in a nonaccusatory manner. I try to deal with problems before they get too big and out of control. This way of handling situations has helped me get along with people whom I work with whether they are my bosses or coworkers."

- "The first thing I do is to try to look at the problem or conflict from all sides. I know that there are always two sides to every disagreement. Then I decide whether this 'battle' is worth losing 'the war' over. In other words, I have to work with this supervisor who has power over my work, and so I have to decide whether it is a matter worth pursuing to the next level of management or human resources or whether it is a matter that should just be forgotten. I then take appropriate action."

- "I have always been taught that the boss is the person in charge and have always shown respect for the position. If, however, the conflict involved something that was a morale or legal issue, then I would have to go to the next level of authority with the problem. I have been fortunate to have supervisors whom I have gotten along well with in my career. I have never had to take anything to that extreme."

Lacking Experience

"Judging from your résumé and your years of experience, I am in doubt that you will be able to step up to this job. What makes you think that you can do the job?"

- "I provided technical problem resolution and ensured effective coordination of activities in every job that I have held. I have also gained a reputation within the manufacturing industry as being a key player when it comes to hard bargaining and negotiations. In my last two jobs I was able to save the companies thousands of dollars through savvy business deals."

- "One of my strengths is being able to explain complicated financial reports to nonfinancial people. I presented a report to a group of managers and executives on a very complicated tax issue. Through my PowerPoint presentation of charts and graphs and my ability to break down the information into everyday terminology, I was able to explain in detail what this situation meant to the future of the company. I was commended on my presentation and for making it easy to understand."

- "My successes in customer service have made me one of the top producers in my company. I have customers who ask for me specifically when they have problems because they know that I will listen and do whatever I can to resolve the problem."

"I notice that you are changing fields. What can you bring to this position from your previous career?"

- "I had to deal with a diversity of customers in my last job, and that is the common denominator in these two jobs.

I've had some very angry customers to deal with in my job as a customer service rep. Those situations are very difficult to handle because we try to make the customer 'right.' Some people can get downright nasty. I have been in the business long enough to know that I can't take it personally, but it still doesn't feel good when I can't resolve a problem. This is the skill that would get me through the transition to this new field."

- "I have worked effectively in three different industries and have been able to make the transition with minimal downtime to learn. My ability to learn quickly and 'hit the ground running' has made a huge impact on my career."

- "There are some skills that I feel transfer to any job I do. Those are some of my strongest skills. I have excellent communication skills and am fluent in Spanish and English. I have a great rapport with internal and external customers. People who have worked with me know that they can come to me with any issues—business or personal. I'm a great listener and really care about people. My attitude is a personal trait that I feel has gotten me through many a tough situation. I am calm under pressure and will do whatever it takes to get the job completed."

"Give me an example of working with diverse groups of people, including those with less experience."

- "One of my strongest skills is my ability to work with a diversity of people. Regardless of the situation, I have the ability to adapt and work under whatever the circumstances may be. In my last job I worked in a small room with 13 people all speaking various languages, and I still managed to stay focused. No matter whom I work with, I treat them as a professional and if I can help them, I will go out of my way to do so."

- "I think one of the more challenging aspects of today's workplace is that there is a diversity of people—all ages, cultures, and levels of experience. I am very aware that there are many feelings involved, and everyone has to respect the role and the space of coworkers. There was a time when a young woman became very upset. She cleared her desk onto the floor and jumped up on top of the desk and started stomping her feet. I stayed calm and eventually talked her down and out of the building as quickly as I possibly could. She had her feelings hurt by a coworker and didn't know how to handle her feelings. Those are the types of problems I can handle because of my maturity and my easy-going style."

- "One of the skills that I take pride in is my ability to listen to people and really hear what they say. I consider this to be key in dealing with people at any age or stage. I was able to help a young man through a very challenging period of his career by becoming his mentor. I have a very patient style and like to teach by explaining with very concrete examples. The young man I helped is now one of the top producers in the department and is very grateful to me for helping him lay the foundation for his career."

Taking Risks

"What has been your experience with taking risks in your job?"

- "One of my jobs in mergers and acquisitions was to research and analyze risks and benefits of possible deals. I discovered some high-risk factors while researching one company and could not recommend the deal based on my findings. I knew that my manager wanted this particular deal to go through and that she wouldn't be happy with my findings. I put together the facts and figures on spread-sheets and made a presentation to her. Although disappointed, she trusted my work and was satisfied that I had exhibited due diligence in getting the facts needed."

- "One example of taking a risk and trying something new is when I was able to lead a cross-functional team in a company that had never used cross-functional teams before. As the lead engineer I decided to try an experiment and took people from various functions and cross-trained them. It was a huge success, and production doubled in a month. The employees really accepted it because it made them feel like they were learning something new that would be of value to them in future jobs. It was received well by management and is now a common practice at the company."

- "There is always a risk when analyzing data and breaking it down so that the customer can understand the facts. I did this for a man who was having a difficult time understanding the numbers and was refusing to buy until he did. I ran several compilations for him—some of which had information we didn't usually share. I thought in this

➡

case it would benefit the sale if he could understand all the data. I spent extra time with him until he was able to recognize the benefit that we offered. I took a risk of putting in extra effort, and it paid off."

"Have you ever not taken a risk and later regretted it?"

- "On the personal side I would tell you that I made some investments that I wish that I hadn't, but nothing of that nature at work. I play it pretty conservative at work."
- "I took a risk by taking a new job that I wasn't really ready for. It was an 'acting supervisor job.' In the beginning, I have to admit I struggled with the position. When they offered it to me as a regular position, I should have said, no, but I was afraid I would get passed over the next time. I took the job and eventually ended up being laid off. That job was not for me, and I knew it. I should have trusted my instincts."
- "I have many regrets in my career, but I consider them all learning experiences. One risk I took was taking a job selling a product that I did not believe would work. Well, it didn't, and I ended up feeling bad about all the people I had sold it to. I am an ethical person who really has to believe in the product that I am selling."

"Tell me about the most successful risk you've taken."

- "I didn't feel I was ready to take on added responsibility in my last job. My boss was a great mentor and coach and encouraged me to try the new tasks. They involved working with the international team, and I was intimidated because of my lack of exposure to the global picture. It turned out that my interpersonal skills allowed me to bond ➡

quickly and make friends almost from the start. Not only was it a successful undertaking, but it allowed me to take a new direction in my career path."

- "I accepted a job in another state where I didn't know a soul. I was nervous about the job and the transition to a new place to live. The job turned out to be wonderful, and among the people I met was my future wife. If I hadn't taken the risk of venturing into a new situation, I would have never had the opportunities I have had in my business life as well as my new personal life."

- "I joined a start-up company as one of the first ten employees. I knew that it could go either way. I could make some money on my stock options, or I could be out of a job rather quickly. It turned out to be the most fun and challenging work experience of my life. We didn't get rich, but we all did well by taking the risk of being first."

Physical Disabilities

"Is there any reason that you cannot perform the duties of this job with reasonable accommodation?"

- "I have read the job posting and description and have all the necessary skills and then some to perform the duties of the job. I would need accommodation with the computer screen. My vision is such that I need a magnifier that is easily purchased and installed so that I can work for long periods of time without my eyes getting irritated. My previous employers have been able to accommodate my needs and have found it worth the effort because of my extensive knowledge and strong ability to work with accounting data and systems."

- "As you can see from my résumé, I have strong computer skills and customer service experience. The fact that I am in a wheelchair would require a ramp to provide me with access to the building. I noticed that you had such a ramp in place, so there shouldn't be any problem for me to get in and out of the building. I have an excellent reputation for my dependability, reliability, and punctuality. I can't remember a single time when I was late for work."

- "According to your job posting, it is a requirement of the job to be able to lift up to 35 pounds. Could you tell me how often lifting would be required? If it were a small percentage, I wouldn't have a problem with the responsibility. If it were a major part of the job, then I would need assistance with the lifting requirement. I have been able to lift at my last jobs with no problem. In fact if you asked my last boss, she would tell you that I am a ball of energy, and I do not let challenges slow me down. I can be ➡

very resourceful about getting around problems
I encounter."

"I see you are in a wheelchair. How will that affect your ability to do this job?"

- "The way I look at it is that I bring my own chair. I have done data entry without a problem for over eight years. If you check with the people I've listed as my references, they will tell you that I am efficient and accurate and that my wheelchair does not affect my work or my ability."

- "The only problem that I have ever experienced in my ten years of working in this industry is when the aisles are too narrow. But that is rare in a business environment where there are buildings that comply with OSHA codes and standards."

- "It's not a problem for me or my performance. Sometimes people have to get used to my being in a wheelchair, but I figure that is their problem. Most people tell me after they get to know me that the wheelchair is so much a part of me that after a while they don't even notice there is one."

"What is the greatest challenge you encounter with your disability at work?"

- "My biggest challenge is with people getting used to my being blind. After a while they are amazed at how well I can get around and how I observe things that they do not. Once they accept me, they forget that I can't see what they can."

- "People are very reluctant to shake hands with a hook. When I put my 'hand' out to shake hands, some people draw back. But my attitude soon puts them at ease. I guess

➡

they figure that if I am okay with it, they are too. I have had very few problems performing at top level in all of my previous jobs."

- "I think attitude is the biggest challenge working with people whether you have a disability or not. If you asked all the people who have ever worked with me, they would tell you that I have one of the most upbeat attitudes of anyone they know. Some people have told me that I inspire them when they get down and feel sorry for themselves. I don't feel sorry for myself, I am grateful for each day and live it to the fullest."

"I noticed on your reference sheet that your last boss is not listed. Is there any reason for this?"

- "I would prefer that you not contact my last boss because I don't think she can supply an accurate reference for me. She was brought in six months ago to replace my boss who went on maternity leave. My boss who was on maternity leave and I had a unique partnership in our work together. Unfortunately, she decided to quit her job and stay home with her baby. The temporary boss was offered the job, and I don't feel she really ever got to understand my role. In fact, my role was entirely different with her from what it was with my last boss. My last boss would tell you that I was her 'right-hand man.'"

- "Yes, I prefer that none of the people at my last job be contacted. My experience there was not a pleasant one. The people I worked with were very nice and a good team to work with, but management was less professional than at other places I have worked. I know that anyone who worked with me or has managed me in the past would be glad to tell you how adaptable and resourceful I am."

- "My current boss does not know that I am planning to leave the company. Unfortunately, I have gone as far as I can go at my current company, and I want to make a proactive move before I get bogged down and no longer have cutting-edge skills. I have been taking classes in the evening and want to apply what I have learned and join a dynamic team such as the one at this company. If you were to talk to my boss, he would tell you that I am very

➡

ambitious and goal-oriented. He would also tell you that he has praised me and promoted me to where I am today."

"We will be doing a background check that includes a credit check. Do you have any problem with that?"

- "I am going to tell you before you see for yourself that I did have a time in my life when my credit was not sterling. It was a time when I was going through a nasty divorce, and it has taken me the last five years to clear up my credit record. I am proud to say that I have been an on-time bill payer since that period ended."

- "I am a person who has high integrity, and any marks you will see on my credit rating are due to hitting some exceptional spending times in my life. Overall my credit has been excellent. There was a time when we were buying a house and furniture that we got in over our heads. We are very conscientious about paying our bills on time and working on being debt-free. I pride myself on my ability to manage money at home and at work. I have always come in under budget on projects that I have overseen in my work."

- "The downturn in the economy has caught my husband and me offguard, and we have not been proud of our credit rating. When my husband and I were laid off at the same time, it was tough to meet all the payments on time. I am proud to say that by writing to the creditors, we were able to negotiate a more lenient payment plan. We are very careful to pay bills on time, even if it is not the full amount due. Things are turning around. My husband has a great new job, and I am confident that I am going to get a great job. We are in the process of pulling resources together to ➥

get our feet back on the ground. Neither of us wants to be in debt to anybody, except maybe the mortgage broker. It will be a while before the mortgage is paid off."

"You didn't provide any references on your job application. What is the reason for this?"

- "I have a separate sheet for references. If you would like that sheet, I would be glad to provide it. I prefer to give the names of references after I have an interview to ensure that these people are called only when there is a potential job at hand."

- "When we are sure that we are both in a position to decide whether I will be a candidate for this job, I will be glad to give you references. I feel references are confidential information to be given out when the time is appropriate. I would not want my references to be unnecessarily contacted."

- "I use a variety of references for different positions, depending on what the job content is. The reason for doing this is that for more technical jobs I think it is appropriate to talk to a technical person. When the position is more people-oriented, I think it is appropriate to talk to persons who have seen me work in that capacity. I will be glad to provide my references when we agree what the job responsibilities are."

Salary

"What do you expect in the way of salary for this position?"

- "I really need more information about the position before I can begin to discuss salary. Can you tell me the range budgeted for this position?"
- "What do you typically pay someone with my experience and education in this type of position?"
- "I'm sure when the time comes and I know more about the facts of the position and how it fits into the bigger picture, we can come to a mutually agreeable figure."

"Can you name a salary range that you would require to take this job?"

- "From the research that I have done it appears to be in the $60 to $70,000 range. Is that the range you had in mind?"
- "Based on my previous experience and education and the 'going rate' for this type of position, I would like to be in the mid to high 70s. Is that a range that fits with your compensation structure?"
- "I would need to know more about your salary structure and how often you review salaries as well as your entire package before I could discuss salary ranges. Could you provide me with more information before we discuss this subject?"

"Would you consider taking less pay than you made in your last job?"

- "I would really need to know more about the opportunity and your whole package before I can give you an answer to that question. My last job had extra perks that this job may not have. Basically, I need more information before I decide."

- "While my highest career value is not money, it is important to me that I be fairly compensated for the work I do. I would be willing to listen to a fair offer based on what I bring to the position in the way of experience and education."

- "Opportunity is valuable to me, so I am always willing to look at the bigger picture. I would always want to be paid according to what I bring to the position, but would be willing to be somewhat flexible when it comes to dollars."

Part III

Perfect Phrases for the Perfect Interview: Specific Types of Jobs

Chapter 5

Perfect Phrases for Executive Management

The higher the level of responsibility, the more detail and examples will be required to demonstrate your ability and accomplishments. Being specific as possible with your examples through stories of your experiences will add to the credibility of your statements.

Leadership

"What was your leadership role in your last company?"

- "In every job I have assumed more responsibility with success. My last position was as general manager of the entire East Coast operation. I built and led new business units, that resulted in lower expenditures and greater returns on investment. My strength lies in my interpersonal relations. I learned early in the game that people are the cornerstone of success, and I am always sure to give credit where credit is due."

- "As national sales operations manager I trained, developed, and lead a 15-person national account sales and support team targeting hospital accounts worldwide. I also provided strategic and tactical leadership and successful technology installations."

- "As CEO of a retail chain I was in full charge of strategic planning and operations. I also had distribution and profit-and-loss responsibility under my management. I led the operation to accelerated growth and nationwide expansion."

Management Style

"How would you describe your style of managing people?"

- "My management style is to lead by example as a catalyst, and role model in achieving results through others. I make an effort to be visible and involved with employees, letting them know that I am available and willing to help in any way that I can."

- "As a manager who came up through the ranks of this company, I keep those who need to know informed and up to date with relevant and useful information. I stay particularly close to the sales representatives who are out there selling the company and the product. I see them as the basic foundation of keeping the company afloat."

- "I believe in the development of those working in any capacity in the company. By offering learning and continuous growth opportunities, I have seen more employee loyalty and motivation. I believe every employee should feel he or she is making a contribution to the bigger picture and that there are opportunities for growth with the company."

Keeping Abreast of Current Business

"There have been a great many changes in this industry in the past year. How have you kept up with the latest industry news?"

- "Every day I take time to read journals and newspapers. I guess you could call me a 'newshound.' I also have an excellent memory for detail and can sometimes relate something that I read to an event that occurred months ago. I make sure that I am up to date with industry news."

- "I find the Internet to be the most valuable tool out there. It's very easy to keep up with what's new, and I can do it on my own time. I'm a night owl and am often on the computer into the wee hours of the morning reading up on the latest trends and issues."

- "Between the TV and radio news and reading various newspapers and journals, I keep up to date on the industry as well as the world news. Globalization makes it necessary to reach beyond local issues. I spend a great deal of time in my car and always listen to news programs on the radio. Those shows allow me to hear snippets of news that I can follow up on the Internet in the evening."

Financial Savvy

"Tell me about a time when your knowledge of finance and business operations made a difference in the company's profits."

- "The key staff members of the last company I worked for all agreed and were committed to a goal of increasing profits 20 percent by the end of the fiscal year. As the CFO I met with the executive team, and we set very specific goals to accomplish this. I was able to get the commitment of individual team members, and we agreed they would receive a percentage of profits at the end of the year if things went as planned. I personally was committed and held accountable to the board of directors. We worked as a team to achieve a very successful campaign rollout. The key was to keep our specific goals in mind and to also keep in continuous communication with one another on the progress of our projects. As it turned out, we exceeded our goal, and every one of us benefited from the team effort."

- "One of the projects that I was most proud of at my last company was the streamlining and enhancing of the corporate budgeting process. I was able to analyze the company's needs and processes and to benchmark activities. The realigning made the process the cornerstone of the way the company's operations are currently measured."

- "When I joined my current company, all the accounting and payroll functions were outsourced. This was not only cumbersome to manage, but also very expensive. By developing and implementing appropriate internal policies and procedures, I was able to convince management to bring the functions back in-house. The overall savings was over 40 percent of what had been spent in a six-month period."

The Big Picture

"How do you manage others day-to-day while focusing on the big picture?"

- "By setting key objectives within the larger organizational context, I am able to stay focused and on top of the management of projects while still maintaining the team's trust. I don't think you'd find anyone that I have ever worked with who would say that I 'micromanage.' I believe in helping others maintain their focus and avoiding 'analysis paralysis.' I have been successful in moving projects forward while not taking away from the leadership of the project."

- "I pride myself on making decisions only after I have considered the 'bigger picture.' That is to say, I am very aware of how the pieces fit together while working with individual team members. Each member of the team plays a part in the success of a project, and I encourage each person to stay focused on the 'whole' project, whether it's a customer's need or a long-term goal. I believe that my open communication style has contributed greatly to my success in managing people."

- "My approach to marketing involves retaining current customers first, and attracting new customers second. One challenge I have faced is customer retention. I work with my staff and members of other relevant departments to retain first, build second. One method that has worked in the past is to send teams to interview 'the customer.' By feeding the data collected to the marketing department, we used 'permission marketing'—ask first, send only upon request for information. The success of a program is our working together as a team to support any campaign from the beginning."

Chapter 6

Perfect Phrases for Managers

Whenever a question begins with a specific request such as "Tell me about a time," or "Can you give me an example…," the answer will require that you relate a specific incident in which you performed an action.

The formula for a strong story is to tell the interviewer—**"Why you did it," "What you did,"** and **"What the outcome was."** In other words, the story needs a beginning, a middle, and an end.

Tip—Remember to listen to the question and determine if the interviewer is asking for **"a"** time or **"an"** example and, if so, then answer the question with a specific example.

"Tell me about a time when you had to make a decision that you knew would be unpopular."

- "I consider myself a strong manager who is open to suggestions. I had one experience in which I had to make a decision that was not well accepted by my staff. It involved cutting one of the benefits they were receiving. I had a meeting and announced the news to the staff. It was greeted with a great deal of anger and frustration. I listened and addressed every question that was asked of me. I had done my research and homework and was able to use facts to demonstrate that the cost-benefit ratio was not in line with good business decisions. They left less upset than when they first heard the news, but it took some time for the bad feelings to go away completely. I believe that talking with them intelligently and using facts made a difference in their feelings in the long run."

- "There was a time when I hired a manager from outside the organization. This was met with hard feelings by some of the contenders for the job who had been passed over. I took a hard stand, even though it was not a popular one. I talked to the disgruntled individuals one-on-one and tried to explain my reasons. Although it is not my preferred style, I had to exercise my authority here. I have to admit there were some tense days to live through at that time, but I firmly believed that I knew what was best for the long haul, and it turned out I was right."

- "As part of management, I realize that my decisions will not always be viewed as positive. One of those times was when I had to make a quick decision to buy advertising at a

➥

490

special rate in order to achieve a quick rollout of a time-sensitive product. I had analyzed the budget and was attempting to gain maximum leverage. I was later criticized for not having consulted the team and getting input. My decision was made based on getting the most value for the least amount of money. Fortunately for me, the project rolled out in a timely manner and was quite successful."

Delegation

"How do you manage through delegation?"

- "At my last company, I had the responsibility of setting standards for the group and for being a role model for the other managers. While others gave appreciated input, it was ultimately my job to meet the goals. I set the course of direction and then made sure the other managers and supervisors were onboard with me. My management style is to let each manager run his or her department as a small business. I stayed in touch through one-on-one and group meetings and by making myself available to deal with issues and problems as needed. Although I led the team, the team itself accomplished the goals."

- "Deadlines are a way of life in my business. We had a publication deadline, and it was not a choice between quality and making the deadline. We had to produce both. I brought in some outside production editors to make sure that the team members weren't stretched so tight that they were making major errors. We made the deadline, and no one ever knew that we almost killed ourselves to do it. I rewarded each team member with a night on the town."

- "One thing I learned early in my career is that no one person makes a project successful. I may lead my team toward the bigger picture or goal, but it is the individual team members who carry out the implementation of the project. My strong communication and organizational skills keep the project on track and moving in the right direction, but ultimately it is my ability to motivate and coach the team members that has made me a successful manager."

Motivating Others

"Tell me about a time when you motivated a team in a unique way."

- "I am a manager who recognizes and rewards hard work. I had a team who came to the rescue with a project that required three months of overtime—weekends and evenings. I made sure that all members of the team talked to me about their family situation and whether it was causing a strain and what they were doing about having some fun outside of work. I rewarded each person with a certificate for a weekend away at a local beach resort when the project ended successfully. I believe in life balance, and I think that is the reason the turnover rate at this company is several digits below the average."

- "As a manager of a customer service team, I have found that competition motivates the employees and they have fun competing. I have set it up so that they earn points for meeting certain goals or plateaus. At the end of the month they cash in the points for merchandise from the 'company store' or for things like movie tickets or dinner coupons. The morale in the department stays high, and there is a great deal of camaraderie relating to these contests."

- "In the sales industry it is very common to have ceremonies to reward top performers. I had been on the receiving end of such rewards when I was a sales rep and found that after a while I had a whole bookshelf full of beautiful trophies that weren't doing anybody any good. When I became the person in charge of selecting awards, I came up with a unique idea to give engraved golf clubs, watches, or luggage as the awards. It was a big change

➡

from tradition, but most people were really motivated by a more practical gift. We had a wonderful year that year, and a lot of people walked away with some great gifts."

Communication Style

"Tell me about a time when your communication style influenced a decision."

- "I was the key contact during the labor negotiations of a contract dispute. As the leader of the negotiations in one particular case I was able to let the opposing side know that I heard its issues and that we were trying to accomplish a compromise. At the same time, we weren't willing to give in completely on some of the key points. Because they saw that I was being open, they trusted me and talked to me openly. In the end we were able to satisfy both sides."

- "I am an experienced presenter and often make presentations to groups of major decision makers. There was a particular time that I spoke to key decision makers in a multimillion dollar investment firm. By finding out what their expectations and needs were in the beginning and letting them know that I understood their expectations, I was able to influence them to buy our entire system."

- "I find the key to successful communications and sales is to see the problem from the customer's point of view. I had a customer who did not think he needed my product. He was only going to hear me out because he liked me. I began by asking him about his business, and once I started questioning him, I found out that he would benefit greatly from the product. I spent almost four hours talking to him about his business and what we could do for him. The problem was that no one had taken the time to listen to his needs. People just started selling to him. I ended up with a good customer as a result of listening."

Ability to Influence Others

"Tell me about a time when you were able to convince others that you had a better idea or way of doing things."

- "I worked with a team of product development people to come up with a new product. I was the liaison between the marketing and product development teams. The ideas had to be communicated back and forth between groups. I was the person who had to come up with creative ideas to appease both groups while not offending egos. It was the most challenging project I've ever worked on, but it was also one of the most successful. We were able to come up with a winning product and a successful campaign launch."

- "While working as a project manager, I analyzed the latest data provided and found a flaw in our system. I put together a spreadsheet and presented it to management as well as to my team. I was able to demonstrate what needed to be changed and to justify the cost involved. My team backed my findings, and I was able to influence management to agree to put in a new system at great cost but that in the end would show excellent savings."

- "My writing ability has allowed me to present the facts, but it also gives me an opportunity to present ideas within my own framework. I worked with a team of graphic designers to come up with the Web site for our company. Although the design was very important, the words I wrote blended to make a complete message. The site has been recognized as a top Web site in the industry."

Chapter 7

Perfect Phrases for Supervisors

Demonstrating leadership qualities during the interview will be necessary if you have had responsiblity for supervising others' work. You should be prepared to talk about how you have related to people and handled people-problems to show your competence in this area.

"What would your coworkers and subordinates say about your management style?"

- "They would tell you that although I am a manager, I am also the type of person who can be counted on no matter what. They know that they can trust me to keep confidential information confidential and to listen to their problems without repeating them."

- "They would tell you that I would never ask them to do something that I wouldn't do myself. I am not above jumping in and helping when the situation requires it."

- "I require results from my team. My team members would tell you that every member is aware and focused on the objectives and outcome of the project as a whole and not as individual contributors. They would also tell you that I am fully committed to the team effort."

Handling Personnel Problems

"Give me an example of a time when you had to handle a personnel problem and what you did."

- "One of the people I supervised was not following the protocol for making requests. I asked him politely to use the forms that everyone else was using, but he became belligerent. I took him aside when the opportunity presented itself and told him that he and I needed to have an understanding so that we could work things out. He knew that I would eventually have to take the problem to the next level and decided it was in his best interest to cooperate. There were no further problems after that, and from then on he followed procedure and acted professionally toward me and the other team members."

- "I had a difficult problem with a supervisor who was taking credit for the work that her team accomplished. Some of the team members came to me and complained. They said it was affecting their attitude. I called the woman in and explained how her taking credit was affecting production and morale. She became very upset that others saw her that way, and she said she was unaware of her behavior or the reactions of others. She wanted my advice as to how to change the situation, and I suggested talking to each person about how much she appreciated his or her team effort. She took my advice, and there was a noticeable improvement in morale as well as in her behavior after that."

- "Selling the concept of change when merging companies has been one of my greatest challenges. When a company of a similar size acquired my current company, it seemed

➡

499

like everyone wanted to be unhappy and complain. By holding a series of meetings with the people affected, I was able to start them looking at the positives of the situation—a stronger team, more exposure in the market, better benefits, etc. Eventually they did begin to see it from the other point of view, but it was a tough sale."

Follow-Through

"You say that one of your strengths is follow-through. When has that made a difference in your work?"

■ "As a pharmaceutical sales rep if I didn't follow through on my promises, I couldn't have survived. I remember there was one doctor who wasn't going to see me or to buy my product no matter what I did. My first strategy was to get past the office manager, who I call 'the gatekeeper.' I went in once a week and chatted with her and said that I was just following through. Eventually I found out that she liked music, and that gave me something to discuss with her. If she told me she was attending a concert or music event, I went out of my way to ask how it was on my next visit. I think she finally decided I was an okay-kind-of-guy, and she was able to get me in to see the doctor. She told me that I was the first sales person to show any interest in her or the workings of the office. When I did get to meet the doctor, I used the same approach on him, finding out what his interests were. It worked like a charm. I was able to sell the most product this doctor had ever bought from the company."

■ "As a human resources supervisor I have to constantly follow through on details of projects for managers. It seems as though everything happens at the end of the year regarding performance reviews and raises. Last year we had a mandatory holiday break, and the data for raises to be effective January 1st had to be submitted two weeks earlier than usual. If you've worked with managers who dreaded completing their performance reviews you will know what I am talking about when I say it can be 'like ➡

pulling teeth.'I was working with two managers who were behind schedule, and I didn't seem to be able to make any progress. I finally made a deal with them. If they would send two a day for a week, we could complete the project on time. Each morning I would call and ask if there was anything I could do to help them make the daily quota. It got so they looked forward to my call and my reminder. I am proud to say that I made that deadline, and the managers actually thanked me for getting them through their dreaded chore."

- "I remember a project on which I supervised seven people. Between the multiple projects going on and the seven people to keep track of, I wouldn't have survived without being very organized with reminders to myself to follow through on certain dates, projects, or upcoming events. My work ethic is that if I say I am going to do something, I can assure you that I will do it, if at all possible. This project was no exception. It was on time with only a minor problem or two to take care of along the way."

Initiating

"Tell me about a time when you initiated an action that brought results."

- "I am a person who tries to plan ahead, and so I usually have a planned schedule for every step of a project. There was a time however when my plan started to fall apart because of a systems crash. It was chaotic for a while until I called and located office space that wasn't being used for a few days. I was able to bring my team into the space and utilize the equipment needed to complete the job. We were back on schedule in no time and met the deadline."

- "As a project manager for my last company I could see a need for a template to guide team members through projects while allowing them to prioritize. I came up with a prototype and presented it to my manager. She liked the idea and suggested I follow through on the development. I did some refining based on her suggestions and then presented it to my team. Members were delighted to have a format to assist them in organizing their tasks. After the template was put in place and used successfully, my boss presented it to management and they okayed it to be used companywide. I received an award for not only the idea but for initiating a more efficient process that will save time and ultimately money."

- "As an officer in the military I had many occasions to initiate action. One time in particular there was a plan of action that went bad, and I had to step in and take the initiative and make a very quick decision. We were in a live fire exercise that should have stopped when a signal was fired. I shot the signal flare, but the firing didn't stop. I had ➡

to make a decision and had my troops hit the deck. I then signaled to the radioman to call in a cease-fire. All fire stopped immediately, and all troops were reported safe. I found out later that the platoon firing the machine guns never got the message about the cease-fire signal and would have just continued firing. My initiative and quick decision saved my troops from being seriously injured or killed that day."

Problem Solving

"Give me an example of a time when your efforts solved a problem."

- "I headed up a project that involved customer service personnel and technicians. I organized a meeting to get every-one's buy-in on a new project that would increase sales opportunities. I held a meeting to brainstorm and get input. One of the problems was that there were technical and nontechnical people involved, and they had different ideas of how the project should run. I drew up a plan, taking the best ideas from both groups and then organized teams, balancing the mixture of technical and nontechnical people. We had a deadline to meet, and I did periodic checks with the teams. After three weeks, we were exceeding expectations, and the team members had a new respect for each others' contributions."

- "One of the most challenging problems I faced as a supervisor was in creating a strategic alliance with a provider of chemicals to use its specialized blending equipment and delivery network. The provider was not interested in a sale because it was such specialty equipment. What I came up with was an exchange. My team would provide marketing, billing, and technical assistance for the use of the equipment. The provider jumped at the opportunity. I convinced my team that this was a win-win situation, and the project moved forward without a hitch."

- "In my last position I faced a challenge of some kind almost every day. One day that stands out was when we had a 'sick out' day when several of the team members called in sick as ➡

a protest against an unpopular decision to change their benefit plan. We were short several key people who were necessary to keep the plant running. I appealed to management for help, and much to my surprise, they volunteered to come forth themselves to run the plant for the day. Some of them had come up through the ranks so it was a bit like 'coming home.' It was a very trying day with so many bosses in one place, but we managed to pull it off. Fortunately the protest only lasted one day."

Part IV

**Final
Preparations**

Chapter 8

Exercises for the Perfect Phrase

Quiz: Writing Your Own Perfect Phrases

Now it's your turn to try writing "perfect phrases." There are no exact answers. The idea is to see if you can turn a "flawed phrase" into a stronger answer with a "perfect phrase." You will find suggested answers later in the chapter.

1. **What are your goals?**

   Flawed Phrase: "I am seeking a challenging job in a growth-oriented company where I can utilize my skills to the best of my ability."

   Perfect Phrase: _____
   _____
   _____
   _____
   _____

2. **Do you have any questions?**

   Flawed Phrase: "No, you've pretty much covered everything that I wanted to know."

   Perfect Phrase: _____

   _____

   _____

   _____

   _____

3. **You don't seem to have any experience in this field.**

   Flawed Phrase: "No, I don't have any experience with that system."

   Perfect Phrase: _____

   _____

   _____

   _____

   _____

4. **How would your current boss describe you?**

   Flawed Phrase: "My current boss inherited me and doesn't really know me or what I do. He's gone most of the time and doesn't have time to give me. That's been a problem for me in my job."

   Perfect Phrase: _____

   _____

   _____

   _____

   _____

5. What do you like best about working with your current company?

Flawed Phrase: "My current company used to be a great company to work for, but since the merger with the other company, things just aren't the same. I liked it better when we were smaller and had more control over our projects."

Perfect Phrase: _____

_____

_____

_____

6. What are your strengths?

Flawed Phrase: "My strengths are my ability to get the job done. I'm a hard worker."

Perfect Phrase: _____

_____

_____

_____

7. What are your weaknesses?

Flawed Phrase: "My weakness is my memory. Sometimes I forget things and have to put little stickies up to remind myself what I have to do."

Perfect Phrase: _____

_____

_____

_____

8. What is your salary expectation?

Flawed Phrase: "I am currently making $40,000 and would like to receive a 10 to 15 percent increase."

Perfect Phrase: _____
_____
_____
_____

9. Why are you leaving your current job?

Flawed Phrase: "I have outgrown my current job and am looking for a challenge. I want to grow and develop and learn new things."

Perfect Phrase: _____
_____
_____
_____

10. Why do you want to work for this company?

Flawed Phrase: "I was searching the Internet for a job and found your posting and thought it would be an interesting and challenging job where I could utilize my skills."

Perfect Phrase: _____
_____
_____
_____

ANSWERS

1. What are your goals?

Perfect Phrase: "I like to think of goals in the short and long term. My short-term goal is to find a company that is a good fit for me and the company. Once I begin to be a contributor, I would like to continue to grow and take on more responsibility for projects."

Note: Avoid using phrases that don't really say anything specific. They don't mean anything.

2. Do you have any questions?

Perfect Phrase: "Yes, I do. Could you tell me about the company culture and how the current economy is affecting your business?"

Note: This is your opportunity to find out important information about the company.

3. You don't seem to have any experience in this field.

Perfect Phrase: "My experience is with a system very similar to that one. In fact, I learned to use the system I am currently using within two weeks of starting my job. Because I like computers so much, new things come quickly to me. I can be up and running in record time."

Note: If you don't have experience with something in particular, think of something similar that you picked up very quickly. Let the interviewer know that you will be up and running in no time and that he won't have to hold your hand through the process.

4. **How would your current boss describe you?**

Perfect Phrase: "My boss would tell you that I work very independently without a lot of direction. He has had to depend on me to run things as he travels a great deal."

Note: Never make your boss look bad. By putting a positive spin on the way you say something, you can emphasize your strengths rather than your boss's weaknesses.

5. **What do you like best about working with your current company?**

Perfect Phrase: "One thing about my company that I really like is the teamwork that is emphasized there. No matter what department I have worked with, there is a sense of partnership and pulling together. That's important to me in my job."

Note: Never bad-mouth a company or person. This reflects badly on you and the company or person you are talking about. The thinking is that someday you will talk about this person or company like that when you leave.

6. **What are your strengths?**

Perfect Phrase: "My strengths are my attitude and my flexibility. I am known for my ability to get the job done;

9. Why are you leaving your current job?

Perfect Phrase: "I have set some career goals for myself to become part of a bigger team in the area of negotiations where I can contribute based on my past experiences."

Note: Words and phrases such as, "looking for a challenge," or "to grow and develop and learn new things," are overused and meaningless to the interviewer.

10. Why do you want to work for this company?

Perfect Phrase: "My goal today is to find out why I would want to work for your company. I know that I have what it takes to do this job, and from what I have read while researching your company, it looks like a good match. I am here to find out more about the opportunity."

Note: By putting the interview on equal terms in which I am "checking you out" while you are "checking me out," you will have a stronger position in the interview.

Your Position—Your Words

Each industry uses "key words," or "lingo," for specific positions. To learn these words, research your specific industry to determine the most current jargon. By using these words in your interview, you will demonstrate your knowledge of the industry, and the interviewer will look at you as a candidate who knows what he or she is talking about.

done right; and done on time. I do whatever it takes to fulfill my commitment to deliver."

Note: By using the same phrase everybody else uses, your words lose their impact. By making a more definite, stronger statement with some punch, your words are more likely to impress.

7. What are your weaknesses?

Perfect Phrase: "I usually have a wonderful memory for details, but sometimes when I am in the middle of several tasks, I have to stop and organize myself and prioritize what has to be done. I make lists and do spreadsheets so that I don't miss anything. This really helps me remember important details as well as the not-so-important details."

Note: Try putting a positive spin on your weakness and tell what you've learned or are learning to improve on a weakness.

8. What is your salary expectation?

Perfect Phrase: "When the time comes to talk money, I am sure that we will come up with a mutually beneficial amount. Could you tell me the range budgeted for the position?"

Note: The unwritten rule is, "He who mentions money first loses." Let the interviewer bring up the subject and then let him or her be the first to mention the dollar amount, if possible.

Here are some examples of key words for specific jobs/ industries:

Engineering process development, quality assurance, testing and failure analysis, field assessment and operations, industrial hygiene, environmental compliance, urban planning

Teaching/Education scholastic standards, academic achievement, curriculum development, lesson plans, college prep, literacy development, dyslexia, academic levels, multicultural, certification, ethics

Human Resources performance management, managed care, headcount, training and development, multidiscipline, efficiency initiatives, expatriate, relocation, competency-based, unions, internal audits

Law briefs, discovery, civil litigation, initiatives, prosecute, reviews, directives, regulations, compliance, mergers and acquisitions, intellectual property, trademark, regulatory compliance

Exec/Management return on investment (ROI), profit and loss statements (P&L), strategic planning, tactical planning and execution, leadership training, business campaigns, growth and expansion, fast track

Sales territory management, quotas, sales producer, sales campaign, gross per unit, renewal rate, team building, cross-functional, sustained revenue, hands-on, emerging markets

Marketing customer relations management (CRM), turnaround, profitability, target market, world class, vision, operating infrastructure, change initiatives, market penetration

Technology information systems management, next-generation products, data mining, online customer support, broadband, turnkey network solutions, customer-driven, prototyping, troubleshooting

These are only a sample of the words you will discover once you begin to make up your own collection of industry words.

Your Position—Your Words: An Exercise

Take time to write down the key words and jargon used in your position and in your industry. This will prepare you for a wide range of questions you'll be asked.

-
-
-
-
-
-
-

Key Words and How to Locate Them

In addition to finding key words through job postings, another source of industry/job words is *The Occupational Information Network* located at http://online.onetcenter.org/. You will find a complete list of occupation keywords, SOC codes, and job families. This site also lists skills required—basic skills, social skills, experience, and tasks.

Another place to look are books at your local bookstore or library. Two great resources are

Key Words to Nail Your Job Interview by Wendy S. Enelow, Impact Publications

1500 Key Words for $100,000 + Jobs by Wendy S. Enelow, Impact Publication